Praise for

SOUL BOOM

"Serving up a delicious smorgasbord of existential philosophy, self-reflection, social science, and *Star Trek*, Rainn Wilson explores the missing role of spirituality in the modern world. It will light up your brain, warm your heart, and tickle your funny bone."
        —Adam Grant, #1 *New York Times* best-selling author of
        Think Again and host of the TED podcast *Re:Thinking*

"This is the insightful exploration of spirituality that we desperately need right now. As we all seek answers amid an unceasing news cycle of chaos and doom, Rainn Wilson's *Soul Boom* funnily but gently and lovingly opens a door to a deeper way to process all that is happening around us. The wisdom in and on these pages will fill your soul and touch your heart."
        —Lisa Ling, coauthor of *Somewhere Inside* and host of *This Is Life*

"Brilliant, humorous, and deeply wise, Rainn Wilson makes the case for spiritual revolution like no other. With humility that lands in the heart, Rainn invites us into a profound conversation on death and despair, God and transcendence, and love as a revolutionary force. The result is an electrifying manifesto on how to transform the world from the inside out. Let *Soul Boom* ignite and inspire you, as it has me!"
        —Valarie Kaur, activist and author of *See No Stranger*

"In *Soul Boom*, Rainn Wilson explores the landscape of the world's faiths and suggests a new and thoughtful spiritual path for seekers. If you're hungry to rediscover what makes your existence divine, this book is for you."
—Arthur C. Brooks, author of *Love Your Enemies, From Strength to Strength,* and *Build the Life You Want*

"A gracious and compassionate (and altogether engaging) book, by someone who truly believes that it is possible to love God, neighbor, and world, and to relate to them and cherish them in ways at once richly spiritual and impeccably rational. He's right, of course: it is."
—David Bentley Hart, author of *The Experience of God: Being, Consciousness, Bliss*

"Rainn Wilson played one of the greatest comic characters of all time, but the crisis we are living through is no joke. That's why you should drop everything you are doing and read this remarkable book. It combines a seriousness of purpose, a depth of intellect, and a warmth of spirit that is desperately needed today. It will lighten your load, fire your soul, and guide you on your way."
—Eboo Patel, founder and president of Interfaith America and author of *We Need to Build: Field Notes for Diverse Democracy*

"A terrific book...makes spirituality accessible in many different ways."
—Al Roker

"It's fascinating.... A great book, I really recommend it."
—Kelly Ripa

"I love the book; [it's] great.... There is a core of hope and optimism that provides the underpinning for all these thoughts as [Wilson canvasses] spirituality and religion and our place in the world and how to think about and approach solving some of the giant problems we face in the world right now."
—Rich Roll

"[A] terrific... thought-provoking, [and] beautiful book.... This is the one you want on your bedside, [for when] you can't sleep.... Lean over [and] read this, especially on those restless nights."

—Tamron Hall

"By the time you've finished reading *Soul Boom: Why We Need a Spiritual Revolution*, Wilson sheds all hesitations and proposes nothing less than the fundamentals of a new faith." —*Chicago Tribune*

"*Soul Boom* is an energized guidebook that argues for more spiritual thinking in our daily lives. Wilson is a funny and self-deprecating thinker who traces the commonalities of the world's major religions, maintaining that embracing the general teachings of their inspirational scriptures can lead to a rich [and] soulful life.... If you're in need of a spiritual shot-in-the-arm from a kind teacher, you've come to the right place." —*The Observer*

"Wilson is a talented writer who is both engaging and direct.... I appreciated the openness he demonstrated right away in sharing his experiences of family and faith... his approach to spirituality is deeply inclusive.... He also demonstrates respect for spiritual wisdom found across various traditions from the major monotheistic religions.... The main thrust of this book is not didactic but invitatory.... This book provides an opportunity for contemporary spiritual seekers—those part of a classical religious tradition, something else or nothing at all—to think through some important themes.... If Wilson's book can get Christians (and Jews and Muslims and Sikhs and others) to think deeply about their own traditions, consider their own spiritual capacities and journeys while coming to respect the spiritual capacities and journeys of others, and invite those not already inclined to contemplate spirituality in these ways, then I think [this] book will have accomplished its goal." —*National Catholic Reporter*

Also by Rainn Wilson

SoulPancake: Chew on Life's Big Questions
The Bassoon King: My Life in Art, Faith, and Idiocy

SOUL BOOM

WHY WE NEED A SPIRITUAL REVOLUTION

RAINN WILSON

hachette
BOOKS

New York

Hachette Go, an imprint of Hachette Books
Hachette Book Group
1290 Avenue of the Americas
New York, NY 10104
HachetteGo.com
Facebook.com/HachetteGo
Instagram.com/HachetteGo

First Trade Paperback Edition: April 2024

Hachette Books is a division of Hachette Book Group, Inc. The Hachette Go and
Hachette Books name and logos are trademarks of Hachette Book Group, Inc.

The Hachette Speakers Bureau provides a wide range of authors for speaking events. To find
out more, visit hachettespeakersbureau.com or email HachetteSpeakers@hbgusa.com.

Hachette Go books may be purchased in bulk for business, educational, or promotional use.
For information, please contact your local bookseller or email the Hachette Book Group
Special Markets Department at Special.Markets@hbgusa.com.

The publisher is not responsible for websites (or their content) that are not owned by
the publisher.

Library of Congress Cataloging-in-Publication Data

Name: Wilson, Rainn, author.
Title: Soul boom: why we need a spiritual revolution / Rainn Wilson.
Description: First edition. | New York, NY: Hachette Go, an imprint of Hachette Books,
   Hachette Book Group, 2023. | Includes bibliographical references and index.
Identifiers: LCCN 2022057224 | ISBN 9780306828270 (hardcover) |
   ISBN 9780306828287 (trade paperback) | ISBN 9780306828294 (ebook)
Subjects: LCSH: Spirituality—Social aspects. | Social change—Religious aspects. | Soul. |
   Religions. | Wilson, Rainn—Religion. | Television actors and actresses—United
   States—Religious life.
Classification: LCC BL60 .W554 2023 | DDC 204—dc23/eng/20230207
LC record available at https://lccn.loc.gov/2022057224

ISBNs: 978-0-306-82828-7 (trade paperback); 978-0-306-82827-0 (hardcover);
978-0-306-82829-4 (ebook); 978-0-306-83262-8 (B&N.com signed edition);
978-0-306-83263-5 (signed edition)

Printed in the United States of America

CW

10 9 8 7 6 5 4 3 2 1

For my dad, Robert Wilson.
Thanks for teaching me about the soul.

CONTENTS

CHAPTER TEN

PREFACE

Instructions for living a life:
Pay attention.
Be astonished.
Tell about it.

—*Mary Oliver*

Here I am. Sitting in my office during the early weeks of the COVID-19 quarantine, furiously outlining the book on big spiritual ideas that I've been wanting to write for years. "Now's my chance!" I say to myself (while wearing the same sweatpants I've worn for the past six days with the little stain where I wiped my cinnamon-raisin oatmeal on my thigh). Here's the big opportunity! Hours and hours of free time to vomit forth a potpourri of ideas on all my favorite topics: the journey of the soul, life after death, the Big Guy Upstairs, and the personal and universal spiritual transformation of society!

The only problem? Me. Rainn Wilson.

Let me be blunt with you, dear reader. I know what you might be asking right now: "Why the *hell* is the actor who played Dwight on *The Office* writing a book on spirituality?"

First, let me explain what I mean by "spirituality."

True story: I recently came across a news headline about some model/celebrity who had undergone some kind of "spiritual transformation." I was intrigued. After all, I *love* spiritual transformations! Have had a couple myself over the decades. In fact, I might be having one right now as I write this. Upon further reading, turns out that this model/celebrity had undergone an actual exorcism of some kind in a remote town in Switzerland. A shaman had released some kind of demon/energy from them, and they were finally, on the other side of it, able to practice "self-care" and enjoy yoga and raw juicing from home. Something like that. Which got me thinking about the word "spirituality." It can mean so many different things to so many people.

To some, spirituality is completely synonymous with religious practice and "organized religion": church, God, and so forth. To others, it can mean rituals involving hallucinogens. To many, because the word "spirit" is in it, it means that ghosts are involved. To still others, like the model/celebrity, it can mean exorcisms by Swiss shamans.

Let me be perfectly clear: I'm not talking about any of that.

The word "spirituality," as the *Oxford English Dictionary* defines it, means "the quality of being concerned with the human spirit or soul as opposed to material or physical things." This is *exactly* what I'm talking about. Way to go, *OED*! I will delve into all these concepts in far greater detail as the book progresses, but if we are to believe, as I very much do, that we have some kind of "soul" that continues on some kind of journey after our bodies fall away, and that this spiritual essence of who we are is just as real (if not more so) than our bodies—in other words, that this "soul" is the nonanimal, nonmaterial, non-pleasure-and-power-seeking dimension of ourselves that continues in some form after our physical existence ceases—and if this soul exists, then there are certain practices, processes, and perspectives that might help to shape our human beingness, the reality of who we really are. This is what I'm referring to when I talk about the word "spirituality": this eternal/divine aspect of ourselves that longs for higher truth and journeys toward heart-centered enlightenment and, dare I say it, God.

But let's go back to the original theme.

Why does a guy famous for playing a weird, officious nerd on one of America's most beloved TV comedies (and many other offbeat characters) want to write about the soul, religion, the afterlife, sacredness, and the need for society to undergo a spiritual reimagining? Why is the beet-farming, paper-selling, tangentially Amish man-baby with the giant forehead and short-sleeved mustard shirts writing about the meaning of life?

Well, I'll tell you one thing: it certainly is *not* because I have anything figured out.

I'm no authority on spirituality, religion, or holiness, and I'm anything but enlightened. Yes, I've read and studied a great deal. I've suffered deeply. I've pondered and contemplated and meditated. I've struggled and many times failed. But aren't writers on spiritual topics supposed to have life all worked out? I'm here to tell you they (we) don't. Although I have some insights from the work I've done, I still get anxious and confused a great deal. I swear too much. I'm impatient with my kid sometimes. I have a big ego that can sometimes subsume me. I compare and despair. I have been (and can be) overwhelmingly selfish and judgmental.

Just ask my wife. (Who, by the way, is far more preternaturally spiritual than I am, believe you me!)

But let's keep digging a little bit. *Why* is a former sitcom actor writing some "big idea" text on spiritual transformation?! And why am I (shameless plug), at approximately the same time, hosting a travel documentary series on finding happiness called *Rainn Wilson and the Geography of Bliss* for the Peacock streaming service?

Before I answer that question, I want to share some context. My life story, the story of my journey toward being an actor, a member of the Baha'i Faith, and a spiritual student/thinker/enthusiast (as told in full in *The Bassoon King*, my serio-comic memoir of 2015), is a complicated one.

My parents, like so many of their generation, were artsy bohemians in the '60s and '70s on a quest for truth, peace, and meaning in their lives. My birth mother, Shay (formerly Patricia) of Weyauwega, Wisconsin, moved to Seattle and became an actress in experimental theater in the late '60s. She did a play once while topless with her torso painted blue, running around in the aisles and swearing at the audience. My father, the recently deceased (more on that later) Robert "Bob" Wilson of Downers Grove, Illinois, was a painter of abstract art and an author of science-fiction novels among various other pursuits. He would often blast opera music from our 1970s stereo system (why were stereos so *big* back then!?) while covered in turpentine and gesso, singing along off-key as he smooshed globs of outrageous color onto canvases. Paintings that very few would actually see because he never really tried to sell any of them, so they would stack up in the basement like multicolored pizza boxes. During the day, he would manage a sewer construction office and dispatch rusty trucks to unclog the leaf-filled drains of Seattle. During his lunch breaks, he would haul out a little portable manual typewriter and clack away onto stacks of paper, unveiling over the span of fifteen years around eleven tomes of sci-fi with such titles as *Tentacles of Dawn*, *The Lords of After-Earth*, and *Corissa of Doom*. My stepmother, Kristin, who was mostly tasked with raising me, wore various vaguely ethnic shawls and capes and made fanciful, animal-shaped silver jewelry that she sold at a stall at the Seattle Public Market.

And as if that wasn't eclectic enough, on their off nights they would attend meetings of the Baha'i Faith, of which they were adherents. They would pray and meditate and study holy texts with other spiritually curious Seattleites. And there were *a lot* of them back then.

An important note about the Baha'i Faith: Personally, after many years of review and reflection, I have come to embrace the religion of my youth and feel like it contains all kinds of relevant wisdom surrounding the issues we face, both as individuals and as a species sharing a planet. And while this book is greatly inspired by the Baha'i Faith and many of the principal writings of its founder, Baha'u'llah, I won't get too deep into the details of the religion in these pages. After all, this is not a book about the Baha'i Faith or for Baha'is; it is merely shaped and influenced by some of its spiritual, mystical, and social teachings.

Any student of history knows the late '60s and early '70s had a completely different energy than the vibe of the previous several decades. When the whole Norman-Rockwell-Eisenhower-lilywhite-American-dream-Doris Day-*Leave-It-to-Beaver*-crew-cut-post-World-War-II skyscraper of American culture and values was taken down by an explosive charge of race riots, Vietnam, various assassinations, rock'n'roll, countercultural love, and LSD, all of a sudden the world as it used to be didn't make sense anymore. People were searching for a different path.

What do you do when the world as you know it falls to ashes at your feet?

Well, the Beatles met with the Maharishi, Cat Stevens became a Muslim, Shirley MacLaine communed with ancient aliens, a young Steve Jobs studied Buddhism in India, everybody was "kung fu fighting," and countless young people sought answers along nontraditional spiritual paths.

Into this milieu was born gigantic pasty baby Rainn Dietrich Wilson.

My dad often told stories of the early '70s, when he would be out and about and see, say, a group of young men on a street corner in fringy leather vests and long hair, passing a "doobie," "jaybird," or "spliff" ('70s terminology) around the circle, and he would approach them, saying, "Hey, guys. Wanna come over tonight to learn more about the Baha'i Faith? To pray and study different spiritual traditions?" And instead of laughing at him and/or kicking the shit out of him, they would respond with great earnestness: "Sure, man. Sounds groovy! What time?"

These spiritual gatherings in our home would include Buddhists and Sikhs and Muslims and Mormons, while our bookshelves became filled with books by and about Buddhists and Sikhs and Muslims.

We would host prayer gatherings and "deepenings" (in order to get deep), and, in addition to the many Baha'i-inspired songs, we would often *literally* sing "Kumbaya." Sometimes while holding hands in a patchouli-scented circle. When Jehovah's Witnesses would come to our door with pamphlets and Bibles, they would be invited in, and we would host an impromptu Bible study replete with pancakes!

I remember one time, when members of a particular sect of Christian Protestant came to our house on a Sunday afternoon, my father asked them to describe their concept of the kingdom of heaven.

A well-groomed man with a Ned Flanders mustache said, sipping some coffee, "Well, sometime in the near future, there will be a great rumbling from above, lightning will strike, and there will be terrible storms. The sky will open up, and down will come Jesus Christ on a cloud with a great trumpet blast. There will be an incredibly beautiful city with gold and silver turrets that descends with angels on it, and this is the kingdom of God. The good Christians will get into the city, and it will float away with Jesus to be with God, the Father, and the rest of the people will be left behind, left on earth to perish."

And then he politely responded with something to the effect of, "What is the Baha'i concept?"

My dad, a wise spiritual teacher and public speaker, responded, "Well, in a lot of ways, it's very similar. There will be great storms and lightning and thunder, and the skies will open up. Down from a hole in the clouds doesn't come a city or Jesus or anything but rather a bunch of bags of cement. Some shovels and hammers. Bricks and mortar and nails and lumber. And finally, at the very end, a note floats down on the breeze and lands on top of all the supplies. It reads: 'Kingdom of God on Earth: Build-It-Yourself Kit.'"

I don't remember what happened after that. But I'll always remember that story, and, I suppose, when all is said and done, that's what it's all about, no? Whether you believe in God or not, whether you're Christian or Baha'i or anything else, we're all down here doing our best to build a more loving, just, equitable, cooperative kingdom on this beautiful and sometimes difficult earth. Or perhaps a more personal, peaceful kingdom of God *within* ourselves? After all, that's how Nietzsche described it:

> The "kingdom of heaven" is a condition of the heart—not something that comes "upon the earth" or "after death."

Basically my entire childhood was filled with two things: art and spirituality.

Oh yeah, and dysfunction. I forgot to mention that. Lots and lots of family dysfunction. And low self-esteem. And a complete and total lack of any conversation about feelings or the fundamentals of basic human emotional interactions.

Because, at the end of the day, as "spiritual" as my family appeared, there was a complete absence of loving expression in our house. Did my parents (including my birth mother, Shay, who took off when I was two and who I didn't really get to know until I was about fifteen) love me? Yes. Most certainly. To the best of their limited, traumatized ability, my parents attempted a piss-poor fumbling love for me and, occasionally, each other.

For my dad and stepmom, there were dinners and TV watching and gardening and dog walking—in other words, all the ingredients of a loving family. But there was no actual bond in their marriage. In fact, when I asked them when they knew their union was a mistake and they didn't actually belong together, they both said that it was within a year of their wedding—in 1969. So they did what any two mature people of insight and level heads would do: *they stayed together fifteen more years* and then got a divorce the *second* I left for college in 1984.

The entirety of this childhood tapestry created in me one cockama-mie suburban cocktail of bohemian weirdness and emotional disso-nance on a galactic scale.

In fact, as a teen I would watch how other kids would act and inter-act while at a restaurant or a school event. I would then copy, word for word, gesture for gesture, *how* they would behave and emulate their seemingly "normal" human interactions in order to learn how to fit in better. Kind of like what an alien in human form would do in order to learn the mysterious ways of the *Homo sapiens*. If, say, a teen would say to another friend-teen, "What's up, my man!" and give him a friendly one-two pat on the back, I would try that same gesture out on a couple friends of mine: "What's up . . . um, my man!" along with matching friendly pats, to see if I could interact with the same effortless casualness.

Needless to say, it worked out perfectly.

So yes, my childhood shaped me this way. This strange petri dish of experiences—this recipe for weirdness—set the stage for the question at hand: Why is the guy who played Dwight writing a book on religious and spiritual ideas?

Another answer to the "why" comes down to this: I almost died. If not for certain tools, concepts, and teachings that I have found on my own spiritual search for balance, healing, and perspective, I would not have made it into adulthood. Or become a successful actor. Or written this damn book.

I'm not going to get into any gory details, but in my twenties and thirties I dealt with many mental health issues that caused me incredible pain and hardship. After graduating from college, I suffered years of debilitating anxiety attacks and to this day have an ongoing anxiety disorder that I have to monitor and work on with great seriousness and care. And therapy. Lots of therapy.

I have undergone long periods of time when I was clinically depressed. There were times I reached emotional lows from which I felt I would never escape. I even seriously contemplated suicide. Thankfully, I always got therapeutic help when I needed it and love from some amazing friends and family members, and I had a profound partner in my wife, Holiday Reinhorn, who supported me with great empathy and strength.

And then there's the other demon of mental (and physical) health: addiction. After some bouts with drugs and alcohol dependency in my twenties, I was able to quit with the help of the Twelve-Step Program of recovery. Pretty much anything you *can* get addicted to, I have struggled with at one point or another: food, gambling, porn, work, codependence, social media, and debt. Even caffeine and sugar. (And now it's my frigging iPhone!)

For me, it all comes back to that perpetual subterranean rumble of anxious discontent, probably stemming from childhood trauma, that I continually attempted to soothe and escape using external solutions. Over and over again, to no avail. Because you can't fix internal imbalance with alcohol or chocolate chip cookies or video games or weed or sex or even Instagram, *Candy Crush*, and Amazon shopping sprees.

It took me a long, long time and a great deal of therapuetic work to discover the spiritual, emotional, and psychological tools I needed to understand and eventually quell that inner discomfort and chronic imbalance.

Like so many spiritual seekers, I "hit bottom" but eventually found a way forward, a path toward recovery and tranquility. Out of this darkness, I went on a spiritual journey to help me in my quest for the truth. I investigated religions and spent many hours reading holy texts and secular works on the spiritual path. Meditating. Searching for God. For meaning. For something beyond the material. For transcendence.

In a nutshell, I spent many years in my twenties and thirties on a private, personal spiritual search, which led me to read most of the holy books of the world's major religions. I'm no scholar or expert by any means, but this quest for the truth compelled me to study the Bible, the Quran, the Bhagavad Gita, and the Dhammapada and other writings by and about the Buddha. I also read up on many Native American faiths and belief systems and caught up on some basics of Western philosophy. I got deeply reacquainted with the faith of my youth, Baha'i. I prayed and meditated profusely, attended various religious services, and dug deep into many central, profound questions: Is there a God? What happens when we die? Do we have a soul? Why do all these idiots watch *The Bachelor*?

Soul Boom is not a gut-spilling, soul-wrenching personal biography by any stretch. (I've already written one of those.) I just wanted, in the preceding pages, to give you a taste, an amuse-bouche, a sampling of my singular and peculiar prehistory. Today, I'm proud to say that the unusual backdrop and breeding ground of art, religion, self-loathing, and social dysfunction made me who I am. Plus, it made me a good candidate for the role of Dwight and the many other misfit parts I've played as an actor throughout the years.

And so the journey continues!

Aspects of this personal spiritual quest are explored in the Peacock television series *Rainn Wilson and the Geography of Bliss*, in which I set off across the globe to see if there might be any lessons on happiness to be learned from other cultures.

The same "Life's Big Questions" that haunted me in my twenties was the inspirational cornerstone that led to my eventual founding of Soul-Pancake, a website, YouTube channel, and production studio that specialized in creating uplifting content and sparking dialogue about the beauty and drama of being a human. Our best-selling book, *Soul-Pancake: Chew on Life's Big Questions*, was a creative workbook based on many of the profound spiritual issues and inquiries I grappled with in my youth and continue to wrestle with in the following pages.

I believe exploring "Life's Big Questions" is an exciting and important part of our fragile and exhilarating human journey. I have seen this again and again—in my study of various religious traditions, in my life as a Baha'i, and in my work with *Geography of Bliss*, *SoulPancake*, and the podcast series *Metaphysical Milkshake*, which I host with the amazing author/provocateur Reza Aslan. And my personal battles with mental health demons have given me firsthand experience in the high-stakes pursuit of meaning, purpose, and serenity from a spiritual perspective.

Besides, none of the other people who are way smarter and wiser and more spiritually evolved than me seem to be writing a book about this stuff, so why the hell not some weird, spiritually curious actor?

So . . . OK to move forward on the old booky-wook? Have a bit of clarity on the personal reasons that led me to create *Soul Boom*?

Good. Just one more thing then. Beyond my personal interest and journey, there's a bigger "why" behind this endeavor. My principal and overriding motivation for writing this book is not as introspectively personal as the tapestry I've just laid out. The truth is found in these words:

We need a change of heart, a reframing of all our conceptions and a new orientation of our activities. The inward life of man as well as his outward environment have to be reshaped if human salvation is to be secured.

—*Shoghi Effendi*

As all the existing organizational systems around us break down, we need answers. We need solutions. We need hope. Unity. Love. Compassion. All that gooey, profound stuff that is so easy to sneer at and dismiss in our cynical, fast-paced, modern world. Yet I sincerely believe that humanity, in order to evolve on both the individual and the societal level, needs a total shift in perspective and a seismic change in how it undertakes pretty much everything. This is the "reshaping" necessary for "human salvation" that the great Baha'i leader and writer Shoghi Effendi references in the above quote.

I hope you'll consider this "big idea" to address the world's problems. *Perhaps* the key to healing the world's chaos and pain lies on a spiritual path. *Perhaps* there are spiritual tools and religious concepts out there that can help us on a societal level, as well as in our own personal transformation. *Perhaps* a spiritual metamorphosis is required for us to not only thrive but to even survive as we sit at the precipice of annihilation.

———◆———

So, gentle reader, what topics are we going to tackle in the ensuing chapters? Some really light material: pandemics, death, God, religion, holiness, consciousness, suffering, social transformation, and the meaning of life. That's about it. We'll go on sacred pilgrimages to Jerusalem and the Baha'i holy land as well as into the distant future of humanity. We'll tackle small topics like death and God and consciousness and the soul. We'll converse with aliens and break down everything that's currently breaking down in society, and we'll even create our own new, awesome religion. Basically, I'll be throwing a lot of spiritual spaghetti against the wall, and hopefully some of it will stick.

I hope this book will ignite discussion and inspire you, gentle reader, to view some universal spiritual ideas through some different-colored lenses. Sometimes silly, sometimes profound and earnest, I will attempt to explore some very old ground with some very new perspectives.

Plus, because I *love* quotes, along the way there will be a myriad of fun, inspirational sayings from dead people far wiser than me. Quotes like this one:

Dost thou reckon thyself only a puny form
When within thee the universe is folded?

—*Imam Ali (Islam)*

And this one:

The ultimate work of civilization is the unfolding of ever-deeper spiritual understanding.

—*Arnold Toynbee (historian)*

This book will be a wide-ranging smorgasbord of ideas—spiritual and otherwise. Take what you like and leave the rest. Some concepts I hope you'll jibe with and others perhaps not so much. But it's the beginning of a discussion, I hope. A touchstone. A spark. And eventually? A much-needed personal and societal transformation.

A spiritual revolution. A boom at the soul level.

But where to begin?

Let's start with television.

CHAPTER ONE

LIVE LONG AND PROSPER, GRASSHOPPER

When I think of spirituality and the 1970s, a particular word comes to mind. It's not "meditation." It's not "LSD." It's not "guru" or "incense" or "chakras."

It's "television."

I spent a lot of time watching television in the 1970s. I mean *a lot*.

Certainly the great sitcoms like *M.A.S.H.*, *All in the Family*, *The Mary Tyler Moore Show*, and *The Bob Newhart Show*. Shows that inspired me to strive to eventually become one of those memorable sitcom sidekick clowns that I loved and laughed at with such zeal in front of our black-and-white RCA.

But I was also drawn to these programs because these were families as real, relatable, and flawed as my own. How I *longed* to not be in my dysfunctional family but instead to live with Meathead and Gloria in Queens, or to be a patient of Bob Newhart in his Chicago practice, or an intern at WJM TV with Mary Tyler Moore. I would even have taken being drafted and having to clean latrines at the 4077th M.A.S.H. unit instead of eating awkward, loveless meatloaf with the Wilson family of Lake Forest Park, Washington.

And isn't that the reason so many people watch TV? Binge-watch our favorite shows on repeat? No matter what the milieu—a police station, a spaceship, a Scranton paper company—we long to spend time with those fictional, loving, flawed, funny families. Perhaps a little bit more than we long to be in our own.

But when I peer back through the yellow haze of time toward that shaggy decade, there were two shows that framed both my identity and my spiritual journey. And, crazily enough, I also believe these two shows—*Kung Fu* and *Star Trek*—define and put into perspective what the reality of our spiritual journey actually is.

The first of these shows was the masterpiece *Kung Fu*, a program that defined the 1970s and reflected its ethos and underbelly. Originally conceived by (and appropriated / stolen from) the great Bruce Lee, *Kung Fu* followed Kwai Chang Caine, the orphaned child of a white man and a Chinese woman, who grew up in a Shaolin monastery in China in the late 1800s, was frequently called "grasshopper," and learned to fight like a badass. As a nineteenth-century adult, he makes his way to America during the cowboy days of the Old West to search for his half brother, Danny Caine. A stranger in an even stranger land.

Everywhere Kwai Chang Caine (let's call him KCC) went, he would bring his moral clarity, Eastern wisdom, and spiritual enlightenment to the rough-and-tumble, violent chaos of the Old West. Each episode would include some kind of moral quandary and some form of social injustice where KCC would stand up for the little guys, peaceably at first, using great reason and compassion and, finally, culminating in a big, ubiquitous "Kung Fu Monk Pushed to the Limit Takes on Racist Mean Cowboy" fistfight.

David Carradine (Bill in Quentin Tarantino's *Kill Bill*) was wise beyond all measure (and had an amazing dragon kick as well). In looking back at the show, however, all one can think now is, "Why the *hell* did they cast a white guy to play a Chinese dude!?" And also, to a lesser extent, "Wait a minute, that's not really him doing all those martial arts moves, is it? It looks like they cut away from him at the last second and are showing someone else's foot making contact with that evil deputy's chin!"

But egregious institutional racism aside, Carradine's depth and believability as a Buddhist monk was still off the charts. Especially for a gawky nine-year-old spiritual seeker in suburban Seattle in 1975.

KCC had a beautiful, soulful repose. A quiet, peaceful, centered energy that shone in stark contrast to the drunken, Asian-hating Western men he was often in conflict with. When someone would say something impulsive, mean-spirited, irrational, and lacking in compassion (which happened about thirty-seven times an episode), his face would flinch, and you could feel the pain inside of his warm, calm Shaolin heart.

(By the way, guest stars during the course of the short-lived [three seasons] show included Jodie Foster, Leslie Nielsen, Harrison Ford, Carl Weathers, William Shatner, Pat Morita, and Gary Busey. I mean, what a cast!)

I cannot describe to you how much I loved this show. I would watch it every time it was on. I searched through the TV listings in the Sunday paper every week to see when reruns might be available. My friends and I would attempt to reenact the fight scenes and would argue vociferously about who would be allowed to play KCC. Although it was equally fun to play the "racist cowboy," because then you would get to swear and spit a lot.

And it was *slooooow*. Man, was it slow. It was slow even compared to the molasses pace of your average 1970s one-hour drama. It made *The Waltons* look like *24*. This was not your modern TV show by any stretch of the imagination. Endless conversations in poorly lit cabins. *Loooong* walks down Western wagon trails that looked suspiciously like roads just off the Warner Brothers back lot in the hills above Burbank. And that flute. There would be drawn-out shots of KCC with his wooden flute playing baleful, vaguely Chinese melodies. And then there was the bread and butter of the show—*the flashbacks*.

When KCC would come up against some dilemma, a gauzy haze would fall over the camera lens, a Chinese flute would play, a candle flame would come into blurred, flickering focus, and we would be back in the Shaolin monastery with KCC and his teachers, Master Kan and Master Po.

Master Po was a blind monk with haunting milk-white corneas who once memorably said, "Never assume that because a man has no eyes, he cannot see." (So true, Master Po, so true.)

Master Kan, who famously called young novitiate KCC "grasshopper," would hold out his palm with a pebble in it: "When you can snatch the pebble from my hand, then it will be time for you to leave." Young KCC would try again and again to snatch the pebble, and when he finally did, he proved his mastery of self. Only then was he allowed to pick up with his bare forearms a giant, flaming-hot metal urn with red-hot coals inside and a dragon emblem on its surface, leaving him with dragon burn-scar tattoos embossed on his arms that forever labeled him as a Shaolin priest. He would then walk on rice paper, laid out on the ground like a rug, without his feet leaving a mark. After passing these tests he was ready, at long last, to venture forth from the monastery.

Every episode dealt with the darkest shadows of human nature and their remedy, the corresponding spiritual opposite. There would be an episode about revenge, for instance, where some persecuted woman on a farm wants retribution against some mean rancher, and we would gauzily, flutily flash back to KCC's master saying, "Vengeance is a water vessel with a hole. It carries nothing but the promise of emptiness. Repay injury with justice and forgiveness, but kindness always with kindness." And then we would see KCC struggle with but ultimately follow his mentor's strictures in said episode. And not only that—KCC would teach others around him the ways of the spiritual guides from his childhood in China. His tranquility and Jesus-like energy would affect and transform those around him. *And* ultimately positively change the millions of polyester-clad audience members watching from their sofas as well.

From that nineteenth-century monastery (which was, fun fact, the castle from the musical *Camelot* where Robert Goulet and his mustache sang "If Ever I Would Leave You," *dressed up* to look like an ancient Chinese religious / martial arts community with ivy and stone paths, waterfalls, bells, and bamboo chimes) streamed wisdom that holds just as true today as it did in 1975 (or 1875). Teachings that could have come from Jesus or the Buddha or the Prophet Mohammed.

So, friends, it's time for us to play a little game:

KUNG FU OR FAMOUS RELIGIOUS QUOTE?

C'mon! Try and guess!

QUOTE		KUNG FU	HOLY TEXT	BONUS: NAME THE TEXT!
1	"Hate is like drinking salt water. The thirst grows worse."			
2	"A bad attitude spoils a good deed just as vinegar spoils honey."			
3	"Reasoning is destroyed when the mind is bewildered. One falls down when reasoning is destroyed."			
4	"All life is precious nor can any be replaced."			
5	"All life is sacred. . . . The thorn defends the rose. It harms only those who would steal the blossom from the plant."			
6	"Real believers walk with modesty; and when the foolish ones address them with harsh words, they reply: 'peace!'"			
7	"Peace lies not in the world . . . but in the man who walks the path."			

(continued)

KUNG FU OR FAMOUS RELIGIOUS QUOTE?

(*continued*)

QUOTE	KUNG FU	HOLY TEXT	BONUS: NAME THE TEXT!
8	"Do not be anxious about tomorrow, for tomorrow will be anxious for itself. Let the day's own trouble be sufficient for the day."			
9	"There is nothing so disobedient as an undisciplined mind."			
10	"Fear is the only darkness. Weakness prevails over strength."			
11	"A tranquil heart gives life to the flesh but envy makes the bones rot."			
12	"Learn more ways to preserve than to destroy."			
13	"Humanity is but a single brotherhood: so make peace with your brethren."			
14	"Carpenters bend wood; the wise master themselves."			

Answers: 1. Kung Fu 2. A hadith (saying) of Islam 3. Bhagavad Gita 4. Kung Fu 5. Kung Fu 6. Quran 7. Quran 8. Bible 9. The Buddha 10. Bhagavad Gita 11. Bible 12. Kung Fu 13. Quran 14. The Buddha

I wish the racists marching around in places like Oregon; Washington, DC; and Virginia could truly allow *all* of these ancient words of spiritual wisdom to sink in. Or the politicians vengefully squabbling in the halls of Congress. The shouting heads on the media talk shows. The angry, fist-shaking, judgmental twitterers. All of us, in fact.

Young KCC would say, "Master, do we seek victory in contention?"

And the wise teacher would respond with, "Seek rather not to contend."

Young KCC: "But shall we not then be defeated?"

And the master would respond again with the Buddhist equivalent of a mic drop: "We know that where there is no contention, there is neither defeat nor victory. *The supple willow does not contend against the storm, yet it survives.*"

Boom! Master Po for the Taoist win!

And isn't that what it's all about? We seek, ultimately, to be the supple willow in a world of storms. And we keep trying over and over, no matter how rarely we succeed in that goal.

Because these are the transcendent lessons of *Kung Fu*: walking the spiritual path with practical feet; seeking detachment from the baser drives of our animal instincts, like rage, lust, and greed; attempting to bring our higher self into every interaction; and turning to wise teachers to guide us when confronted by tests and difficulties.

Those teachers exist in all our lives. We have spiritual guides in the form of parents and grandparents, professors, and mentors that help us along the way. We also have great historical religious teachers, like Jesus, Lao-tzu, Mohammed, Baha'u'llah, Lord Krishna, Confucius, the Buddha, Moses, and the prophets of the Torah—all guides whose teachings have helped millions along this same path.

And only when it is our last recourse, when our backs are up against the wall, do we need to kick some mean cowboy ass with our humble (bare) feet.

I carry *Kung Fu* with me and think about it often. And I bring up the show in this here first chapter to, perhaps long-windedly, set out one of the principal notions underpinning this book:

We are all on a spiritual path.

—◆—

Whether we are aware of it or not, we are each KCC in our own way. We seek to gain wisdom, nurture our virtues, and master the darker, more ego-filled parts of ourselves. Every single reader draws on the wisdom of his or her past, the teachings of one's parents or faith tradition or important mentors. We all want to become better people, to have our hearts be true and our souls radiant. And we seek this in spite of the vicissitudes of the world that we confront on a daily basis.

Let's try a simple little exercise. Imagine yourself in 2023 America (or wherever you may be) as a contemporary monk. A wise disciple of both an ancient philosophy and a martial art practice with roots thousands of years old. You are lean and adept in your body. Calm of mind and open of heart. You step out the door of your house/apartment/building and go to your car/subway/bus. You have your keys, your wallet, your phone, your coffee sippy mug. You are on a journey. A journey of the day that lies in front of you and the greater journey of your search for meaning and purpose.

You're off to seek to make a living for your family or become educated in a school, perhaps. Maybe you're going to go shopping for the household or to a job interview.

What will you encounter in our modern world? Countless frenzied people rushing about their lives? Staring at their phones in their cars, on sidewalks, on buses, on elevators, and at desks? Ingesting an ever-refreshing fountain of news, emails, images, memes, videos, and updates from family and friends? Updates that, while they refresh on your phone, never really seem to refresh your mind, heart, and soul.

But from this frenzy, just for today, you take a break. You have enough information and updates and memes and images in your head for the time being.

And if you let those distractions go, what else will you encounter in the outside world? Not a drunk, angry cowboy, but perhaps some forces equally as toxic. Someone being rude or judgmental, perhaps.

Self-centeredness, probably. Conflict. Anxiety. Rage. Things not going as planned. People behaving badly. Some type of suffering. Rejection. Or, perhaps, disappointment (one of the most difficult and complex feelings for me personally to encounter).

And how will you meet these challenges? Will you be buffeted around like a leaf in a storm? Or will you accept them as part of life? As the Buddha (supposedly) said, "Pain is certain. Suffering is optional."

Will you allow the unevolved cretins around you to affect your serenity and determine what course of action you take? Or will you deftly, metaphorically slip by them, seeking not contention but to "win not by fighting"? Will you wisely, placidly, draw on your deep well of inner wisdom and navigate these issues like a willow tree in the wind?

We are all, after all, little KCCs on the road through the Old West, beset by tests and having to overcome both external obstacles and the insistent cries of the wants, needs, and unchecked passions of the inner ego.

In many religious traditions, we are on the planet for basically two reasons. Our mission / purpose / raison d'être has two components, two paths. In the Baha'i Faith (and I just love this guidance because it is so simple and clear), we call it our "twofold moral purpose."

On the one hand, our spiritual journey is about our personal transformation. Spirituality and religion should make our lives better and show us a path toward personal peace and enlightenment. If it doesn't do either of those two things, then we should all jettison it. The wisdom of faith either makes our lives better, increases serenity, and makes us better people, or there is really no reason to have it in our lives.

Kung Fu is an expression of this first part of the twofold path. The personal, internal one. As we seek to walk the spiritual path with practical (occasionally ass-kicking) feet, we are frequently daunted by the hurdles thrown at us by the outside world. And, more importantly, we are often overwhelmed by the obstacles that we ourselves create. Ones that arise from within to keep us stuck and immobilized, and occasionally to throw our lives into chaos. We let "overwhelm" and "resistance" keep us from achieving the goals we've set for ourselves. We often have negative internal voices that consistently and corrosively tear us down and hold us back. We become slaves to addictions that sabotage us and blow up our lives or insidiously eat away at us from the inside. Negative character traits like envy, jealousy, anger, and resentment oftentimes toxify our lives, moving us ever further away from the life we dream of—a rich, satisfying one filled with joy and contentment. The list goes on and on.

Spiritual traditions and teachings, I believe, are like the Shaolin training of KCC. They are a set of tools that, when practiced (sometimes over and over and over again), can help us navigate the rocky shoals of an uncaring, overwhelming outside world. A world that requires rent and work and health care premiums. A world fraught with rejection, stress, idiot bosses, and crazy roommates. External temptations and seductions from drugs, alcohol, sex, power, prestige, status, money, and the endless screen-fueled distractions that live in our pants pockets.

When you can snatch the pebble from the hand of your *self*, that is when you will pass the ultimate test. When you can effortlessly walk the rice paper of your own *ego* without leaving a mark, *that* is when you can leave the symbolic monastery as a *master*—a master of your darker, more selfish impulses. A spiritual warrior-monk emerging into the world in order to face dark and dangerous adversities and dark and dangerous temptations.

Most people's spiritual paths end there, at the personal. When most people think of spiritual tools for change, growth, and finding peace, they think of themselves working internally to increase serenity, perspective, and wisdom. In contemporary American culture, we rarely view a spiritual path as having much, if anything, to do with the peace, serenity, and wisdom of the *totality of humanity*.

This leads me to the next part of the journey—the other branch of our twofold moral purpose: our spiritual journey *not* as an individual but as a collective, a species on a planet—a planet that we are on the verge of destroying.

———◆———

Enter *Star Trek*. That great 1970s TV show that addresses this very issue. Gene Roddenberry's original masterpiece. (Note: I am very aware that *Star Trek* was a '60s TV show. But it didn't achieve relevance and popularity until the '70s. So bite my phaser.)

Star Trek is a difficult mythology and cultural phenomenon to encapsulate. Perhaps, dear reader, you have seen every episode and, like me, have every other line memorized. Or, more likely, you've only seen one or two and have only the vaguest idea of what the show is about, aside from knowing some of its venerated pop-cultural phrases like "Beam me up, Scotty," "To boldly go where no man has gone before," and (Scottish accent) "I'm doing the best I can, Captain!"

To summarize. In the twenty-third century, humanity is boldly seeking out new life and new civilizations with its navy of starships called Starfleet. The show follows the starship USS *Enterprise*, helmed by Captain James T. Kirk, played by the legendary William Shatner. He and his stalwart crew, including the half-Vulcan Spock (Leonard Nimoy), are exploring star systems on the outskirts of the galaxy, responding to distress calls, and generally having all sorts of fun, dangerous, science-fictiony adventures in snazzy form-fitting uniforms.

Their humanity is put to the test in each episode. The cast and crew of the *Enterprise* are challenged both personally and professionally, morally and intellectually, metaphorically and practically.

What may be *most* important about *Star Trek* is that the human race has worked out its problems on planet Earth through both science and an emotional wisdom comprised of restraint, reason, and maturity. This spiritually and intellectually awakened humanity then seeks to spread and share its evolved nature while exploring the galaxy in a peaceful manner.

The viewer can watch *Star Trek* simply on a basic level, as a science-fiction action show with laser beams, spaceships, cool aliens, and memorable characters. Many people do. To a large extent, that's what drew my six-year-old fanboy self to the show in the early '70s. (And, unfortunately, the most recent series of J. J. Abrams–produced films function almost exclusively on this level.)

But the miracle of *Star Trek* and why it stands the test of time as a paragon of great television is how it lives on a symbolic level. In *Star Trek*, everything is a metaphor. (As is everything on this physical plane. Just ask Plato. More on that later.)

The show metaphorically tackled all of 1960s society's greatest challenges—war, racism, technological advancement—from the point of view of an enlightened human race. This wasn't a show about personal growth; it was a show about collective transformation.

Take racism, a scourge that has killed millions over the centuries, incited hate, and kept humanity divided since the dawn of time. Roddenberry and his cracker-jack sci-fi writing staff tackle this issue in multiple episodes of the show. Why? Because Roddenberry believed that this was an issue that humanity would inevitably overcome in its eventual maturation.

"Intolerance in the twenty-third century? Improbable!" Roddenberry said. "If man survives that long, he will have learned to take delight in the essential differences between men and between cultures."

He also said, "We must learn to live together, or most certainly we will soon all die together."

Delight in the essential differences between cultures? Cool! ("Unity in diversity" is one of the central teachings of the Baha'i Faith, and as a young Baha'i, my Ba-mind was officially blown.)

As an example, in the episode "Let That Be Your Last Battlefield," a man who is black on the right side of his body and white on the left side is fighting a man who is white on the right side and black on the left. Bele and Lokai.

For *tens of thousands of years*, the people of the planet Cheron have been at war, simply because of the reverse nature of their shiny complexions. Bele and Lokai have been chasing each other in the galaxy for fifty thousand years, locked in hatred. When they board the *Enterprise* and are taken back to Cheron, everyone there is dead. Consumed in the fires of an intense war of racism. And Bele and Lokai can't see what is patently obvious—that they are from the same stock. Just look at this exchange:

BELE: It is obvious to the most simpleminded that Lokai is of an inferior breed.

MR. SPOCK: The obvious visual evidence, Commissioner, is that he is of the same breed as yourself.

BELE: Are you blind, Commander Spock? Well, look at me. Look at me!

CAPTAIN JAMES T. KIRK: You are black on one side and white on the other.

BELE: I am black on the right side!

CAPTAIN JAMES T. KIRK: I fail to see the significant difference.

BELE: Lokai is white on the right side. All of his people are white on the right side.

Before leaving, Bele accuses Captain Kirk of being an "idealistic dreamer," and the two enemies "beam down" only to continue their deadly battle on the planet's surface, the only members of their species left alive.

A bit silly and dated, perhaps. A bit obvious, maybe. But for a child in 1970s Olympia, Washington, it was profound and powerful. And, like it or not, it's still relevant.

It provided me and millions of others great inspiration around humankind's future ability to solve these massive issues of race and prejudice. Captain Kirk would say lines that most people would probably think naive. Lines like, "The prejudices people feel about each other disappear when they get to know each other." There is nothing truer than that.

However, nothing tackled the issue of race better than a historic episode entitled "Plato's Stepchildren" in which the first interracial kiss in television history was broadcast to millions of homes. Kirk and the gorgeous chief communications officer, Uhura (played by the late, brilliant, beautiful Nichelle Nichols), are forced to kiss by an alien race on some adventure or other. What was big about the moment was that the kiss was simply no big deal to the crew of the *Enterprise*. Humanity had long moved past any ill-conceived concerns about people of different races having relationships. That "no big deal-ness" of the kiss was what made it revolutionary.

That one kiss, viewed by millions, opened the doors for an acceptance of interracial marriage and helped mature and elevate the issues around civil rights and race in a volatile time. All made OK because it was viewed through the lens of fantastical, "pretend" science fiction.

There are many other examples of episodes as metaphorical mirrors for the dark social spasms that were convulsing planet Earth in the late '60s.

The idea of understanding the other—finding empathy with species different from yours—was a recurring theme in the show. Wherever they go in the galaxy, the crew of the *Enterprise* is called on to deepen their compassion and understanding toward "the alien." To go beyond what is safe and comfortable and "human." The episode "Metamorphosis" is a love story between a human and an alien cloud. There's "Arena," where Kirk fights the reptilian Gorn, only to realize that the evil Gorn believed all along that it was humans who were the aggressors. And "Devil in the Dark" tells the story of humans who have been killing the babies of a weird creature called the Horta, and we come to understand through empathy and reason that the Horta's violent actions are actually those of a protective parent.

Another theme was the idea that science and reason (and, ultimately, technology) could overcome all obstacles. In perhaps the greatest of all the episodes, "The City on the Edge of Forever," the hero, Edith (played by Joan Collins) speaks from Earth's past (the year 1930) about its future:

> One day soon, man is going to be able to harness incredible energies, maybe even the atom . . . energies that could ultimately hurl us to other worlds in . . . in some sort of spaceship. And the men that reach out into space will be able to find ways to feed the hungry millions of the world and to cure their diseases. They will be able to find

a way to give each man hope and a common future. And those are
the days worth living for.

She essentially sums up Roddenberry's utopian vision for the future.
(Spoiler alert: Kirk falls in love with her. She dies. She *has to* in order to
prevent an alternative reality in which the Nazis win World War II.
Bummer. So it goes. Note to self: time travel = tricky. Avoid at all costs.)

And all of that technological potential Edith alludes to is summed
up by a device that lives in every room of a starship: *the replicator*. A
machine in the wall that looks like a microwave but can pretty much
assemble from random molecules anything you want to eat. Soup. Boy-
senberries. Beet chips. Hot dogs. You name it. Not only that, but in
later iterations of the show, the replicator can make pretty much any-
thing one could want. Weapons, human organs, a crescent wrench, a
Dwight bobblehead. You get the idea.

Can you imagine a world in which every family has a replicator? Need
a lightbulb for a refrigerator? Press a button. Need a sandwich? Press a
button. A new pair of wool socks, AirPods, or a pet lizard? Press a button.

Boom. Technology wins. Hunger solved. Instant abundance.

Having the science of the replicator, humanity is then able to progress in profound ways and work toward achieving lasting peace.

In *Star Trek: The Next Generation*, which takes place a hundred or so
years after the original series, the sociological/spiritual/emotional evolution of humanity has reached an even greater level of maturity. Conflict itself has been eliminated.

Apparently, this was quite a challenge for the writers of this *Star Trek*
spin-off when it was being created in the late '80s. Roddenberry insisted
that on this show, humanity had overcome all of its baser instincts—
greed, lust, power. Which could make for some very boring television. I
mean, how is a television writer supposed to make great drama if no
one ever disagrees with anyone else?

Somehow they managed, and it became a great series in its own
right.

It was not only conflict that was eliminated by the twenty-fourth century but also money. The economic system was hinted at being completely liberated from wealth and poverty, from greed and profit and acquisition. Sometimes referred to as "Trekonomics."

Captain Jean-Luc Picard (played by the baldest knight in the history of the realm, Sir Patrick Stewart) was once quoted as saying, "The economics of the future are somewhat different . . . money doesn't exist in the twenty-fourth century . . . the acquisition of wealth is no longer the driving force in our lives. We work to better ourselves and the rest of humanity." (Sound familiar? That's the old twofold moral purpose in action!)

In another episode, Picard says to a time-traveling, greedy '80s Wall Street tycoon, "People are no longer obsessed with the accumulation of things. . . . We've eliminated hunger, want, the need for possessions. We've grown out of our infancy."

When I read those quotes, something touches me deeply. Perhaps it's my inner idealist/utopian/optimist longing for a resolution to all this unnecessary strife on our lovely, feverish little planet. It gives my sour little heart some measure of hope for our species, our world, our future. Like the *Enterprise* itself streaking into the distant galaxy, *Star Trek* shows us the way toward humanity's future.

Although faith and religion are never overtly mentioned in the show, and *Star Trek*'s central focus is the glorification of science and exploration, to me the core message is essentially a spiritual one. *Global unity for our human family, founded on increased compassion and universal equity.*

And this brings me back to the origin of this conversation—how two 1970s TV shows illuminate the two spiritual paths in front of us: the personal journey (*Kung Fu*) and the spiritual evolution of a species (*Star Trek*).

You might be wondering at this point, What does any of this have to do with me? Well, like the hippies said, "Let there be peace in the world, and let it begin with me." And as the frequent Subaru bumper sticker reads: "Think Global, Act Local." Meaning we all bear some individual responsibility for the collective good. And, believe it or not, that has everything to do with the techno-futurist, sci-fi mythology of *Star Trek*.

Again, for most people in the modern world, spirituality as a whole belongs firmly in the first *Kung Fu* category. Most don't actively consider a spiritual path that would focus on service to the greater needs of humanity, even though most spiritual traditions emphasize this idea repeatedly.

For instance, Buddhism is often reduced to "being in the moment" and "releasing attachment" and "eliminating suffering" and other tools that lead toward personal transformation and inner peace. But remember, Buddhist teachings also refer to building good "karma" by serving others, especially the poor. There are countless stories of the Buddha himself feeding and educating the downtrodden, calling out for service to others, and saying,

> So long as the sky and the world exist, my existence will be here for the eradication of the miseries of all beings.

And he sent forth his OG crew of apostle/monks with the following:

> Wander forth for the good of the many, for the welfare of the many, in compassion for the world.

Which sounds suspiciously like writings from the Torah:

> Give justice to the weak and the fatherless; maintain the right of the afflicted and the destitute. Rescue the weak and the needy; deliver them from the hand of the wicked.

And Jesus:

> Whoever is generous to the poor lends to the Lord, and He will repay him for his deed.

And the Prophet Mohammed:

The best of you is he who is of most benefit to others.

Obviously, at first blush, these writings are simply about sacrificing one's own needs to alleviate the suffering of others.

But to what end? *Why?* Why serve others?

To make ourselves feel better? For some personal benefit? Karmic rewards? No. Rather it is, with our eyes on a far bigger prize, to create a world filled with less suffering. To create justice, equity, love, and a reduction in unnecessary pain for the inhabitants of our beautiful planet. To build the kingdom of God on Earth.

The founder of the Baha'i Faith, Baha'u'llah, writes,

Let your vision be world embracing rather than confined to your own selves.

And:

All men have been created to carry forward an ever-advancing civilization.

And to quote that renowned sage science officer Spock,

The needs of the many outweigh the needs of the few.

And that, dearest reader, is what the *Star Trek* modality of spiritual growth is all about.

What good is a spiritual path that only enriches our own inner peace while hundreds of millions go hungry? And conversely, how do we sustainably serve those millions if our hearts are hard, empty, cold, and filled with selfish ego or materialistic motives? How can there be peace without justice? There is an ongoing dance, a conversation between the

twofold moral paths that lie ahead of us. We seek personal enlightenment so that we can serve more, have an outward orientation, and help
create a better world. And when we undertake this service, we are in
turn internally awakened and fulfilled to an even greater degree.

Because, ultimately, we sojourn forth with two forces in our hearts—
two icons from the 1970s holding hands like the yin and yang—two
ass-kicking guides to our spiritual journey, ushering us along the mysterious road of the soul, one leading us toward inner tranquility and the
other toward the progress of humanity itself: Master Kwai Chang Cain
and Captain James T. Kirk.

CHAPTER TWO

A PLETHORA OF PANDEMICS

It is difficult
to get the news from poems
yet men die miserably every day
for lack
of what is found there.

—*William Carlos Williams*

This is a famous fragment from a longer poem, "Asphodel, That Greeny Flower," by the great William Carlos Williams—he the poet of "The Red Wheelbarrow," perhaps my favorite poem of all time.

Here that is in its tiny, perfect entirety:

so much depends
upon

a red wheel
barrow

glazed with rain
water

beside the white
chickens.

To me, the poem encapsulates the perfect intersection of language, memory, and a specific American vernacular—breaking poetry free of the shackles of any academic strictures or classical formalism, any fanciness or floweriness, any need to be "poetic."

But that's for a different book. I leave the poem here merely for your enjoyment. It has nothing to do with the point I'm making. In fact, I probably shouldn't have even put it in the book in the first place. You know what? Forget you even read it. Cross it out with a Sharpie if you like. Moving on.

To go back to those lines from the *first* Williams poem—"it is difficult to get the news from poems"—the two ideas that are presented in opposition to each other are, obviously, "news" versus "poems."

Ezra Pound, the famous writer (and fascist), once said in a similar vein, "Literature is news that stays news."

In other words, great fiction and poetry address core universal human issues.

W. H. Auden, echoing the idea, said, "Poetry makes nothing happen." But in the same poem, an ode to Yeats, he also describes poetry in this way: "It survives, A way of happening, a mouth."

In the case of the Williams quote, my thesis is this: I would humbly submit that one could easily substitute the word "spirituality" for the word "poems." It is difficult to get the news from *spirituality* . . . Meaning it might be difficult, at first blush, to get something seemingly tangible, practical, and readily applicable to one's day-to-day life from poetry or spirituality. But men die *miserably* every day from *lack* of what is found there. In other words, we humans suffer needlessly from an absence of what can be found in poetry and in spirituality.

And what is found in both spirituality and poetry? I would submit that the only thing to find therein is "what matters." What's important.

You know . . . Truth. Beauty. Serenity. Heart. Vision. Meaning. Inspiration. Soul. A shift of perspective away from the menial and toward the profound and transcendent.

According to Williams *and* great spiritual teachers like Krishna, Jesus, and the Buddha, men die miserably every day for *lack* of connection, meaning, devotion, spiritual perspective, and God-consciousness. As well as a plethora of other universal, soul-ripe issues that spirituality explores.

And, similarly, as per Auden, spirituality like poetry "survives." It is also "a way of happening, a mouth."

This discussion reminds me of a Zen teaching: "A finger pointing at the moon is not the moon."

We humans are capable, through language and image and art, of indicating something beautiful and mysterious. It is the pointing that guides us *to* the mystery. Language and metaphor are the finger. Poetry and music are the finger. Holy writings, divine texts, and religious wisdom are the finger. A spiritual teacher is the finger. Pointing to where? To the ancient, luminous moon of the essence of truth/God/beauty/wisdom. But be careful not to mistake the finger for the moon.

It is difficult to make money from poetry. It's a challenge to fit spirituality into one's iCal, weekly planner, spreadsheet, Slack channel, or Zoom call. It is impossible to use poetry or spirituality as collateral for a loan to repair your garage roof. It is really challenging to get something tangible and practical, like the information one might find in a local headline or a news app, from something that points toward the moon of truth and beauty and love.

Yet men die miserably . . .

But do they really? Are people actually dying for this lack of spirituality that I've been describing? Let's dig a little deeper. Let's take the temperature of humanity in the midst of its current challenges.

We are currently in a global mental health crisis that is ruthlessly affecting teens and young adults at a rate unlike anything the world has ever seen. In the dozens and dozens of talks and presentations I've given at colleges and universities, this fact seems to be abundantly well-known by those under fifty and almost completely, cluelessly *un*known by those over fifty.

Here are some sobering statistics around what experts are calling "deaths of despair," a catch-all phrase that includes alcohol and drug abuse as well as suicide. It was the name to describe a marker that explained how and why the lifespan of the average American had been falling over the last decade. I'm widening the usage of that evocative umbrella to also include some other aspects of the mental health epidemic, including, and I know this is pushing it, *social media*! As I said, I'm no expert, but as a concerned nerd, I wanted to share some staggering statistics I found online while looking into these issues.

DEATHS OF DESPAIR

According to Brookings, around seventy thousand people in the United States died annually from suicide or drug- and alcohol-related deaths between 2005 and 2019. Mental health specialists call these "deaths of despair."

DRUG ADDICTION

- In 2020, the CDC reported that 68,630 people died from opioid-related overdoses. (And that's down from previous years!)

- More than 932,000 people have died from a drug overdose since 1999. Two out of three drug overdose deaths in 2018 involved an opioid.

- In 2019, an estimated 9.7 million people misused prescription pain relievers and 745,000 people used heroin.

SUICIDE

- The rate of suicide-related thoughts and outcomes among young adults increased by 47 percent from 2008 to 2017.

- Suicide is the second leading cause of death among people aged ten to fourteen and the third leading cause of death among those aged fifteen to twenty-four in the US.

- Annual prevalence of serious thoughts of suicide, by US demographic group:

  - 4.9 percent of all adults

  - 25.5 percent of young adults aged eighteen to twenty-four

  - 18.8 percent of high school students

  - 23.4 percent of LGBTQ+ teens

  (Stop and take this in for a moment, will you? Almost one in five high school students have thought seriously about suicide this year!)

ANXIETY AND DEPRESSION

- According to the National Institutes of Health, nearly one in three of all children and adolescents will experience an anxiety disorder. These numbers have been rising steadily, increasing 24 percent from 2016 to 2019. By 2020, 5.6 million children had been diagnosed with anxiety.

- In 2020, depression was prevalent among nearly one in ten Americans and almost one in five adolescents and young adults.

- According to the Boston University School of Public Health, depression among US adults *tripled* in the early months of the COVID-19 pandemic (2020)—jumping from 8.5 percent before the pandemic to a staggering 27.8 percent.

- Over 280 million people around the globe suffer from the mental illness of depression.

LONELINESS

- According to the 2020 Census, 37 million adults ages eighteen and older now live on their own, up from 33 million in 2011. Loneliness has the equivalent negative effects on health as smoking fifteen cigarettes a day.

- A recent Cigna study shows that senior citizens (those seventy-two years old and older) have historically been the loneliest demographic. But in 2018, young adults ages eighteen to twenty-two reported feeling lonely at significantly higher rates than seniors, who are now the *least* lonely generation, while members of Gen Z are lonely at rates of almost 50 percent.

- A recent Harvard report suggests that 36 percent of Americans—including 61 percent of young adults—feel "serious loneliness." Forty-three percent of young adults reported increases in loneliness since the outbreak of the COVID-19 pandemic.

SOCIAL MEDIA

- The National Library of Medicine reports that since 2018 there has been a nearly 13 percent rise in loneliness. Heavy users of social media were lonelier as compared to light users. Feelings of isolation were prevalent, with Gen Z (ages eighteen to twenty-two at the time of the study) having the highest average loneliness score.

- According to a study published by the American Psychological Association, a possible contributing factor in the nation's rise in mental illness could be the increasing use of social media. Online interaction has taken precedence over face-to-face communication, perpetuating isolation and loneliness. Youth between the ages of eighteen and twenty-four who experienced psychological distress increased to 74.9 percent in 2020.

This tiny sampling of stats is supported by what students are increasingly focusing on in college these days. Take the most popular class at the University of Southern California, which is called "Making Meaningful Relationships" and is about the basics of how to make a friend. The most popular class in Yale University history is taught by the great Dr. Laurie Santos and focuses on happiness—it's entitled "Psychology and the Good Life."

The bottom line is that young people are suffering greatly. They seem to be lacking in the tools, skills, and ability to find solutions to these difficult issues. To befriend, to bond, to connect, to self-soothe, to find joy. To create community. They are seemingly cut off from what nourishes them, suffering from diseases of despair, and oftentimes feeling there's no way out.

Why am I going over all this depressing information in such detail? Because I often wonder why we don't call this sweeping problem of millennial and Gen Z mental health issues what it is—not just an epidemic but a *pan*demic. After all, it is spreading around the globe exponentially, and it's killing a great many more of us than the COVID-19 pandemic is. It needs to be taken *far* more seriously than it currently is, and it needs to be conceived of on a far larger scale.

Mental health is but one of many of these global pandemics that are eating away at the fabric of society and tearing it apart. It's crucial, before we explore a number of spiritual themes that await us, that we get a sense of what the enemy is. After all, that's what Captain James T. Kirk would do in *Star Trek*. Identify what we're up against. In this way we can see how high the stakes are and what tools and weapons we will need to progress.

Speaking of taking a global perspective, let's now look at the various problems we are facing from the broadest possible vantage point. Let's pull back to a thirty-thousand-foot view and ponder our goofy little species, *Homo sapiens*, inhabiting a remote blue planet, facing some of the greatest challenges of its brief existence.

PANDEMICS APLENTY

Professors Merriam and Webster define a pandemic as "an outbreak of a disease that occurs over a wide geographic area (such as multiple countries or continents) and typically affects a significant proportion of the population."

Besides the decline in our mental health, as well as the obvious COVID-19 pandemic of our modern times, which has claimed seven million lives by the close of 2022, our globe is being rocked with a myriad of other catastrophic dark forces at work on the world's population today.[1]

RACISM

At the same time that the COVID-19 pandemic was ravaging hospitals around the world, here in the United States, cities erupted after witnessing the brutal, slow, public murder of George Floyd by a police officer

---

1 Disclaimer: I am not any kind of expert on the following topics. I'm certain that within each of these categories, I have missed vital elements and summarized ineffectively. Also, it must be acknowledged that I am among the most privileged and entitled of humans (white, male, tall, wealthy, famous, outrageously handsome, world-class athlete), and my all-too-brief and superficial encapsulations of some of the world's most virulent issues must be taken with a grain of salt. Apologies in advance.

in Minneapolis. A rage that had been rightfully percolating for a couple of centuries once again exploded onto streets across the country. Passionate protesters of all races sought both justice for innocent black lives as well as a definitive change in the corrupt systems that surround us.

It was a poignant expression of another great pandemic of our time—racism.

> To me the earth's most explosive and pernicious evil is racism, the inability of God's creatures to live as One.
>
> —*Malcolm X*

Whichever country one goes to, one can find the markers of racism: its inherent qualities of contempt, distrust, and arrogance, as well as the resulting injustice and anguish that it inevitably causes for those it disenfranchises. Due to a particularly dark, violent, and complex history, it may be difficult to find a place where racism is as virulent as it is in the United States, but all across the globe there are tribes that feel themselves superior to other tribes, races that have conquered and enslaved other races, and peoples that have a long, violent history of socially and economically subjugating other peoples.

Because at racism's core is the idea of *otherness*. Like many other human behaviors that might have once served some kind of initial survival purpose but are now obsolete and destructive, otherness, one could potentially argue, is something that might have aided humanity in earlier epochs.

For instance: Our tribe, which has curly hair and big feet and lives in *this* cave, is far better than the tribe that has straight hair and little feet and lives in *that* cave. Our people in this valley are *way better* than the idiots who live in that other valley. Our village is so much better than that other village. Our skin color and the way we make our clubs is far superior, so let's conquer them, rob them, and take them as slaves! Our city/culture/nation has a prerogative to subjugate them because of the disgust-inducing otherness of that other city/culture/nation.

Then, eventually, those racist impulses become systematized and insti-tutionalized and much more difficult to unravel. Racism goes hand in hand with the power, militarism, and domination in historical human expansion. (*Especially*, it should be noted, with the Spanish *Requerimiento* of 1513, in which the conquistadors read a screed to "less than human" natives, informing them of the Spaniards' God-given right to conquer and enslave justified on a misreading of Catholic principles. Look it up.)

In actuality, when you examine human DNA, you *cannot determine the race* of the person. Social scientists see race as nothing but a construct, a classification created with the ultimate goal of oppression and othering.

Our outmoded social structures have evolved alongside us, from cave to tribe to valley to village to town to city to fiefdom to kingdom to state to nation to the entire world! And yet we cling to ancient hatreds and prejudices that still cause untold suffering. This racist oth-ering needs to be reexamined and dismantled, with a prime focus put on restitution and healing.

But how?

I have no idea.

We'll dig into this in greater detail later, but essentially by healing the spiritual disease of otherness *as well as* making broken systems more just and fair, we can eventually envision and create the big, diverse human family most of us long for.

SEXISM

Now, if you'll allow me, buckle up your seat belts and let me "man-splain" sexism for you.

Gender-based discrimination is another of our current societal pan-demics and one that has existed for millennia.

Despite the recent progress made with the #MeToo movement in Hollywood and the workplace, women around the world continue to be routinely belittled, abused, held back financially, and disempowered. Whether they are being sexually degraded, objectified, or paid less than their male peers (as in the United States), or treated like broodmares without any basic human rights, as in some areas of the world, one thing is certain: discrimination against women is one of the great global evils of our time and of times past.

In 2013, my wife and I and some Haitian friends started an education initiative in rural Haiti called Lidè Haiti, which centers around providing arts and literacy, scholarships, tutoring, and many other benefits to young Haitian girls. Our students are some of the poorest in the world, working in the farmlands of the Artibonite region. The word "subjugated" doesn't really do justice to how the average Haitian girl is treated. Starting at age nine or ten, they are made to get up before dawn to boil water and make breakfast, a meal they themselves rarely get to enjoy. Haitian girls do all the cleaning and childcare while most of the grown men relax and chat away much of the day. Young girls are expected to work the fields and sell the food in markets. They rarely get any schooling beyond the basics of a second- or third-grade education and are frequently sexually abused as well as trafficked to the nearby Dominican Republic. Often these young girls are "sold" or "loaned" to uncaring families in the city as *restaveks*, unpaid domestic workers who, like indentured servants, receive room and board (and only in the rarest of circumstances an education) in lieu of compensation. Although the lives of adolescent boys in the region can also be incredibly difficult, they do not undergo near the amount of exploitation, disrespect, and overwork that their sisters do.

This is a portrait of your average rural Haitian girl, but it is also a comparative snapshot of the more than 130 million girls around the developing world who are not in school.

Fortunately, we have found education to be a path not only out of poverty but also out of subjugation. It creates resilience, hope, and community as well.

Meanwhile, in parts of the world with higher living standards, there are also severe problems: we see reproductive rights being rolled back in the United States, wives being beaten legally in Russia, and Iranian women and girls arrested and killed for not wearing the hijab. "Women! Life! Freedom!" is being shouted at the police on the streets of Tehran. It is clear that we have a long way to go before this pandemic is healed.

There is far too much to say about the countless generations of subjugation of women by men throughout history to do this incredibly important topic any kind of justice in a couple of brief paragraphs.

As we bring ever greater justice into our laws and governments as well as instill in our young ones the vital importance of girls' education, the power of motherhood, and the sacred awesomeness of the divine feminine, women's rights and empowerment will inevitably flourish.

MATERIALISM

Our next world-encompassing disease from the *Soul Boom* pandemic buffet is that of materialism and its chief expression—consumerism.

> Materialism, noun: A tendency to consider material possessions and physical comfort more important than spiritual values.
>
> —*Oxford Languages*

Like racism, materialism comes from an ancient, base desire to survive in a treacherous world. Accruing stuff could mean the difference between life and death for many millennia of humankind's existence. A tribe who had a cave filled with corn, pointy sticks, furs, and deer jerky had a better chance of making it through the winter and surviving until the next harvest. A village with the best goods, like butter churners, windmills, anvils, and sturdy fences, might become more desirable and attract a better "clientele" to be a part of its community. Status would be increased for the chief, warlord, or king who had the shiniest objects.

> Steal a little and they put you in jail; steal a lot and they make you king.
>
> —*Bob Dylan*

This isn't that different from wealth and consumerism in the modern world. Accruing stuff. Showing it off. Stockpiling. Gaining power, status, and self-esteem from ownership.

Down in our ancient caveman brainstems there lies a series of deeply embedded synapses that deal in the instincts, fears, and impulses that inspire the amassing of goods. Pleasurable dopamine is released when we feel we have accumulated enough things, afforded ourselves increased comfort, and are safe with all of our "stuff."

I remember when the COVID-19 lockdown first started and things like toilet paper, canned goods, and pasta *flew* off the shelves. My wife, Holiday, was at the store during that first week, and she showed me on her phone how the shelves were empty except for a few bags of strange, obscure, expensive foreign beans. I told her, "BUY THE BEANS! ALL OF THEM! BUY THE EXPENSIVE FOREIGN BEANS!" I felt a twinge of that prehistoric panic. I didn't want to STARVE! TO! DEATH! in my nice house in leafy, suburban Los Angeles! Can you imagine? So she came home with strange-shaped navy beans and sorghum and crazy expensive black Japanese soybeans, which, even as I write this, are sitting in my cupboard gathering dust and will probably never be eaten. But dagnabbit, my ancient caveman deprivation brain-terror had been placated. Soothed with weird Japanese beans.

These same tendencies play out to this day on the pages of *Vanity Fair*, in music videos, and on reality shows. Increased status, sexual dynamism, power, and esteem—all achieved through the accumulation of things.

And let's not forget that some of the most popular videos for young people on YouTube are "unboxing" videos, which regularly rack up hundreds of millions of views. In these vomitous, glossily lit entertainments, the host is literally narrating the unwrapping and showcasing of a toy, an electronic good, or a high-end designer fashion accessory for the camera with rapturous awe.

When mass public consumerism gained momentum in the twentieth century, especially with the rise of advertising on radio and television, ad agencies began their reign. They figured out rather quickly how to stimulate those deep human brain synapses in order to manipulate us into wanting to buy more and more, to convince us that we needed stuff that we had previously been just fine without. Following the findings of behaviorist B. F. Skinner, the "Mad Men" learned about dopamine responses and reward stimuli and used it to affect consumer behavior. (Later, this same psychological map would be tapped by social media companies as well as app and game developers to harness the same "uncertainty" and "variability" reward system that a slot machine uses.)

That same panicked FOMO (fear of missing out) that I experienced at the beginning of the pandemic with those weird Japanese beans has been fostered and cultivated in board meetings on Madison Avenue for decades. How are we going to get Joe Smith to buy Colgate instead of Crest, or Chevy over Ford, or this floor wax versus that floor wax? Will we use sex? (This particular brand will make you more attractive.) Fear? (This brand will stop dangerous things from happening.) Status? (This brand will make you more well liked and revered.) Well-being? (This brand will make you feel sated and content.)

These same manipulations are also used to make people want to buy things they "never knew they needed!" Things they had never bought previously! How often have we perused ads online and been tempted by the picture, description, or emotional aura around a new object?

A few years ago, everyone was talking about the Instant Pot. My wife and I don't really cook anything but the basics (i.e., scrambled eggs), but I *had* to have an Instant Pot. I saw ads and read articles about how easy it made cooking and how simple it was to make a nourishing and tasty meal. I mean, look at the name—it even has the word "instant" in it! It's like the replicator from *Star Trek*—you just *think* what you want, and it will emerge, steaming and delicious, right?

And now? My Instant Pot literally has not been plugged in for three years. (Actually, now that I think about it . . . I could cook some of those weird Japanese beans in it. Crisis averted! Win, win!)

My hope is that as we develop an understanding of our spiritual reality, and seek ever greater levels of community and an economy based on sharing, our ancient primal need to amass and obtain at all costs will be replaced with that other primal need: to lend, give, sacrifice, and collaborate.

UNJUST ECONOMIC EXTREMES

Related to this unchecked consumerism is the grotesque pandemic of global economic inequality. The statistics are staggering. A symptom of this disease is that the world's eight richest men currently own as much wealth as the poorest 50 percent of the world's population, according to Oxfam International. That's almost four billion people! The top three billionaires own as many financial assets as the poorest *forty-eight countries combined!* The haves are getting havier and the have-nots are getting increasingly have-notier.

This grotesque wealth disparity affects health care, education, nutrition, food security, child mortality, and countless other issues that devastate the world's poor.[2]

While increasing taxes on the rich in order to give more social services to the poor is certainly good in theory (and occasionally in practice), it isn't the panacea for this extremely complicated and systemically ingrained issue.

Besides increased taxation, I suppose we as a culture need to reach a spiritually evolved state where a mega-rich multibillionaire *could not sleep at night* knowing there was hunger somewhere in the world. They would voluntarily seek to give away their fortunes to improve the lot of

---

2 There's absolutely nothing wrong with someone like Jeff Bezos, Bill Gates, or Mark Zuckerberg founding an amazing, innovative company and profiting from it. However, it is *not* just or right for these men to be able to amass, ruthlessly protect, and frivolously spend this staggering wealth while hundreds of millions of other humans suffer. The immensity of the income gap between billionaires and the impoverished is, quite simply, unjust and unsustainable.

the destitute. And, conversely, if the rest of humanity could not tolerate the remorse in their hearts while economic injustice ravaged the poor, then some substantive change might finally be enacted. In addition, from a spiritual perspective, we need to shift our view of true success away from the accumulation of wealth and toward nobility, selflessness, and generosity.

You may say I'm a dreamer, but like Gene Roddenberry (and John Lennon), I may not be the only one.

NATIONALISM AND MILITARISM

Many believed that after World War II, the formation of the United Nations, and the success of the Marshall Plan, we would enter a new world order of peace based on the interconnectedness of countries and continents. Then, despite the Cold War and nuclear proliferation, in the late '80s and early '90s, the Berlin Wall fell, and the European Union grew and strengthened. Perestroika was enacted, and many again thought that we *finally* had the opportunity to bring about the unity of the world's nations. But that utopia has yet to manifest. Instead, a large number of countries around the world have moved in the other direction, toward authoritarianism and a toxic obsession with nationalism.

And with the 2022 invasion of Ukraine by Russia, war once again is burning away and killing hundreds of thousands along the edge of Europe.

I do believe there *is* such a thing as "healthy patriotism"—a measured pride in one's country and culture—but that should not be confused with the kind of "my country always, right or wrong" that goes hand in hand with leaders seeking military superiority and attempting to whip their populace into a frenzy. George Bernard Shaw wrote about this absurdity by saying that patriotism was a "conviction that a particular country is the best in the world because you were born in it."

Unfortunately, nationalism arrives in unison with militarism. The threat of war (or proxy war) is, at the time of writing, at its highest level since the early 1960s, and it's unclear as to where the next potentially devastating nuclear flashpoint could be. China and Taiwan? North Korea and the United States? Pakistan and India? Israel and Iran? Russia and practically everyone else? It's anybody's guess. But stockpiles of weapons (including about twelve thousand nuclear warheads worldwide), military posturing, and increasing nationalistic furor and fervor are bringing the world once again to the brink of unimaginable conflict.

The *Bulletin of the Atomic Scientists* is an organization and a publication that includes, most notably, the Doomsday Clock, a symbolic device that measures human-made threats to our species and planet and is regularly summed up with the following question: "Is humanity safer or at greater risk this year compared to last year?"

For the year 2022, this Doomsday Clock was the closest it's ever been to its metaphorical midnight: one hundred seconds away.

The bulletin describes the threat in the following terms:

Humanity continues to face two simultaneous existential dangers—nuclear war and climate change—that are compounded by a threat multiplier, cyber-enabled information warfare, that undercuts society's ability to respond. The international security situation is dire, not just because these threats exist, but because world leaders have allowed the international political infrastructure for managing them to erode.

In the early days of the COVID-19 pandemic, I remember seeing videos of entire cities cheering and banging pots in unison every evening to show support for frontline workers. And images of sequestered neighbors in Italy playing music together across their balconies. It was a glimpse into what the world could look like if it was truly able to unite and come together in solidarity. Perhaps therein lies the antidote to nationalism—to find the deeper, more meaningful, and less random and transient bond of unity between humans.

CLIMATE CHANGE

And now we get to the granddaddy—and by some accounts, most complicated—of all pandemics: climate change.

On one level, it's quite simple. Man-made CO_2 and other greenhouse gases released predominantly by the energy sector, manufacturing, commercial agriculture, air conditioning, construction, deforestation, and transportation are creating a heat-trapping blanket layer around Earth.

The repercussions of this "global warming," such as extreme weather systems, ocean acidification, glacial melt, and loss of biodiversity (i.e., extinction), take a deadly toll. Also complicating climate change is that its impact first affects the poorest populations (usually people of color) and the tens or hundreds of millions of climate refugees that are already surging from the south to the north.

As a matter of fact, the entire Syrian civil war and its resulting refugee crisis, which had a devastating effect on much of the Middle East and Europe, was initiated by a climate change–induced drought, the worst in Syria's modern history. That drought, combined with record unemployment, moved the country toward a brutal civil war and subsequent humanitarian disaster. There will be many more of these human disasters to come.

If you dig deeper, addressing climate change is far more complicated than simply reducing CO_2 emissions. The underbelly of this pandemic reveals many forces at work: consumerism, capitalism, competition, profit, and greed. Ultimately, the climate disaster is caused by the corrosive disease of gluttonous consumption and an addictive need for nonstop economic growth that sucks resources into the ever-smoking crack pipe of "economic progress." It is "money-making über alles" that trumps any kind of connection to and respect for the sanctity of nature and the balance of the universe. Mother Earth being used as both an endless mine for exploitation and a garbage dump. Climate issues are intricately and inextricably intertwined with, into, and around social justice issues as well as the have-ish-ness and have-not-ishness I outlined in the earlier pandemics.

And yet *this* particular pandemic is preventable. Or at least salvageable. *If* (and this is quite a big "if") the world, in its strongest possible committed action, comes together around the international accords of the Paris Agreement of 2016. *If* we ban coal. *If* we cease exploring for oil. *If* we tax polluters. *If* we plant a couple billion trees. *If* we limit beef consumption and stop deforestation. *If* we develop renewable energy sources like wind, solar, and geothermal.

That's a lot of "ifs."

But the most important of these "ifs" is *if*, as part of a spiritual revolution, we work together to live in modest harmony alongside the natural world and with right-sized economic growth.

⇒◆⇐

When you stop and deeply consider these insidious pandemics of injustice, disease, and imbalance, you start to see connections between them that make it much more difficult to examine them individually. Climate change is intricately connected to GREED and its resulting MATERIALISM, which eats away at most every culture in the world. Greed is connected to SELFISHNESS, which is a vice that lies behind, beneath, and around the economic injustices that dovetail into RACISM and SEXISM. Selfishness also links up with the NARCISSISM and EGO that fuels militarism and NATIONALISM and contributes to the alienation that triggers LONELINESS and MENTAL HEALTH STRUGGLES, which are made worse by materialism, bringing us right back to where we started!

Fortunately, there is hope.

I return to the early days of the COVID-19 health crisis and the concurrent racial uprisings sparked by the murder of George Floyd. At that time, the world community of human beings were "all in this together."

Compassion was at an all-time high as we suffered alongside communities as diverse as Italy, Brazil, and grieving black moms in, say, Minneapolis. The world seemed so interconnected.

We *Homo sapiens* are struggling to emerge from our turbulent adolescence into our inevitable maturity and wisdom. However, our species, like a pill-popping, porn-obsessed, cocktail-swilling, cocaine-fueled teenager, may need to "hit bottom" and go to some kind of metaphorical rehab before any significant change is ultimately made.

What does that look like? Well, just like with an addict, all the chickens of denial need to eventually come home to roost. All the issues that keep getting pushed to the back burner and swept under the carpet will rise up, and we will be forced to face the various pandemics I've outlined here.

But how? How do we solve these overwhelming issues? Through increased legislation, voting, and changes to jurisprudence? Through modifications to economic policy and social welfare on the national and international level? More global treaties? More regulation? More international cooperation?

Of course, these legislative changes are crucial. In the United States, we *needed* to abolish slavery with the Thirteenth Amendment. It was imperative that we, as a culture striving for ever-increasing justice and equality, uphold *Brown v. Board of Education*, approve the Voting Rights Act, and eliminate Jim Crow laws. We've passed plenty of much-needed laws to try and eradicate the gross injustices perpetrated against America's black citizens. All of that legislation was crucial. But did it heal us? Did it do anything about white America's tendency toward racism?

Not even close.

In 2009, we even elected a black president who left office eight years later with an approval rating of 57 percent. A president who (according to most of my secular/urban/liberal friends) was supposed to unite our nation, provide *hope*, and build bridges between the races. And yet, somehow, the backlash to his presidency fueled even greater division and actually increased a virulent prejudice against immigrants, Muslims, members of the LGBTQ+ population, and many types of those aforementioned "others." The cultural, psychological, and yes, spiritual roots of the cancer of "otherness" are still very much alive and well.

The fundamental cancer doesn't have an immediate political solution because, as much as they might appear to be at first glance, the problems themselves are not essentially political.

They have only a spiritual cure, because when you examine them deeply, the issues, imbalances, and diseases are actually spiritual in nature. As long as we have a competitive, antagonistic, self-centered way of interacting with each other, we will never be able to overcome any of these toxic, life-threatening pandemics.

And this, my friends, my readers, my fellow humans, brings me (finally!) to my thesis and the ultimate purpose of this book. A thesis that, I hope, will gradually unfold and become clear over the coming chapters.

This is why we need a spiritual revolution!

The solutions to the global pandemics that face us as a species don't lie in the halls of government but in every human heart and soul.

Jesus asked us to "love thy neighbor as thyself."

The Buddha once said, "Whoever would think, on the basis of a body like this, to exalt himself or disparage another: What is that if not blindness?"

The Quran states, "Allah loveth the just dealers."

Baha'u'llah writes, "Let your heart burn with loving-kindness for all who may cross your path."

The Hindu teacher Sri M says, "Love is a many-splendored entity. . . . You want to give, want to sacrifice your personal convenience for the sake of your beloved. . . . I plead, please, that we fall in love with humanity as a whole."

In Judaism, *tikkun olam* refers to the divine prerogative, or a type of *aleinu* (our duty), toward repairing the world.

Again, as Mr. William Carlos Williams, the poet who launched this chapter, so pointedly brought to our attention, men die miserably every day for lack of what is found in poems. And I propose that *humanity* suffers every day from lack of spirituality—the nourishment that can be found in the ancient wisdom-based writings for the soul, those achingly beautiful words that stream from the one Divine Source. Teachings that have been around in one form or another for a very long time—inspired, holy wisdom we desperately need to revolutionize and transform how we approach, consider, and ultimately address *everything* we humans do on planet Earth.

Because the keys necessary to this much-needed transformational change can be found in the core of spiritual writings, holy texts, and essential teachings of the various religious faiths throughout history.

Do not fear, skeptics, atheists, antireligionists, and agnostics. We don't need to ascribe to any particular faith in order to put these practices to use individually or collectively. There is, after all, a significant difference between "spirituality" and "religion." It's why "spiritual but not religious" is the largest, fastest-growing belief system in our country.

However, while we don't need religion per se, we do need to be in a humble enough posture of learning to admit the following:

As a species, we are quite lost right now, and perhaps the systems, beliefs, practices, and behaviors that society is currently operating under are simply not working. Maybe they are founded on some faulty, unsustainable assumptions. Maybe political parties, international intergovernmental organizations, and our Washington, DC, leaders, won't fix us. Maybe our existing economic systems, nonprofits, and social movements don't have the answers either.

We need another way forward. A soul-inspired revolution.

But before we can understand what that looks like, we need to gain the vastest possible perspective and go all the way forward. As far forward as we can go. Forward to the very end.

To the Big Sleep itself.

CHAPTER THREE

DEATH AND HOW TO LIVE IT

When you are in doubt as to which you should serve, forsake the material appearance for the invisible principle, for this is everything.

—*Alexandre Dumas*

Live as if you were to die tomorrow. Learn as if you were to live forever.

—*Mahatma Gandhi*

I was screwed. My father was dead, and his body was laying on a metal table at a funeral home. We only had an hour to wash it in preparation for burial, according to the Baha'i funeral rites. However, there wasn't any kind of appropriate bowl to hold the water for said washing. Sweat pouring off me, I jumped in my deceased father's pickup truck and tore out of the funeral home parking lot, on a quest for this holy grail of bowls in the remote farming town of Wenatchee, Washington.

Preparation of a body for burial in the Baha'i tradition involves ritually washing the corpse, saying prayers, wrapping the body in a shroud, and placing on the deceased's finger a special ring, which reads,

I came forth from God, and return unto Him, detached from all save Him, holding fast to His Name, the Merciful, the Compassionate.

Having played the offbeat mortician Arthur on HBO's *Six Feet Under*, I was actually a little familiar with the strangeness of morticians and the funeral business in general. I did not, however, foresee myself in a situation like this.

I had arrived at the funeral home wracked with grief and wet with sweat, as there was an epic heat wave at that time in that area of central Washington State. The mortician, Michael, was a very nice and accommodating man with a trim mustache who looked like someone who collected things in his basement—things like wind-up toys and vintage '70s porn. However, when I entered the hushed, air-conditioned sanctuary of the funeral home, he made it clear that he didn't have an appropriate vessel to put the water in for us to then wash and purify my father's body.

"I could see if we've got a take-out bowl from like a Chinese restaurant in the back or something," he offered, kindly. And I agreed to let him look. He shuffled down a dark hallway and started banging around in some cupboards in what was obviously some mysterious, hidden mortician's back kitchen.

I had no idea morticians even had or needed kitchens. But I suppose it made sense. I mean, preparing bodies has got to be some tough work, and a mortician's gotta eat! What a strange and specific location when you stop to think about it. A good candidate for one of those comedy improv shows where they shout out, "OK, we're gonna need a location for this next exercise!" Next time we all go to an improv show at some college campus, church basement, or rinky-dink theater, let's all respond, "Kitchen in the back of a mortuary!"

Anyway, back to the story.

The funeral was in about an hour and a half at a remote cemetery. The clock was ticking. My new friend Michael the mortician was digging and clattering around in that mortician's kitchen. I heard a female employee enter and say, "What are you looking for?"

"A bowl. I don't know. A cereal bowl or a Tupperware one maybe?"

"Let me help you look," Mortician No. 2 said. More clanging and clattering.

Then it hits me. Wait. I'm going to use an old take-out bowl or Tupperware tub to hold the water to wash my father's now-deceased sacred human vessel as we wrap it in a shroud of sacred white linen and say sacred prayers over him for his sacred eternal soul?!

"Never mind!" I shouted down the hallway. "I'll go get a bowl."

"Hey, how about a teapot?" I heard him call back. "Would that work?"

"That's OK, Michael! Be right back."

"OK, but hurry! We have to get going to the cemetery real soon!" he yelled after me.

I ran huffing across the parking lot and jumped into the truck. After tearing around the sweltering metropolis of Wenatchee, I found a Target store, screeched to a stop, and bolted inside.

Panting, sometimes sobbing (and masked because of COVID), I asked a lady where they might have some nice glass bowls.

"Aisle 37B!" she chirped at me and gestured toward the far side of an endless fluorescent maze. I started to jog, ever deeper into the bowels of this museum of "stuff."

This is truly absurd, I thought to myself: a minor television celebrity is jogging through a Target the size of an airport in a black suit, sweaty hair pressed to his head, trying to track down a bowl nice enough to use to wash his father's dead body, which is laying on a table in a basement a few miles away. Thank God no one shopping at this Target knows who I am or what's going on. I thought of my dad's spirit, looking down on me and chortling heartily. I smiled. This would have been *exactly* his sense of humor. He would have loved telling this story. In fact, he's probably telling it to some weird angels as you're reading this:

"Get this! My son, the big TV hotshot, was racing through the Wenatchee Target in a sweaty suit and snotty mask in order to get the perfect dead-body-washing bowl from aisle 37B!"

My father was an amazing man. A painter. A writer. A sewer construction manager. A deeply thoughtful contemplator of spiritual thoughts and ideas. An artist.

He died of heart disease a few days before the preceding events. Didn't make it through a major quadruple bypass surgery due to all the blockage in his arteries.

My stepmom, Carla, and I were there when he was eventually unplugged from the machines. We gave the OK. What struck me about the moment was how it was *exactly* like one of those scenes in a sappy hospital show: the beeping machines; the hushed doctors and nurses; the squeaking of shoes on the linoleum floors; the tangle of wires and tubes descending toward a still, grayish body; the flick of a switch; the emotional goodbye.

The doctors were losing him. It was time. They gave a rough estimate of one to two hours before his blood pressure lowered to such an extent that his heart would eventually stop beating.

We stood over him. Weeping. Praying. Aching.

And as the breathing tube was removed from his trachea, and his lungs stopped lifting in his chest, a small truth about life and death became incredibly clear to me. It was a lightning strike. *Of course!*

This body, this vessel, was *not* my father. The reality of Robert George Wilson—abstract painter, sewer truck dispatcher, science-fiction writer, Seahawks fan, student of spirituality, he of the twinkling eyes and chuckling laughter—was not contained in or defined by this, for lack of a better word, *corpse.* Yes, his sweet face was there. His occasional stray eyebrow hair, jutting up like some weed from a sidewalk crack. His mustache was there. Recognizable scars and moles on his arms and hands. But that wasn't him. That still, vacant body on that hospital bed in the ICU was simply a suit he once wore.

To the materialist or physicalist, our "life" (i.e., the consciousness that is bouncing around like a neuro-electric pachinko ball in our brains) is physical in reality and electrochemical in manifestation. So when the heart stops, the brain stops, and the electrical impulses stop, that, my friends, is the end of the story. The candle has been snuffed. Personality, life, thought-sensation, and all awareness are done with. Lights out. Fade to black.

I, however, felt there was something more than these scientific theories. Armed with nothing other than thousands of years of mystical writings, a deep gut feeling, a belief in the majesty of the universe, and wild respect for the mystery and complexity of human consciousness, I knew in that moment that there was something deeper afoot. That a *life*—mine, yours, my father's—could not simply come to an end because brain-centered activity ceased.

Consciousness, you see, is one of the last frontiers of science. It's kind of like the big bang: ultimately unknowable and yet filled with complexities, revelations, and mysteries that radiate out from it.

In fact, scientifically, this fundamental human mystery is often called the "hard problem of consciousness." Scientists, try as they might, have a limited understanding of what consciousness actually is, how it works, or more importantly, *why it's there.* They don't even know some of the basic building blocks, like why our memory seems infinite or why it resides in multiple parts of the brain. Why we dream. Why we need emotions.

Yes, researchers can track electromagnetic and chemical pathways and different flare-ups of brain activity when one is, say, playing ping-pong versus reading Proust, but they are still trying to figure out how any of it puzzles together with DNA to make you *you*. Your thoughts/emotions/personality/will are in a constant state of buzzing, bouncing, reflecting, pondering, wondering, and evolving. Yes, that seems to be *somewhat* attached—and related—to the big, gray human brain matter, but it is also true that human consciousness is one of the greatest mysteries in the known universe.

To a scientific materialist, such as scientist and philosopher Daniel Dennett, the only way to explain consciousness is to say that it is all an illusory trick of the brain. For Dennett and many others, this is what happens: A kaleidoscope of impressions incessantly pour into our sensory portals. They are cataloged and sorted, and responses need to be continuously meted out. In order to make sense of all this stimulus and information (including potential dangers), the synapses of our brains fill in the gaps and create the cinematic, emotional, and interactive narrative sensation we call consciousness. All these thousands of stimuli are effortlessly, seamlessly, and instantaneously woven into a single, integrated, emotional, personality-filled, subjective experience. But it's merely an illusion (or delusion) of consciousness.

And, materialists continue, if this consciousness thing *is* more than some electromagnetic pulses in our brain, then shouldn't there be, from a purely scientific point of view, an evolutionary reason why it developed? Shouldn't there be some kind of *proof* that consciousness helps us survive and multiply?

Well, oddly enough, there isn't. There is zero evidence of how contemplation, emotion, self-awareness, reflection (not to mention poetry, art, and prayer), and the internal cinematic experience of consciousness help or have helped humanity propagate and thrive. Wouldn't we do just as well if we had monkey minds up there? A more limited cognitive perception that might be only slightly more evolved than our closest relatives, the chimpanzees?

Respectfully, and without any hard science to back me up, I and many others disagree with this purely physical assessment of the most profound of human experiences.

My consciousness, as well as yours, is a mysterious, ineffable, dancing diorama of emotions, memories, perceptions, triggers, and thoughts. We take in, blend, and yet transcend senses, creating a peculiar alchemy of the awareness and sensation of being a human, of having a moment-by-moment experience of living. In the philosophy and science of mind, these little bites of memorable conscious experiences are called "qualia." In one second my consciousness is making a decision on what kind of tennis balls to buy, the next it's remembering my first date with my wife, then it's worrying about something I have no control over like how late my mother-in-law's plane is going to be. Then, all of a sudden, my uber-mind is still, quiet, and has an all-encompassing spiritual insight. Suddenly, it focuses on a bird singing from a cactus. How does it sit on those thorny branches, I wonder? It adds, subtracts, contemplates, and laughs, ponders, and reacts. It is constantly illumined with the ongoing flickering of feelings swirling around the human heart and peppered by beautiful flashes of memory, of qualia.

Another aspect of consciousness that science doesn't well explain is that it *evolves*. What is the mind awareness that a fetus has in the womb? An infant at birth? A toddler? And how does it differ from the thought awareness and self-reflection of a kindergartener? A fifth grader? Our minds seem not to be fully "online" until somewhere around our late teenage or young adult years. Does consciousness itself continue to grow throughout our adult lives? Or rather does it fade as we age? Does this matterless, energyless, boundless, mysterious "experience" of *being-ness* continue after our bodies stop working? Would there ever be a way to prove that?

All of this human experience would be so much easier to explain if we could definitively conclude that our minds worked simply as cold, predictable, robotic, computer-like tools of perception used only for immediate problem solving and survival. But unlike what the B. F. Skinner behaviorists might lead us to believe, we don't have fleshy Spock-like calculators in our head bone, tabulating our next move for no reason other than to procreate, socialize, and feed ourselves.

To quote neuroscientist and philosopher David Chalmers, the king of consciousness studies, "Why is the performance of these functions accompanied by *experience*?"

Although we have insistent, animal-like impulses and reactions that originate deep in our brainstem and pull us toward certain behaviors, our emotions and thought processes are not simply a slightly more advanced version of the cognitive experience of a bear, dog, or ape. These scientific/physicalist explanations of how we perceive and process fail to accurately explain the totality of our living, breathing experience.

Scientists might be able to prove they can locate the feeling of love in the brain. A synapse. A chemical. That little junction in the gray matter that lights up under an MRI or CAT scan. But that particular electrochemical transaction would simply *not* be the same as the *experience* of love.

Science studies the *notes* of consciousness, but what we actually live is *the music!* We write operas. We hold our babies and weep at the beauty of it all. We smell a leaf and are transported to a time when we were smelling that exact same type of leaf on a dreamy summer's day when we were seven years old. We *adore*. Deeply. We are profoundly sad. We commune. We draw/write/create from places of inspiration deep in our essence. We struggle. We ponder our death. We compose books and poetry about all the amazing qualia we've experienced.

The red wheelbarrow of consciousness, glazed with rainwater, beside the white chickens of experience.

It simply doesn't compute that it all adds up to nothing.

In fact, when someone asks about "the meaning of life," aren't they really asking about "the meaning of consciousness"? What does this complicated, personality-filled life experience *mean*? *Why* do we have it? Why were we shambling, goofy mammals gifted with it? Why does it do what it does, the way it does? Toward what end shall I use its tools, powers, and perceptions? Does this consciousness really end when my heart stops? Can it be expanded? If there is a God, what would God's consciousness be like? Is God simply the consciousness of all living things?

The questions continue to pile up!

If you believe, as many do, that consciousness resides solely in the brain, consider the story of Noah Wall, who was born with only 2 percent of his brain and whose survival was deemed by doctors to be "impossible." You would think that would limit his consciousness to that of a potato, but little Noah's brain actually *grew* (which medical science had previously deemed impossible), and his mind, personality, and interactivity are in a seemingly normal range! He speaks almost at age level, and all this *without having a cerebral cortex*, which is, according to biological science, considered the seat of consciousness itself!

Many studies are finding that a great deal of our decisions and feelings are actually based in our intestines, our guts, and the bazillions of bacteria and the two hundred million neurons that line our digestive tract. In fact, many scientists are now referring to our guts as our *second brains*! Talk about the advice to "go with your gut" or the question "What does your gut tell you?" taking on new meaning!

In the book *The Expanded Mind* by Annie Murphy Paul, her thesis is that the brain merely acts as the conductor, and a majority of our thinking is done by the entirety of our body, internal organs, gestures, and sensory perceptions.

Now why the hell am I talking about all this? Why did I start out talking about my dad's death only to dive into the mystery of consciousness?

Because I believe that to see the world through spiritual glasses, we have to start at the very end. If my previous observation/supposition is true, and we are *not* just our bodies, and, in fact, our consciousness transcends our physical limitations, then what does that mean for how we live our lives until the body's final breath?

—•—

The first evidence of humanity having some kind of spiritual journey is seen in some of the earliest human settlements, more specifically the burial mounds of thirty thousand to one hundred thousand years ago. In almost every single ancient culture around the world (including in pre–*Homo sapiens* species like Peking Man and Neanderthals), bodies were buried in shallow graves, and alongside those bodies were regularly placed items and objects that the deceased individual might need in the afterlife: swords, jewelry, pets, canoes, tools.

Why? Why would humans, from the beginning of time, not just toss bodies aside the same way animals do? It's a hell of a lot easier. Plus, the time, expense, and difficulty of digging ceremonial graves without backhoes or even shovels, and burying bodies alongside still-usable items, makes *zero* financial sense. An ax might take *months* to make, and its materials would have been incredibly valuable. It would be *far* more useful to the tribe or family to keep and recycle jewelry or weapons rather than to have them interred with a body and lost forever. *Unless* the items weren't seen as being lost forever and were instead viewed as essential tools for whatever awaited the dead man on the next chapter of his mysterious, ongoing journey.

What kind of rituals or ceremonies were carried out as the dead were placed into the ground? What kind of communion with the "souls" of the dead took place?

This so-called ancestor worship (also commonly known as veneration of the dead) is perhaps the first real religion humanity ever knew. Archaeologists have documented that *Homo sapiens* from every corner of the world call on the spirits of their ancestors to intervene on their behalf, to send blessings, and to watch over their families. Perhaps this was even a precursor to a belief in gods. Before we would pray to a supernatural sun or rain god, maybe humans prayed to our deceased wise grandfather's soul to aid with the hunt or crops or fertility or help in finding the equivalent of a prehistoric parking space.

What is it in our ancient DNA that tells us collectively there is something beyond this physical realm? That we need to ritualize the burial of a body, inter it in a sacred place, and provide items to help it along its journey? Are we wired for a spiritual connection to our lost loved ones? And if so, why? I mean, from a sociological perspective, it provides zero benefit to the species.

Was this ancient connection to the afterlife due to dreams? After all, dreams are bizarre and surreal, existing outside of the limitations of time and space—one moment you're in a grocery store, the next you're yelling at your mother in your childhood bedroom when she suddenly morphs into your best friend Carl and is wearing a football helmet. They are a window into a world beyond the limitations of time and space. They sometimes contain inexplicable, mystical correlations to what happens in the "real world."

Both consciousness and dreams give us a portal into viewing death in a slightly different context. Here are some other ways of looking at it:

Death is not extinguishing the light; it is putting out the lamp because dawn has come.

—*Rabindranath Tagore*

What happens after death is so unspeakably glorious that our imagination and our feelings do not suffice to form even an approximate conception of it. The dissolution of our time-bound form in eternity brings no loss of meaning.

—*Carl Jung*

Die happily and look forward to taking up a new and better form. Like the sun, only when you set in the West can you rise in the East.

—*Rumi*

Death is simply a shedding of the physical body like the butterfly shedding its cocoon. It is a transition to a higher state of consciousness where you continue to perceive, to understand, to laugh and to be able to grow.

—*Elizabeth Kubler-Ross*

Everything science has taught me—and continues to teach me—strengthens my belief in the continuity of our spiritual existence after death. Nothing disappears without a trace.

—*Wernher von Braun*

I'm not afraid of death because I don't believe in it. It's just getting out of one car and into another.

—*John Lennon*

I wonder what car John Lennon is in now. I'm guessing an Aston Martin DB3.

———◆———

The great British documentarian and philosopher Adam Curtis talks about how in Victorian times people spoke about death constantly but never about sex. In contemporary society, the reverse is true: we *never* talk about death but are *obsessed* with sex. I think that's why the COVID-19 pandemic was especially terrifying to us. As body bags were stacked and hospitals were brimming, it forced us to seriously examine the topic that, culturally, we least like to face.

Yet death is a perfect lens through which to view life itself. It's the ultimate framing device. It puts everything into perspective. In fact, historically, death has always been used to reframe how we see life in practically every culture around the world.

Think of the famous Sioux saying, proclaimed by Crazy Horse as he led men into battle: "Today is a good day to die." A phrase apparently not only used in battle by many tribes but also in everyday life as a reminder of the preciousness of "living for today."

In early Buddhist writings, the term *maranasati* translates as "remember death." It's a mindfulness meditation through which the urgency of living in the present moment is cast into focus by contemplating one's mortality. There's even a meditation where one tracks and ponders the nine stages of a corpse decomposing, from "festering and blue" all the way to bones turning into dust.

In Mexico, there is Dia de los Muertos (Day of the Dead), a wild celebration to help us drink in our mortality, rife with profound and humorous rituals and shrines. And lots and lots of skeletons.

The essayist Michel de Montaigne spoke of an ancient Egyptian custom where, during times of festivities, a skeleton would be brought out, and it would be said, "Drink and be merry for when you're dead you will look like this."

Sufi (Muslim) mystics were sometimes referred to as "people of the graves" because they would spend so much time in graveyards pondering their mortality.

In the country of Bhutan, happiness is a central focus of life and culture. The government doesn't solely measure economic improvement but also its citizens' well-being, with its tracking of GNH or Gross National Happiness. And yet, in the same culture, one is expected to think about death at least three times a day. Incredible for any nation, but especially for one that is so linked to fostering its happiness.

In Tibetan Buddhism, there is a long, rich "death meditation" history. The renowned eleventh-century teacher Atisa had nine meditations on this theme:

1. Death is inevitable.

2. Our personal life span is decreasing continuously day by day.

3. Death will come, whether or not we are prepared for it.

4. Human life expectancy is uncertain.

5. There are many causes of death.

6. The human body is fragile and vulnerable.

7. At the time of death, our material resources are not of use to us.

8. Our loved ones cannot keep us from death.

9. Our own body cannot help us at the time of our death.

The Tibetan guru Padmasambhava says,

Thine own awareness,
shining, void, and inseparable
from the Ground of Radiance,
hath no birth,
hath no death,
and is the Immutable Light.

American poet Walt Whitman supports this idea too:

All goes onward and outward, nothing collapses,
And to die is different from what any one supposed, and luckier.

Think of the ancient Roman Stoic ritual of memento mori, the daily practice of remembering our mortality. When there was a parade through ancient Rome, the general, senator, or caesar at the center of the procession would have someone following him, holding the laurel crown over his head and whispering "memento mori" in his ear as the crowds shouted their praise. Translation: "Remember, you are going to die."

But what, exactly, does death put into perspective?

Why, the preciousness of life, you big silly willy!

At my aforementioned SoulPancake media company, we took a big gamble in the early days of launching our programming and produced a show tangentially about death called *My Last Days*. We tried pitching it as a TV show and were flat-out rejected. *No one* did shows about death, we were told. In fact, in many cases, we would pitch the show to a room filled with TV executives who would be sobbing by the end of our presentation, moved and humbled. And then they would mumble something through their tears to the effect of "Sorry, we just can't do a show about death. *But thank you! It's so beautiful!!!*"

So we made it as a short-form docuseries for our YouTube channel (created and directed by the great Justin Baldoni)—a show about what we could learn about life from those who are facing death. This was a *huge* risk. It was a taboo topic in the media. But we made it—a couple dozen portraits of courageous, radiant, beautiful souls who were in their "last days."

Was it sad? A little. Was it inspiring? *A lot!*

Hundreds of millions watched. And we did eventually turn it into a TV show on the CW Network, because sometimes media executives don't know a damn thing.

But back to my point: The show encapsulates so much of what I'm delving into in these paragraphs. The many dozen subjects of this ongoing series would always come back to the exact same handful of essential human truths. The rush of gratitude they felt for every miraculous moment of life they had left. The flood of love they felt for those who were precious to them. The sanctity and fleeting nature of time itself.

Connecting with nature. The need to *slow down* and breathe into every single invaluable moment. Sharing their hearts. Increased compassion. And, finally, regret for the time spent *not* being grateful, loving, and "in the moment."

Not a single subject of the *My Last Days* series said, "Damn, I wish I had *worked more!*" Or spent more time online. Or mindlessly scrolling on their phones. Or gossiping. Or comparing themselves to others. Or in a fog of self-interest, pursuing superficial carnal pleasures and material comforts.

I had a friend named David who was dying of cancer as I was working on this book. He was swimming one day at the age of fifty and felt a pain in his side. Thought nothing of it. It kept coming back. Went to the doctor a week or two later and, out of the blue, was diagnosed with stage 4 stomach cancer, the second-deadliest and the first most painful of cancers. Doctors predicted that he would survive about eighteen months. He lasted about twenty-four. David had a ten-year-old daughter and was completely devastated. Overcome with sadness and fear and yet, at the same time, living his life with a focus, clarity, and joy that I'd never seen from him before. We used to take weekly walks on the beach, and the thing he kept saying to me is, "It's all just static! The noise, the emails, the calls, the bills, the demands, the texts, the to-do lists. You've got to *cut through the static.* None of it matters—see your life with as much clarity as you can. Life is *sooo* short!"

It should be noted that we're all dying of something. In one way or another. For many of us, it'll take a grand total of like eighty-seven years before whatever it is finally gets us. For David, it was two. For me? Who knows. Twenty? Thirty? Forty if I'm lucky? Shakespeare himself says, vis-à-vis the character of old Capulet in *Romeo and Juliet,* "Well, we were born to die."

What is this *static* David is referring to? Are you in it now? Maybe all this talk about death and perspective has quieted it for a short spell.

There is an analogy I heard once about twins in the womb having a conversation. (Which is *ridiculous,* I know. I mean, fetuses can't talk!

They don't even have working lungs!) One says to the other, "I can't wait to get out of here! What adventures await! I bet it's amazing on the other side of that trap door." The other says, "Are you *out of your uterine mind*!? On the other side of that vaginal hatch is nothing but death and blood and screams and chaos! Enjoy your life *in here*! Nothing to do but kick back and enjoy this amniotic fluid and poke your elbows around every once in a while. We'll just keep growing our organs and chillin' in the sac, bro! Oblivion awaits out there! Fight it! Don't *gooo*! *Stay inside at all cost!*"

Isn't that kind of what we do in this life when thinking about the next?

Speaking of babies, there is a terrific spiritual metaphor from the Baha'i teachings that relates babies in wombs to the afterlife.

As we know, the fetus, cells splitting like crazy, is growing all kinds of organs, limbs, and various accoutrements that will come in quite handy in a few short months. Now, if you were able, as in the previous "womb-versation," to converse with said baby in utero and ask it what it was doing with these newly grown eyelids and elbows and ears and knees, the baby would have zero idea. It is quite content just floating and growing, feeling cared for and connected to the all-encompassing motherly presence that quite literally surrounds it. It has no idea what its nascent eyes are for and how important they are and will someday be. It is utterly clueless that its sensory organs, for the most part, will drive its ability to make sense of the physical world. And not only that—they will be portals through which ceaseless wonders will pour into the consciousness of this ever-expanding little being. Paintings by Cézanne, sunsets over deserts, nightingales singing, loved ones whispering that they love them. The smell of Cinnabon in an airport at dawn. Symphonies of light, sound, color, music, art, and inspiration. And from what? A few mushy, weird-looking organs growing on the front and sides of their little heads.[3]

---

3 I don't mean to be ableist here. Those born blind or deaf can use other senses to more than make up for their sensory experiences, and when asked, more often than

Now let's, for a minute, examine ourselves in our physical, post-utero universe through a similar lens. Imagine, if you will, that we are undergoing a related process while walking, talking, learning, laughing, struggling, while in our bodies on womb-planet Earth. What metaphorical "organs" could we possibly be growing here and for what use?

Well, to carry the metaphor forward, on this physical plane, we are growing what we need for whatever realm lies beyond this physical one. (I'm not talking about heaven or hell—more on that silliness in later chapters.) We are continuing the saga of our soul's journey. One transition was from the womb to birth to life (in this material dimension) and then we journey forward to the next transition, which is life to death. (Which is in itself a kind of birth.) In this upcoming metamorphosis, we move onward to the infinite worlds beyond time and space, where we suddenly realize why we needed our souls in the first place! So this world, basically, has to be viewed as a soul-enriching factory! A physical laboratory for developing and nurturing our spiritual essence.

And what will we take with us when we leave? What do we need in the afterlife? The soul dimension? The kingdom of light? Heaven. Bliss. Nirvana. Eternity. The Happy Hunting Grounds. Whatever you want to call it. What will we use there? Certainly not the "stuff" we've accrued over our lives. Probably not even our "personality," at least not how we understand it, as so much of who we are is circumstantial. What would the miracle of consciousness need from an earthly experience?

If, and this is a big supposition, the next world is some sort of heavenly, eternity-and-light-filled state beyond our comprehension, then we will need eternity-and-light-filled things to function effectively there. What are those things? Well, to carry the metaphor forward, the *spiritual* eyes and ears and knees and elbows that we are growing on Earth

---

not, would choose *not* to have missing senses given to them after the fact. I merely use the example of these organs growing in utero to create a larger metaphor.

are actually the attributes of divine light and power. Love, certainly. But also qualities of the Creator.[4]

Many call these divine attributes "spiritual virtues." For some more secular types, they might be referred to as "positive qualities" or "character traits." Virtues are the God-like attributes within us. The same qualities of the saints and the angels, the enlightened and the wise.

Here are a few:

---

4 By the way, I'm doing a whole chapter on the Creator just a few dozen pages from here. It's called "The Notorious G.O.D." Don't let all this God talk throw you. I know it can be off-putting. We'll get it all sorted out. Relax and have a Cinnabon.

The list goes on and on. Literally:

Some of these virtues come easily to us, others not as much.

In this virtue-nurturing context, we are neither living only for this world (as the atheist/materialist/physicalist might aspire to) nor living only for the next world (as the heaven-seeking fundamentalist might be). We are living for both. Because, it seems, both are connected. Are one, actually. Our overarching purpose is pure and simple: *soul growth*. Developing our virtues is about cultivating that part of ourselves that is, at its essence, divine. This ongoing growth process requires a complete and total commitment to the physical plane of existence—this gorgeous, difficult planet, its ups and downs and trials and challenges, its beauty and sorrow. At the same time, it requires a long-tail view of the eternal—knowing that we're in this whole game of life for a very, very, very long haul. As in, like, infinite worlds of existence.

Speaking of the game of life, when I was a kid, we used to play the actual game called the Game of Life. It was and still is preposterous. And just a little bit fun. You started on a square called Infancy and ended on one that read Happy Old Age. The point was to drive around the board and live a truly American or Western way of life. You bought a car, got married, went to college, had kids, and worked a job. Money changed hands. A lot of it. You paid bills and taxes. You "got revenge" against the other players.

And how did you win?

Well, according to the Milton Bradley official rules, "After all players have retired, all players at Millionaire Estates count their money. The richest player takes the 4 LIFE Tiles at Millionaire Estates. All players then count up their money, and add the two figures together (LIFE Tile value plus cash value). The player with the highest dollar amount wins!"

In other words, everyone retires as a millionaire. The person with the most toys wins. Game over.

And don't even get me started on the most popular American board game of all time, Monopoly! You win by bankrupting all the other capitalists of Atlantic City and owning, developing, and exploiting every single existing scrap of property. Guess what, America? Monopoly, created during the Great Depression, came true. It (the game) won.

The Game of Life was America's first parlor game hit. It was originally created in 1860 and eventually rebooted in 1960. The superficiality of the American dream incarnate being unknowingly injected into countless febrile young American minds. It's even displayed in the Smithsonian!

Now, of course, there's nothing wrong with having a car and getting married and responsibly paying your bills and whatnot. I've done a lot of that in my days. And still do. Perhaps the game is even a trifle educational and allows fourth graders to begin to understand the complexities and hurdles that await them in the rush toward maturity. But the Game of Life is a symptom of a much deeper disease of our culture: materialism. (Remember that pandemic from Chapter 2?)

What would it look like to create a theoretical "spiritual" Game of Life that also includes the aforementioned spiritual qualities? In that version, in order to "win," it wouldn't be about ending up on a retirement square with the most cash but instead ending your earthly life with the richest, deepest, and most sincere set of divinely inspired virtues. These could be game cards one acquired through the many ups and downs and highs and lows of navigating the board.

And how does this particular version of the game end? There is your little player peg, stuck in his little car peg-hole, moving *past* the retirement space on to the "death" section of the board, saying goodbye to all his little peg loved ones, tossing away all of the cash and stocks, bonds, and property, only able to take his stack of spiritual quality cards. Cards that read: Enthusiasm! Truthfulness! Joy! Wisdom! Selflessness! Lovingkindness! Compassion!

And that there's your *real* life lesson for fourth graders—the true reality of human life is our soul's expedition.

My favorite quote of all time (and one of Oprah's as well) is from Father Pierre Teilhard de Chardin:

We are not human beings having a spiritual experience; we are spiritual beings having a human experience.

Another great quote (often mistakenly attributed to C. S. Lewis) is:

You don't have a soul. You *are* a soul. You *have* a body.

Because what is the real game of life, dear human brothers and sisters? What is the point of all this sweaty, gooey reality—the obstacles we strive to overcome, the dysfunctional families, the trials we undergo, the horrible jobs we sometimes have to work, the times of tremendous stress and sadness, the annoying people we bump up against, all the tests and difficulties that lay strewn along our life's path?

I believe it's to generate these spiritual eyes and ears and elbows that we will need on the other side of this physical dimension, beyond the veil.

And the hardships we suffer in this world are what, unfortunately, make us wiser, humbler, softer, kinder, more loving.

Sometimes you meet someone in their later years who has such a kindness, light, and perception in their soulful eyes that it is quite moving. I often make a mental note and think to myself, "Rainn, strive to be like that! What a cool senior citizen!" And sometimes you meet an octogenarian who is flinty and mean, emotionally cut off, shut down, and cold. Oftentimes, I'm sorry to say, surrounded by great material luxury, like Mr. Burns from *The Simpsons*.

I do the same thing in those instances. Say to myself, "Rainn, don't end up like that! Don't be a flinty old jerk senior citizen!"

Now, of course we don't know the road that anyone has walked (and being judgmental is one of my worst character traits), but I use these examples to make a point: What kind of old human do you want to be? That is, if my perspective is right and your consciousness and its corollary—your soul—exists beyond your physical body, who is the person you are taking with you when the old age segment of your life is finally over?

What did my father, Robert George Wilson (who definitely fell into the first category of older folks), take with him?

He certainly left behind his 78.5-year-old body on that table near the mortician's kitchen. He left behind a few hundred fantastic abstract paintings, a collection of rare books, his truck, and various drafts of novels and essays. A closet full of old-man clothes. A toothbrush. He also left behind hundreds who loved him and were deeply touched by his spirit, life, service, and art.

And what did he *take with him*? He took his wisdom. That spark of mischievous fun. His positive, inquisitive nature. His gentleness. His vast, colorful imagination. The patience he showed to the octogenarians to whom he volunteered his time and read to regularly. The love he showed to the teens he taught art and painting classes to. The profound, humble devotion he had to his faith.

——◆◆——

So there we were. Back at the funeral home in that back room just off the mortician's kitchen. Water filled the lovely glass bowls I had just purchased at Target. My father's body was laid on an open white linen shroud on the table. My stepmother, Carla, and I were standing over him, and we read some prayers from the Baha'i writings:

> Thou hast joined that precious river to the mighty sea, Thou hast returned that spreading ray of light to the Sun of Truth . . . and led him, who longed to look upon Thee to Thy presence in Thy bright place of lights.

We washed his precious body. One dab of water at a time. The human vessel that had held my father's essence for nearly seventy-nine years before it broke down. We wept. We grieved. We held each other.

We placed the ring on his finger and slowly, carefully wrapped his now clean body. And later that day, that same body, laying in a plain box, was placed into the ground.

Rest in peace, Dad.

CHAPTER FOUR

THE NOTORIOUS G.O.D.

Be still, and know that I am God.

—Psalms 46:10

There is a Secret One inside us;
the planets in all the galaxies
pass through His hands like beads.

—Kabir

If there is a thing that exists in the world, there is probably a reality TV show *about* said thing. Drunk housewives. Kardashians, Vanderpumps, and Chrisleys. There are "unscripted" pottery competition shows and sword-making shows and tattoo shows and Lego shows and shows where people compete for the best fingernails or the worst plastic surgery. There are naked people running around in the woods (sometimes dating) and weirdos bidding on abandoned storage lockers. American ninja warriors (who, spoiler alert, are actually schoolteachers, personal trainers, and firefighters). And shows where sexy trainwrecks get married after meeting in a hot tub and knowing each other for a couple days and giving each other a flower.

There was, however, one topic that I really wanted to explore that wasn't terribly well represented in this smorgasbord of "entertainment."

God.[5]

True story. Armed with a terrific sizzle reel and pitch deck, as well as a great team from my SoulPancake production company, I headed into the conference rooms of every network, streamer, and cable channel in LA to pitch a show about God. It was called *The Notorious G.O.D.*

What I wanted to do via the medium of television was to explore the *idea* of God in today's cultural landscape. Is He still some light-skinned, bearded, old man Sky-Daddy™? Is He a gumball-machine deity, dishing out personal favors, good parking spaces, and lottery tickets to His favored children? Or, if no one believes in those versions of God anymore, then what exactly *is* He?[6]

In this TV show, I wanted to examine the "big ideas" behind science, death, life, psychology, sociology, and philosophy through the lens of there being a possibility of a divine force or presence behind our great big beautiful universe. A show for everyone: believers and skeptics, scientists and religionists, born-agains and atheists, agnostics and seekers.

We had outlined some amazing sample episodes about artificial intelligence and strange funeral rituals and rockin' atheist churches, but, needless to say, as you are not currently seeing said program on the air, *Notorious G.O.D.* was summarily rejected by all of Hollywood.

---

5 Yes, true, Morgan Freeman once had that program *The Story of God* where he jetted around the world to delve into the world's religious traditions. And writer / public philosopher Reza Aslan hosted that tragically short-lived show on CNN entitled *Believer* where he experientially participated in diverse spiritual beliefs and ceremonies. But both of these worked more as travelogues with colorful rituals and a smattering of theology than a specific exploration about how to redefine a Higher Power in the modern world.

6 Please note: I'm going to use "He" when speaking about the Creator. I know this pronoun is loaded in this context and has a difficult, challenging history to it. But "It" sounds kind of "icky" (to quote Carl Sagan), and as much as I'd love to use "She," it feels like reactively assigning gender identity to an all-powerful creative force that is beyond all personal gender labels. So—many apologies—in these brief pages I'll be using "He."

The strangest note was one that we received from Netflix and several others: the topic was not good for their brand because it was deemed too "controversial."

God? Too controversial? Seriously?

You can have a show about drunk housewives throwing garbage at each other but you can't have a show about God? You can have countless action shows where people are being riddled with bullets and having limbs sliced off in torturous ways, yet digging into the concept of the divine is too explosive? You can have teen dramas where there's an endless revolving door of hook-ups, drug binges, and violent rapes, but you can't explore spiritual transcendence in the modern world?

And after all, I thought controversy was supposed to be good for TV.

So how did we reach this point? Why are we at a juncture where either (a) nobody wants to watch a show about potentially the most important subject in the history of humankind, or (b) a show about the most important subject in the history of humankind is deemed too controversial?

How did G.O.D. become a four-letter word?

Let's start at the very beginning—with me. This is my book, after all.

ME AND GOD

God help me.

My longing-filled search for meaning, for the divine, for the Big Guy Upstairs has always been a constant, active part of my life. It's a relationship that I've been in a continuous state of struggle with. Not exactly sure why. Some people, even from religious families, don't ever give the Celestial Being a second thought.

In the preface, I wrote about growing up as a young suburban Seattle Baha'i nerd with a strong sense of and belief in God. The Creator, from the Baha'i perspective that I was brought up with, was not your typical Old Testament Sky-Daddy™. Instead, God is described as "the Unknowable Essence" by Baha'u'llah, the prophet/founder of the Baha'i

Faith. From my faith's perspective, the reason that holy teachers like Jesus and Mohammed and the Buddha bring their divine messages to humanity is that God is *so* far beyond human comprehension and interaction (being outside space and time, etc.) that these "messengers," "prophets," or "manifestations" of God are much-needed intermediaries to help guide humanity to its ultimate spiritual maturation.

God is also described as being "closer to man than his life-vein," a line from the Quran. What a delicious, mystical quandary: unknowable and yet so, so close. The God of my suburban Baha'i youth was loving and reasonable, as relayed to dorky young me, and had absolutely no fire-and-brimstone qualities—that is, He was not keen on damning or burning anyone in a sulfuric lake-o-fire for eternity or anything like that.

So that was nice.

Nonetheless, as I became a teen and started to do things that were not in alignment with Baha'i moral teachings, God started to strangely morph in my mind and heart into that culturally pervasive, all-seeing, judgmental Sky-Daddy™, frowning down on me having fumbling pseudo-sexual activities with my seventeen-year-old girlfriend in the backseats of cars.[7] At that point in my life, I suppose God became more like the God from *The Ten Commandments* starring Charlton Heston, bellowing in a sonorous basso voice from beyond the clouds, "*Moses!*" Or in this case, "*Rainn! Stop trying to take your girlfriend's bra off in the back of that Volvo!*" I suppose it was the impossible-to-ignore torrent of societal imagery about the role of God in a Judeo-Christian world at work in my adolescent head: Santa Claus–God scornfully watching us struggle with our naughtiness and niceness from His angelic heavenly abode.

---

7 Yes, Baha'i, like most of the world's religions, has moral laws about premarital sex. I won't get into the ups and downs and pluses and minuses about morality and/or its reason for existing in a religious/spiritual context, as that's a *doozy* of a topic to unravel—the subject of another book, perhaps?—and far beyond my feeble mental capabilities (as well as my feeble moral compass).

Let's face it. The God of the Hebrew Bible (Old Testament) is more than a little, shall we say, "all over the place." This anthropomorphized entity occasionally flies into rages; can be vindictive, envious, and violent; and is filled with irreconcilable contradictions. How could this view of an angry, judgmental Creator, who has been worshiped, sermonized, studied, and portrayed in countless works of art, *not* seep into our collective Western psychology, and subconscious?

But back to our story. Fast-forward to me in my twenties, having moved to New York to study acting, where I promptly jettisoned anything having to do with God, morality, religion, and spirituality. During my time in New York City, while I attended acting school and the years thereafter, I rejected anything and *everything* related to spirituality. For a couple of years, I even tried on atheism like some jaunty, rebellious cap!

I transitioned to skeptically seeing God as someone or some*thing* grandmothers might need to believe in so that they feel better about their lives. Religion was for old conservative types who weren't capable of creating a rich, vital life of their own and needed some outside supernatural belief system to provide structure and meaning in a chaotic world.

At the same time, I started to see hypocrisy all around me, in most religionists, and even in the Baha'i community. Like a suburban Seattle version of Holden Caulfield, I reacted, however immaturely, by thinking, *What a bunch of phonies.* And I turned away from anything having to do with religion, God, and the faith of my youth. As so many young folks in America's big cities do.

This new universe-view in place, I promptly threw myself into my acting studies. I spent years studying the craft of theater for fourteen hours a day: memorizing Shakespearean sonnets, doing scenes in acting class and tongue stretches and long vowel sounds in voice and speech seminars, and wearing red noses in clowning workshops. (A class, by the way, that would greatly benefit me as Dwight Schrute in later life!)

But (and this is most important), under the tutelage of Zelda Fichandler, one of the grand dames of American theater and founder of Arena Stage in Washington, DC, and head of NYU's graduate acting program, I started to see the pursuit of being an artist as noble and transcendent. Being an actor and a storyteller was a potentially life-and-world-changing vocation. We were not just being trained as actors; we were being inspired and cajoled, expanding our view of theater training as more of a *mission* than anything else. Why was it a mission? Well, because throughout world history, there have always been shamans—those who have a deep connection to the spirit world. And that was, in essence, the role that a great actor played.

This was a revelatory idea for me. Usually, an actor is simply hired to bring dialogue to life. The director is the puppet master, and the lines themselves are sacrosanct and usually can't be altered. It's the equivalent of being in an orchestra. You play the notes as written on the page, and the conductor makes all the real creative decisions about the piece.

But a shaman!? Truth be told, we don't actually know what the duty of a shaman was ten thousand years ago. There weren't Ring cameras up on the walls of caves, documenting what went on when a tribe gathered around the nightly fire. But we do know that the shamans were a combo platter of a lot of different roles. They played the part of truth teller, certainly. Also, mage. Priest. Storyteller. Mystic. Diviner. Perhaps a little sprinkling of social commentator, stand-up comedian, and clown. They were part griot or medicine man, passing down the legends from the past and truths from the ancestors who guide us into the future. Certainly, dancing and singing were incorporated into their ceremonies and presentations. Could there have been a touch of "gadfly to the Athenian nation" in the role they played? Perhaps, like Lear's Fool, they entertained, cajoled, and at the same time had one eye fixed on the mysterious realms beyond.

Thinking of an actor as playing this societal role was transformative. I could be a truth teller, holy man, and fabulist all in one.

This idea would be the central guide in our theater training over the coming years, and it has influenced my thinking ever since.

Now, you might be rolling your eyes at this juncture, and I wouldn't blame you. As in: Wait, how was Dwight a shamanic role? He was just an annoying idiot sitcom sidekick. Don't actors mostly just look pretty and say their lines in a vapid way? Sell beer and cars and tennis shoes on the side? Seek Instagram followers and complain about their agents? Stoke their egos and hold court on things they know nothing about?

Yes, true. All of that.

But—and hear me out—think about when you see a performance that transcends the ages and becomes a voice of the time. A performance that lifts the story from the banal and traditional to the sublime. A performance that you remember your entire life. That's when we get a glimpse of the actor-as-shaman.

Think of Brando at his best. De Niro in *Raging Bull*, *King of Comedy*, or *Taxi Driver*. Daniel Kaluuya in *Judas and the Black Messiah*, Frances McDormand in . . . well, anything. But also think of the times when you've seen breathtaking performances in the theater. Brave. Bold. Unpredictable. Riotously funny. Fierce. And I've seen far too many great ones to share here.

Sorry to wax pretentious, but in these instances, an actor is far greater, far more revelatory than a hired musician simply playing the appointed notes within the boundaries of a symphonic orchestration. The actor reveals the human condition searingly, with truth and fearlessness, humor and vulnerability.

So here we were. A bunch of little shaman wannabes in acting school, treading the boards in the world of professional theater.

As I continued on my acting journey, casting away my Baha'i past and finding a new, exciting shamanistic religion in *the theater*, I hit a few roadblocks.

Long story short, in the '90s, many of my friends and I were fighting devastating internal battles that really had no name, no way of categorizing them. Today, we recognize and label these as "mental health issues." But no one was talking about mental health in 1992. At least no one I knew. Mental health is what Jack Nicholson in *One Flew Over the Cuckoo's Nest* and Leonardo DiCaprio in *What's Eating Gilbert Grape* were dealing with. (Two other shaman-like performances, by the way.)

But mental health was what I was in a battle with in my early twenties. I first went into therapy in 1990 because I was so depressed I couldn't get out of bed. I was frequently beset with anxiety attacks that left me on the ground in a puddle of sweat with a rapid heartbeat, and I was using various levels of drugs, alcohol, porn, food, and whatever else to attempt to escape and numb my feelings. I was lost. And when you can't name something, it becomes even more daunting and overwhelming.

This is not the book for me to relay all the ups and downs of my mental health story and its many battles. (I reveal a bit more of it in my 2015 comedic memoir, *The Bassoon King*.) The reason I bring this chapter of my life to light in this context, however, is because it was these mental health tests that brought me to seek out a relationship with the Creator in a newly minted way. Or rather, these challenges and their resulting emotional earthquakes *forced* me to look for a Higher Power. For a greater sense of meaning and purpose in my life. For balance and perspective. For something bigger than my mixed-up self. For hope.

I echo what the great teacher and writer Julia Cameron once said: "Necessity, not virtue, was the beginning of my spirituality." I was no saint being visited by some Holy Spirit. Nor was I some bodhisattva finding enlightenment through intensive contemplation and revelatory insight.

I needed to seek spirituality because I was really frigging unhappy.

I would have a lot of conversations with myself. Look at me, my incessant thought spirals would spin. I'm a working actor. Broke, but working. Great girlfriend (now wife). Awesome apartment in Brooklyn. Kick-ass van. But I'm so unhappy? Why do I wake up at 3:00 a.m. and stare at the ceiling? Why do I despise myself so much of the time? Why do I cry myself to sleep on occasion? What gives?

Then I continued, *Was I rash to have thrown out everything and anything having to do with God? People with God in their life sometimes seem happier, after all. Maybe I threw the baby out with the bathwater?*

I started talking to friends about the concept of a Creator, but no one really ever wanted to get into it. When I would ask my friends and workmates if they believed in a Higher Power, after some awkward hemming and hawing and some uncomfortable, stumbling silences, they would respond with some version of, "Kind of. I guess. Sort of. Maybe." They would say that they certainly didn't believe in the previously referenced Grampa God with a flowing beard on a cloud with a telescope and an agenda. But they also didn't think that creation was nothing but meaningless molecules bouncing around, either.

They remained, shall we say, noncommittal about the whole thing. They all "kind of" believed in God, but their answers were the vaguest milquetoastiest answers possible.

This didn't work for me.

The existence of God was kind of like being pregnant. It is or it isn't. You can't be "kind of" pregnant. I mean, there either needed to be an all-knowing, all-loving, all-seeing creative force behind and above and within everything *or* consciousness was purely a random and meaningless accident of an even more random and meaningless assemblage of molecules bouncing around in a random and meaningless physical plane of existence. There's really not much in between those two options. As it says in the AA Big Book, "God is either everything or else He is nothing. God either is, or He isn't."

So I went on a journey of spiritual and religious rediscovery. I dug deep into the holy books of the world's great faiths. The Bible, certainly. The Quran, yes. The Baha'i books that I had noticed on my parents' bookshelf but had never cracked open as a teen. But also, the Bhagavad Gita of Hinduism and the Dhammapada and other teachings of the Buddha.

And, finally, some books that truly changed my life: *The Gospel of the Redman, The Sacred Pipe, Black Elk Speaks, God Is Red,* and many other mystical but accessible tomes about Native American spirituality. (Books, by the way, that dove even deeper into the meaning of the role of the shaman!)

It was there, at long last, that I read about a conception of God that was going to change my life: Wakan Tanka, a title for God in the Lakota Sioux tradition. A concept that led me on a road to ever greater understanding and helped me steer (very gradually) out of the vortex of my mental health struggles.

But before I dig more specifically into this life-altering spiritual discovery, there's a lot of ground I want to cover in this chapter's quest to reimagine, explore, and explode this concept of the Notorious G.O.D.

First, I want to begin with a shout-out to the atheists.

YO, ATHEISTS!

In case you were wondering, this section is not going to be like one of those videos where a God-believer and an atheist sit on a stage in front of a partisan audience (who already have their minds made up) and have an argument about whether God exists or not. Those discussions are pointless. Just read the comments sections underneath the videos. No one has ever changed their mind about something as colossal as *the Supreme Being* because of who scored more points in an argument on YouTube, no matter how articulate the speakers might be.

I'm not here to change anybody's mind. Just to provide some (hopefully) interesting, fresh perspectives. I absolutely love, admire, and respect atheists. Seriously. If I wasn't a dyed-in-the-wool theist, I would definitely go back to being an atheist.

Why? Because atheists, by and large, *love* science and its method of understanding the universe. And I can totally relate because I love science too. I certainly don't consider science to be in any kind of opposition to faith and spirituality. That's the epitome of a false dichotomy. Both are effective, albeit different, modalities for understanding the same ultimate reality.

Science is an incredible methodology and set of tools for studying the material world. Through its systematic focus, it has unlocked, especially over the past two centuries, what one could consider miracles. The quality of our lives has been made infinitely better thanks to it. (He says, drafting this book on his *laptop*, on which he can watch videos of cats playing the piano, calculate advanced math equations, research *anything that has ever existed ever*, record music tracks, schedule his calendar down to the minute, listen to podcasts about beekeepers, and talk face-to-face in crystalline clarity with someone in Mongolia.)

Science. I mean, who doesn't love the *systematic study of the structure and behavior of the physical and natural world through observation and experimentation!*

Unfortunately, throughout the ages science has frequently been positioned as being in opposition to faith. If one looks at a thumbnail history of God, He (God) was an ever-present figure with us *Homo sapiens*, appearing in various incarnations, both pantheistic and monotheistic, since the dawn of humanity. Every *Homo sapiens* culture has some kind of relationship with a divine power that exists beyond space and time—a relationship that many believe helped early civilizations answer questions about the world that couldn't be answered in any other way. This, historically, is called the "god of the gaps." Anything science can't explain *is* God or is *of* God.

We early humans don't know where that scary-sounding thunder comes from? Well, let's put a divine face or label on it and, by creating a god of thunder, like Thor (Norse) or Ba'al (Phoenician) or Set (Egyptian), *BOOM!* Problem solved. (See what I did there?) The answer to the mysterious noise must be that there's a powerful *being* in the sky that occasionally gets angry and makes a thunder crash with his hammer or sword or what have you. Then, eventually, through the tools of science we humans discover that thunder comes from the rapid expansion of the air surrounding the path of electricity discharged through a lightning bolt, and all of a sudden, there's no longer any need for Thor or Ba'al or Set. The powerful "god" is then relegated to colorful ancient mythology, and science holds the new explanation for said phenomenon.

Some religious folk would continue to draw this "god of the gaps" idea forward to the modern day and say (using the example of some event we don't have an explanation for as of yet), "Well, since we don't have a clue how life started on planet Earth, or how a bunch of chemicals and molecules suddenly transformed into single-celled organisms and bacteria, their de facto creation must be God's finger zapping the oceans of our planet billions of years ago!"

However, to the materialist / naturalist / person of science, everything can *ultimately* be explained by a scientific theory. So it's not that we don't know the answer to why chemicals and molecules evolved into live organisms four billion years ago . . . we simply don't know the answer *yet*.

Now of course this whole paradigm is ridiculous. It pits religion versus science in an incredibly simplistic way. Everything proven belongs to science and all things mysterious and undiscovered belong to God? Um, no. God is either within and without and interwoven throughout *all* of nature and natural phenomenon, or there is no supernatural presence whatsoever and there is only matter, energy, and their physical laws bobbing and throbbing about purposelessly in a vast, empty space.

Again, it's impossible to stereotype an entire population based on what they believe, but on the whole, I think it's safe to say that atheists are naturally skeptical. As a whole, they try not to inherit beliefs handed down from their childhood, culture, media, or family. They pride themselves on examining things with an eye on the individual investigation of truth and demand to be shown proof, usually repeatable and provable. Those admirable, sometimes pesky, atheists delight in knocking down sacred shibboleths, challenging all assumptions about the supernatural. They reason things out on their own, with their own eyes, their own brains. I greatly admire these traits and attempt to hold myself to the same exacting, skeptical standard. We all should.

In fact, I would say that if you blindly and incuriously believe in *any* religious faith, especially the faith of your parents, you are kind of an idiot. There, I said it.

Atheists have rejected so many of the obvious hypocrisies, corruptions, and especially nonsensically literal interpretations of symbols and metaphors in most of the world's religions. At tremendous risk of pissing off every single religious faith in the world, I would simply offer you some examples of these superstitions:

- Elephant-shaped gods
- The reincarnation of "bad" human beings into cockroaches
- People being turned willy-nilly into pillars of salt
- Magical enlightenment under trees
- Burning bushes that talk to you
- Jesus's body floating away after three days to be with his dad
- Mohammed riding a winged horse back and forth to Jerusalem in a night

Besides all the mythological stories, atheists have *sooo* many very good reasons to *not* believe in God!

For instance, from the dawn of time, religion has caused innumerable wars and incalculable deaths. All in an "all-loving" God's name! From the crusades to the mass exterminations of "nonbelievers" during the first centuries of colonialism to the Spanish Inquisition. From 9/11 to the Iran-Iraq war to Hindu mob violence against Muslims in India to armed Buddhist terrorists setting off bombs in Sri Lanka. No religious faith has escaped this violence. Not to mention the endless list of holy genocides, holy wars, and holy pogroms that have preceded recorded history.

And let's not forget that God-people seem to be so weirdly anti-science at times! I mean, why this recent bizarre connection in evangelical circles between believing in Jesus and disbelieving in vaccines?!

God worshipers frequently seem to just *believe* in stuff that makes little to no sense, and they never seem open to investigating the truth for themselves. They then label this as having "faith."

Also, God, as we have come to understand Him through the Abrahamic mythology, is so toxically *male*! It's patriarchy personified. Big, disapproving, bearded, warlike, anthropomorphic, *masculine* daddy-man who is going to spank you with plague or lightning or locusts or damnation if you don't do his bidding. A ton has already been written about how all the glorious ancient feminine and matriarchal spiritual traditions were stomped down and shoved aside to make way for this domineering patriarchal conception. And how this oppressive religious patriarchy forced more "traditional" roles on women, which in most cases, for countless generations, kept our innately powerful women subservient, abused, and undereducated.

Also? In so many faith traditions, God seems narcissistically obsessed with people bowing down and worshiping Him and sending those who don't do so to burn in the fiery pit of hell for all eternity. (Which, by the by, is a very, *very* long time!) What a jerk! I mean, *who does that*?!

Like I said, it makes total sense to reject some or all of this God nonsense.

THE SIMULATION HYPOTHESIS

Interestingly, atheists have come up with a cutting-edge theory of their own that is one of the most spiritually minded tools for viewing the totality of reality ever invented! It folds beautifully into Christianity and Buddhism and connects science *and* religion into a feasible and awe-inspiring speculation. I'm speaking of the simulation hypothesis, of course. Popularized by Elon Musk and Neil DeGrasse Tyson. Subject of the popular *A Glitch in the Matrix* documentary. Potentially believed in by millions. A supposition that can be embraced by theists *and* atheists around the globe.

This simulation theory basically postulates that we are all living in a perfect simulacrum of a three-dimensional universe and that when we "die," in actuality we are ending our relationship to the illusory world that seemingly surrounds us, and we then wake up in our "real" bodies in the "real" universe. In other words, what, how, and where we have been living—our flesh tuxedos walking around on good old planet Earth—is like *The Matrix* and *Avatar* combined! Our bodies are virtual avatars, and the world outside our windows is a hyperadvanced 3D simulation of real life!

For many who engage in such a belief system, this entire apparatus of reality is overseen by a giant supercomputer or AI that keeps track of each individual in the midst of their computer-generated, sensory-illusory experience. This infinite digital overlord also oversees the "real world" that one wakes up into following death. It "backs up" our souls on the much more real "cloud" in servers that are above and beyond the limited space-time continuum of this plane.

Sounds suspiciously like another way of thinking about the Notorious G.O.D., no? In fact, this template of the illusion of reality syncs up perfectly with many religious traditions.

The Imam Ali says in a famous hadith (sacred saying) from Islam, "People are asleep as long as they are alive. When they die, they wake up." In other words, this saying uses the exact same metaphor of life as a dream with death being an awakening from that dream/illusion into a completely new "reality."

You may have heard of the term "maya," the ancient Hindu concept for the illusion of the material world. It also refers to the illusory nature of any kind of duality between the physical and spiritual realms. Maya, as far as I can grasp this incredibly complex and nuanced concept, means not only "illusion" but "magic," and also has a sprinkling of the definition of "foolishness" in it.

Shankara, the great Hindu philosopher, once used the example of the rope and the snake as an allegory of maya. You're walking down the road at dusk, and you see a snake in front of you. Your pulse quickens, and you start to panic, but then you realize the snake is actually a rope. You've seen through the illusion, and as your breath stabilizes, you are back in "reality." That is maya. And it is applicable to the world we see around us.

Maya is also frequently seen (especially in Advaita Vedanta, the predominant Hindu philosophical branch) as an illusionary way of seeing the world that is personally summoned from the worst facets of our own selves. It can be thought of as the clouds of "selfishness" that obscure the reality of the sun. When we contemplate our true spiritual nature and do selfless acts, only then will the clouds of ego disperse, allowing us to witness the beautiful power and purity of the sun. Then we are in brahman and no longer in maya.

Brahman (which is in opposition to maya) is the true spiritual reality of everything, the cosmic soul or universal spirit of all creation. (Yet another way of conceiving the Notorious G.O.D., perhaps?) Although there truly is no duality between the two. No either-or. In my feeble understanding of Vedic thinking, there is no material versus spiritual. All is spiritual. The material world, a manifestation of the divine, simply magically tricks us into thinking that it's the only game in town.

This idea is foundational in the Baha'i Faith as well. Baha'u'llah says, "Verily I say, the world is like the vapor in a desert, which the thirsty dreameth to be water and striveth after it with all his might, until when he cometh unto it, he findeth it to be mere illusion."

'Abdu'l-Baha, Baha'u'llah's eldest son, a Baha'i leader and great spiritual teacher, says, "Know thou that the Kingdom [of God] is the real world, and this nether place is only its shadow stretching out. A shadow hath no life of its own; its existence is only a fantasy, and nothing more; it is but images reflected in water."

In other words, we are physically living in the equivalent of a mirage, a vapor, a vision, a shadow, a fantasy . . . and the spiritual world, which we will all end up in, is *true* reality, or "the real world."

All roads lead to the simulation hypothesis!

The one place I am guaranteed never to
find God is in my thinking.

—*Anonymous*

THE CASE AGAINST GOD

There are many reasons to not believe in a Higher Power, and I often hear them from various people I cross paths with.

I was once shooting a movie in England, and the director, who we'll call Benedict, and I were visiting a church, and he turns to me and says, "So I understand you believe in God and all that?" I responded in the affirmative. He then replied with, "Well, I don't!" I said, "Oh no? Really?" And Benedict went on. "No way! When I was a kid, I was dragged to church practically every day of the week. It wasn't enough to just go on Sunday; we had to go to daily mass. I was a choirboy and helped with the painfully long ceremonies and had to participate in all the god-awful church activities. It was just the worst. I hated it. So I just can't believe in God or any of that."

I would argue there are some holes in that argument, but I'll let you decide.

Another actor friend of mine once said to me as we were traveling in Spain on a movie shoot, "Rainn, I'm sorry, but I can't believe you buy all of this God and religion garbage! I mean, *look* at all the hypocrisy! Look at all the evil that has been done in the name of this 'loving' God. How can you possibly get with that?!"

We pretty much covered that topic earlier. (See "Yo, Atheists!")

A TV writer friend once said, "Rainn, I just can't get with any religion that thinks that people are going to burn in hell for all eternity if they don't 'believe.' I mean, how evil can you get?!"

And I completely agree. Also, covered. (See "Me and God.")

I have another friend, named Chip. He also spoke to me about God and a Higher Power and relayed to me, "When I was a kid, I was raised in the evangelical church, and we were taught that if we accepted Jesus, and were good people, that we would be showered with blessings and be saved and that good things would happen to us. Well, I did all that, and then my wife got breast cancer and had to get a lumpectomy. I just can't believe in a God where I did everything right and then we're getting punished like this!"

This aligns with another friend of mine, Dave, who used to have quite a strong relationship to God but has struggled with it after both his daughter *and* his wife developed brain tumors. His anger at God overwhelmed him, and he cut off any relationship he might have previously had. He was devastated, furious, and emotionally wounded by these horrific events.

Understandable. How do we rectify a Creator that would hand out so much personal tragedy? Grotesque, painful things happening to good and kind people. Heartbreaking.

This brings us to one of the grandpappy arguments against a Divine Creator that I would like to take a little time to address on these pages.

A DIGRESSION ON THE NATURE OF SUFFERING

This long-standing argument against God was very effectively made by the actor/writer/atheist Stephen Fry. When asked in a now viral video, what if he was wrong about God's existence and then he died and met God at the pearly gates, what would he say to Him, Fry replied, and I quote, "I'd say, bone cancer in children? What's that about? How dare you? How dare you create a world in which there is such misery that is *not our fault*? It's not right; it's utterly, utterly evil. Why should I respect a capricious, mean-minded, stupid God who creates a world that is so full of injustice and pain? That's what I would say."

A very compelling argument indeed.

This is a very complicated topic that Mr. Fry and the aforementioned Dave and Chip raise, all in their own fashion. With the limited space I have here, I will offer my perspective on this question, which is ultimately this:

Why do bad things happen to good people? Why is there so much suffering in the world, especially inflicted on the innocent?

We all experience pain and suffering. Death is a constant. Even childbirth is grotesquely painful—excruciating and miraculous all at the same time!

Needless to say, sickness and illness are everywhere. Natural disasters abound. Accidents occur constantly. Hundreds of millions go to bed hungry each night. And as we grow older, there's the ever-increasing "thousand natural shocks that flesh is heir to."

My short response to this conundrum is threefold:

#1. Where exactly does human responsibility end and God's hand begin?

Imagine how much effort, research, and technology we've put into creating missiles, guns, warships, bombs, mines, drones, nuclear subs, fighter jets, and other countless horrific weapons of mass destruction. What if humanity spent the same amount of time, money, and energy working on actually healing and curing diseases (like cancer) that it puts into warfare? Perhaps we wouldn't even be *dealing* with cancer today, as well as so many other diseases. And tell me again, how is this *God's fault* and not our own doing? We have all the basic scientific tools we need to find treatments and cures for so many diseases that needlessly kill and cause untold pain to hundreds of millions. Yet we, as a species, have always chosen war, profit, and division over real humanitarian progress.[8]

And it's not just disease and bad health care that are negative by-products of our misguided societal priorities. Agriculture. Clean water. Nutrition. Distribution systems and transportation. Mosquitos.

---

8 Note: World military spending in 2021 was more than *$2 trillion*—with the United States making up more than a third of that. This is what $2 trillion looks like: $2,000,000,000,000. One trillion dollar bills laid end to end would stretch out *farther than the distance between Earth and the sun*!

Vaccines. We cause climate change and then raise our fists and curse God when extreme weather events destroy our forests and cities. There is a list of entirely preventable ways in which innocent people suffer and die that we humans—especially the wealthiest among us (see the "Unjust Economic Extremes" pandemic in Chapter 2)—could *easily* be taking a far, far stronger stand in proactively treating/fixing/solving/healing. And the fact that we aren't should horrify and outrage every single one of us until we want to scream. But instead, we just putter along. Or lazily blame the Big Guy Upstairs.

So there's that.

#2. Could suffering have an intangible upside?

Let's look at suffering itself as a concept.

Perhaps the Buddha was right in one of his central theses, that *life is suffering*: "I teach one thing and one thing only: suffering and the end of suffering."

Suffering, due to attachment, is one of the "four noble truths" and a central tenet of Buddhism.

It should be noted that the Buddhist Pali/Sanskrit term "dukkha," which loosely translates to "suffering," also means discontent, irritation, anxiety, frustration, and craving. In other words, negative emotions. The Buddhist path is to eventually free oneself of dukkha. More on that later.

But what would the world look like if there were no pain? No suffering? No death, no stubbed toes, no broken bones or illnesses or natural disasters? This might be the universe that Stephen Fry longs for with an almighty God at the helm. What would that physical universe be like? How would it operate? Let's take a peek.

A baby is born, gently, without any crying. The mother's vagina magically opens to allow the child out without any pain to her or the baby. And postpartum stitches, recovery, and bleeding? None of that. Children mature without ever getting skinned knees, growing pains, or broken bones. No child ever gets their feelings hurt. Pain receptors only operate as pleasant internal warning systems. Accidentally staplegun through your finger? Mild tingling only. There is zero disease and no genetic mutations. There are no earthquakes, tornadoes, or natural disasters. Death comes automatically at age one hundred without any grief or discomfort to either the person passing or their friends and family. And, most of all, no pain or death could ever possibly come to anyone innocent or younger than, say, thirteen years of age.

But as the great sages ever remind us, without ever experiencing pain or hurt or sadness, how would we then learn to appreciate joy or exhilaration or ecstasy?

When you consider this as an option for our material plane, an option seemingly desired by Mr. Fry, it paints an absurd picture. And a portrait of a hollow world.

#3. Is there a scientific case for suffering?

Which brings me to my final response, which is, of course, *science*!

A physical universe without pain, accident, disease, or death simply makes *zero* scientific sense. We are bodies composed of chains of vulnerable DNA. We live on a rock, hurtling through space with billions of other organisms, many of which (including viruses and bacteria and crocodiles) want to feed on us in various ways. Like all organic species, our bodies decay and deform. The list goes on and on.

There is a false dichotomy that somehow the existence of God would mean that the laws of science would be abrogated and tossed out the window. Santa Claus Father Odin—who is, after all, like the Bible says, "all loving"—would make *allllll* our boo-boos go away. Or, like Chip brought up, this Sky-Daddy™ would *only* allow *bad* people to get bone cancer, *not* the believers who hadn't done anything wrong. Certainly not innocent babies.

What a preposterous idea!

The much larger question is *why* is there suffering, and what purpose does it serve in this physical plane?

If you accept my humble proposition that we are spiritual beings inhabiting material bodies for a few handfuls of decades, then maybe, just maybe, pain and suffering, both physical *and* emotional, might perhaps be connected to both our biological *and* our spiritual journeys.

And, once again, wisdom on the purpose of suffering can be found in the great spiritual and religious traditions.

The apostle Paul writes in Romans,

> We also rejoice in our sufferings, because we know that suffering produces perseverance; perseverance, character; and character, hope. And hope does not disappoint us, because God has poured out his love into our hearts by the Holy Spirit, whom he has given us.

The Buddhist tradition doesn't speak much about the *benefits* of suffering per se but more of the *overcoming* of suffering through nonattachment as our life's purpose and eventual path to spiritual enlightenment or nirvana.

In the Buddhist tradition, suffering also allows us to increase our empathy for others that suffer, and this also helps us on our personal journey of compassion.

> Like a mother who protects her child, her only child, with her own life, one should cultivate a heart of unlimited love and compassion towards all living beings.
>
> —*Gautama Buddha*

In Islam, one gives thanks to God (Allah) for the tests and pain we are given, and these things bring us closer to Him. Those who are able to see God's hand, will, and presence in affliction are the most spiritually evolved. The Holy Quran says,

> Surely We will *try* you with something of fear and hunger, and loss of wealth and possessions, death, and the loss of fruits of your toil. Yet, give glad tidings to those who are patient who, when they are

visited by an affliction, say, "Surely we belong to God, and to Him we return." (2:155–157)

And finally, in the Baha'i tradition, tests and difficulties, similar to Paul's statement, are "given" to us for our own perfecting and maturation.

> The more difficulties one sees in the world the more perfect one becomes. The more you plow and dig the ground the more fertile it becomes. The more you cut the branches of a tree the higher and stronger it grows. The more you put the gold in the fire the purer it becomes. . . . Therefore, the more sorrows one sees the more perfect one becomes.
>
> —'Abdu'l-Baha, *Star of the West*

Personally speaking, I have had tests in my life that I wasn't sure I would make it back from in one piece, but looking back on the torturous suffering I experienced, I emerged incredibly grateful.

I'm sure there is some truth in this for all of us. Take a brief moment during your perusal of this paragraph to look back on your life and give a brief witness to the calamities you've survived and the growth, humility, wisdom, and perspective that you carried with you out the other side.

Helen Keller, someone who endured unimaginable tests, said, "Life is full of suffering; it is also full of the overcoming of it."

In summation, perhaps suffering, tests, and difficulties are actually the *reason* for this material existence, and finding joy while in the midst of them is our life's greatest and most important challenge.

But let's get back to our story.

WHY I AM NOT AN ATHEIST

If I respect atheists so much, then why am I not one, you might be asking yourself.

I will dodge that answer with a poem:

To be alive: not just the carcass
But the spark.
That's crudely put, but . . .
If we're not supposed to dance,
Why all this music?

—*Gregory Orr*

And I will back that artsy-ass poem up with a well-known science-based quote from Albert Einstein: "The most beautiful and most profound experience is the sensation of the mystical. It is the sower of all true science. He to whom this emotion is a stranger, who can no longer wonder and stand rapt in awe, is as good as dead."

Now, bear with me. I know many atheists hate it when they simply and clearly ask for proof of this supernatural entity and the theist immediately gets all cryptic and grandly poetic and uses that to deflect the question at hand.

Let me start by saying that when in conversation with an atheist, I always ask about the God they *don't* believe in, and they usually, to a T, describe a God that I *also* don't believe in. I'll then get to respond with one of my favorite sentences:

"I don't believe in the God that you don't believe in."

If one holds that the existence of a Higher Power must be based on a scientific standard of hard proof—an experiment in a laboratory or an algorithm on a computer screen—can we all agree that we're screwed? The old "*show me verifiable and repeatable evidence* that there is something other than matter, energy, and the laws of science" is quite a task. Impossible? Perhaps. But not if one is open-minded enough to shift one's way of looking at and thinking about the topic. Not if you give yourself loving, imaginative permission to recontextualize your conception of the question itself.

And by the way, what exactly would that hard proof look like? Let's say there was profound evidence of some inexplicable, never-before-seen mysterious force that preceded and even initiated/guided the big bang. Well then, of course scientists would simply be looking for evidence of a scientific understanding of said force. As well they should! Because that's how things work in this physical universe. But again, I believe this is a false dichotomy, of God existing *separately* and apart from science and nature or *above* science and nature. It's a dead-end street.

Would the proof a materialist/naturalist/physicalist needs be a verified photograph of a ginormous God-like face peering over the Andromeda galaxy and holding a lightning bolt while eating a churro with crumbs in His enormous beard?

So back to the question I've been dodging. Why am I not an atheist? Because, according to materialist doctrine,[9] at the end of the day this would mean that there is only "stuff." Things. Specks. Atoms. Chunks. Molecules. Matter. Plus a little dark matter thrown in. Energy flitting about in between. Stuff that seemingly created itself. A universe that came into being on its own for some completely unknown and ultimately unknowable reason some 13.8 billion years ago.

This leads me down the rabbit hole of, "Well, why is there anything at all? Why is there something? Why is there not just nothing?"

Butt-loads and butt-loads of stuff just popping into existence on its own for no reason simply makes no sense to me. It feels like its own kind of science-based superstition. I "believe" that matter, heat, energy, neutrons, protons, electrons, light, gravity, and time just burst forth from a single point because . . . well, it just did. That's just how it is. There is stuff. Period. Case closed. An entire universe of infinite

---

9 Note: I'm referring to the second dictionary definition of "materialist," not a person who seeks consumerist comfort but one who believes that existence is comprised entirely of the material.

complexity was born in a heartbeat because . . . science. Really? Sorry, but it feels like a bit of a stretch.

Plus, then it's all so meaningless! And in a world where we humans are wired for some unknown reason (thanks, consciousness!) to be incessantly searching, questing, longing for meaning, it just doesn't add up!

Author and theologian David Bentley Hart makes an incredibly salient point. In the atheist worldview, there is a distinct and concrete way to measure success: *whoever can get by in their daily life and pretend not to notice that life is utterly meaningless . . . wins!* In a world without a divine spirit of the universe, you just have to plunk along day in and day out without noticing the inherent lack of meaning too often or letting the overall purposelessness of life bother you overly much. People who are good at that will do just fine and have a relatively happy life.

That's not me. I lose in this scenario. I tried for several years, but I just couldn't accept being surrounded by all this awe-inspiringness that is completely devoid of purpose.

Again, this *experience* of being alive is so wondrous and mysterious, isn't it!? Can "The Force that through the Green Fuse, drives the flower" really just be narrowed down to nothing more than a series of accidental electrochemical impulses in our neurons?

I simply can't abide being an atheist because of the reality of the great, glorious miracle of consciousness itself! The fully interactive, all-consuming, scintillating, transcendent, overwhelming 3D Sensurround™ movie that's running nonstop in my body, heart, and head! I am having much, much more than just a biological experience as I motor along fretfully being the consciousness of Rainn Wilson while writing this ridiculous book.

And one of the centerpieces of this whole miraculous experience is love.

Let's (again) look at "love" as an analogy connected to the conception of our old chum, the Notorious G.O.D.

If I were to say to someone who is deeply, madly in love, "Hey—love doesn't exist," they would say, "Nonsense." They are having a tangible *experience* of love—its power, its transcendence, and its many sumptuous and difficult nuances.

I would then say to them, "Show me *proof* of this 'love' of which you speak. Where is it?" I want to see it replicated and demonstrated in a laboratory or in an equation or in an experiment or on a computer, I tell them. Where is the formula or algorithm for said love?

Certainly, there are CT scans in which a region like the ventral tegmental area of our brain lights up when we look at a picture of someone we love, but that isn't proof that this singular, indescribable feeling exists. Those scans don't illuminate *one single thing* about that rapturous, transformative emotional surge one gets when tearfully holding one's newborn child. (And, in all actuality, that exact same area of my brain that lights up when I see a picture of my wife or son would also probably light up if I saw a picture of a strawberry-rhubarb pie or a kitten in a teensy-weensy cowboy hat.)

What if we needed actual *proof* that love exists? That it is glorious and all-consuming. Drives our impulses and is a condition, experience, and state of being toward which we can set our personal and collective north star!

One might, as a real-time, hands-on sensory experiment, walk hand in hand with someone along the Seine in the rain, watch *The Notebook*, listen to Marvin Gaye, eat chocolate-dipped cherries, sniff roses, ride on a Ferris wheel while gazing longingly into another's eyes and tenderly touching lips—but then ultimately feel nothing, nada, zip. I could then say, "See? There's no such thing as love!"

I mean, even the great musician Nina Simone once said, "You can't tell someone what it feels like to be in love."

There is simply no way to scientifically *prove* that the most exquisite, gut-wrenching, and transcendental of all human experiences exists. And yet it is most certainly quite real and has driven a sizable number of human impulses for most of recorded history.

Hell, this idea is even in the words of the hippies *and* the Bible: "*God is love*. Whoever lives in love lives in God, and God in him" (1 John 4:16).

Let's undertake the same kind of spiritual analogy with the concepts of art and beauty.

Let's say, for example, an alien comes down to Earth and says, "Greetings, earthlings. We don't have this thing you call 'art' in our culture on our home planet. What is it, exactly? Prove to me that art and its resulting beauty, as you know and experience it, exist."

Said art-curious alien could then be shown statues and paintings and symphonies and poems and dance performances. But the alien would simply proffer that those were certainly tangible examples of modes of human expression, but that's not what it was explicitly asking for. How does said alien *know* that a Radiohead concert or a Monet painting or a Shakespearean sonnet or a Brazilian capoeira demonstration is moving and beautiful? When does mere expression attain the station, status, or transcendence of "art"? Can we ever point directly to what comprises the "art-iness" of certain music, words on a page, movements on a stage, or filmed stories on a screen? Where is *proof* that said artistic works truly rise above humdrum reality and move emotions and perspectives in a radiant demonstration of elevated aesthetic pleasure? Where is the repeatable experiment that irrefutably *proves* that said works reveal the human condition, are verifiably beautiful, and quantifiably provoke longing, compassion, and sublimity as great works of art and beauty supposedly do?

For most of us, defining art is similar to Supreme Court Justice Stewart's famous refrain about porn. When asked what makes something that contains nudity "porn" or not, he famously said, "I know it when I see it."

The inability to *prove* art or love or beauty does not mean that those concepts don't exist. They may be on a higher plane of human perception but are just as real as a toaster oven or a shrimp burrito.

I accept your judgment, judicious reader—comparing proof of the existence of God to proof of the existence of love, art, beauty, goodness, and truth might be a bit of a stretch. But is it any more of a stretch than considering a God that compares in some fashion to a omniscient superhero in the sky? Wanting proof of a "being" or "entity" that "exists" somewhere? That "looks down" on us from above? That judges us nonstop and tabulates naughty and nice?

The scholar David Bentley Hart points out that what most atheists describe when they talk about God is an abovementioned "demiurge," a being among other beings—only this particular demiurgic being is a kind of deity who fashioned the physical world and meddles in the affairs of the denizens it created.

Couldn't God, in fact, be far more comparable to a concept than a being? Hart speaks of thinking of the Divine as less of a being than of "being itself."

Just as we have a little bobbing 3D movie of our consciousness in our heads as we trundle about our lives, couldn't God be conceived of as the consciousness of the universe itself? God as nature? As science? As light? As pi?

Scientists do backflips trying to find a unified theory of everything, a hypothesis that can connect all of physics—from gravity and general relativity to quantum physics and electromagnetics. From the subatomic principles to the very limits of astrophysics and the big bang itself. And if you've ever tried to take a peek into string theory or M-theory and their preposterously countless dimensions of reality and hyperspace, one comes back to Occam's razor—"sometimes the simplest explanation is perhaps the best one." In this case, isn't it simpler to infer that a Creator Spirit explains the underlying unity in all things?

The Nobel Prize–winning physicist Max Planck put it this way: "All matter originates and exists only by virtue of a force. We must assume behind this force the existence of a conscious and intelligent Mind."

As I write this, I realize that attempting to define the undefinable, especially with the limited resource of mere language as our toolkit, is somewhat a fool's errand. How can one use a tool as deficient as language to attempt to express the inexpressible? Language is merely the flitting of the shadows on the wall of Plato's cave in the grand scheme of things. A finger pointing at the moon. But nonetheless, we forge on.

I was speaking to Dr. Varun Soni, chaplain at the University of Southern California, and he had an outrageous comparison for God that truly made me chuckle. He suggested that perhaps we should think of God as being like the internet. What precisely *is* the internet? Can you point your finger at it? Is it circuits? Servers? Websites? No, it's so much more! It's a plane of being unto itself. Think *Tron*. Think *The Matrix*. It's beautiful and horrible. It contains love and hate and the beauty of human expression. It's both a tool *and* a destination. It can be harnessed for good or twisted for evil. It's a world of malignant hackers and imaginative digital artists. It's a world of ones and zeros and also of scintillating pixels. Mindless diversion and unifying, gorgeous entertainment. But there is power there. Running in it, through it, behind it. A microcosm and shadow of our physical universe.

To extrapolate on this absurd metaphor, Wi-Fi is then analogous to the Holy Spirit. And our individual computers (Macs or PCs) are our souls. All interconnected. And these laptop souls of ours can be trained and harnessed for either good or evil. They are tools that can be used for writing beautiful poetry or distributing paranoid lies on Facebook.

Again, Dr. Soni is not saying that God is specifically "like" the internet, but he is simply drawing another analogy that allows us to shift perspective *away* from anything remotely demiurgic or anthropomorphized.

'Abdu'l-Baha writes,

People have pictured a god in the realm of the mind, and worship that image which they have made for themselves. . . . Consider then, how all the peoples of the world are bowing the knee to a fancy of their own contriving, how they have created a creator within their own minds, and they call it the Fashioner of all that is.

That Essence of Essences, that Invisible of Invisibles, exists above all human speculation, never to be overtaken or fully comprehended by the mind of man.

This concept exists in every culture and faith tradition.

The Tao that can be told is not the eternal Tao. The name that can be named is not the eternal Name. The unnameable is the eternally real. . . . Free from desire, you realize the mystery.

—*Tao Te Ching*

In the Fourth Gospel, Jesus prays "that they may all be one, as thou, Father, art one in me, and I in You, that they may be one in Us" (John 17:21).

Zeno (great name!), the founder of stoicism, said beautifully, "God is not separate from the world; He is the *soul of the world*, and each of us contains a part of the Divine Fire. All things are parts of one single system, which is called Nature."

"Soul of the world." I just love that.

Western thought has been maniacally focused on God as the *source* of creation, a founder, an instigator. There have been countless debates, discussions, and philosophical treatises in this vein. My friend the great Baha'i philosopher (and PhD in physics from Princeton) Steven Phelps reminded me that the discussion has unfortunately been far less focused on God as a *goal*, a destination, a way of life, a rich garden of qualities to emulate, or an energy to both draw from and align with. Perhaps we ought to spend less time thinking of this creative force as a *what* and more like a *how*—how to live in this world with radiance, humility, a spirit of service, and a sacred harmony. A God that emanates divine qualities in the same way that pesky spiritual metaphor in the sky, *the sun*, emanates light, heat, and healing.

Perhaps God could not even be considered as something distinct or separate from what He has fashioned but rather as the sum of creation.

The fifteenth-century philosopher Nicholas of Cusa had an indelible and unforgettable way of framing the conception of the Creator. He once said, "Divinity is in all things in such a way that all things are in divinity." He spoke of a God "whose center, so to speak, is everywhere and whose circumference is nowhere."

Kind of like Wakan Tanka.

ME AND WAKAN TANKA

So here I am in the 1990s in New York City, in my turbulent adolescence, rebelling against most everything. Including God.

(And isn't that what humanity is doing, really? Individuating in the midst of its collective turbulent adolescence? Eight billion of us pushing back against the perceived "father," God, the great big patriarch in the sky? I certainly was.)

But I was also searching for something.

And it was during this fumbling stage that I stumbled on the concept of Wakan Tanka, which translates as "the Great Mystery." When this gawky, confused mid-'90s soul-rebel came upon this Indigenous American idea of divinity, my mind opened like a sunflower. After all, I loved mysteries. Not of the Agatha Christie or true crime podcast variety but of the mystical sort. I saw the making of art itself as a great mystery and was excited to dig into an even bigger one. My eyes were opened to new possibilities as I read about this Great Spirit of the Lakota Sioux.

I spoke a while back with the late Kevin Locke, a Lakota artist and elder, and consulted with him about what I had studied all those years ago.

From my feeble understanding, this concept of Wakan Tanka is *the* creative force that binds and generates life. That exists beyond time and space. It is in no way anthropomorphic. Wakan Tanka is not a dude, being, entity, or demiurge. It is the mysterious power of the seven directions: north, south, east, west, up into the sky, down into the earth, and, finally, the seventh direction, the internal (inside the chest, the heart, the soul). Wakan Tanka is the God of our ancestors and binds us to them and is experienced in connection to the wind, the sunlight, the grasslands, and the water.

I came to understand that this loving power is completely and irrevocably welded to and within nature and cannot truly be understood as anything separate from the natural world.

Consider this excerpt from a book that in all honesty I have not read but am excited to quote—Rosalyn Marie Amenta's *The Earth Mysticism of the Native American Tribal Peoples with Special Reference to the Circle Symbol and the Sioux Dance Rite*:

> The mystical experience indigenous to the native North American tribal peoples stands out uniquely in the history of religions in that it is grounded in the vision of a Sacred World which underlies, envelops and is manifestly present within the entire empirical order. The sacred dimension, although being qualitatively different from the phenomenal realm is not regarded as "otherworldly" or "transcendently beyond" in the same way as it is meant in a monotheistic or monistic apprehension of the Divine. In this sense, the Native American does not "transcend" the world in the Christian or Vedantic or Neo-Platonic manner; rather, he "plunges into" the world and experiences himself and the earth with all its myriad phenomena as being totally immersed in and revelatory of the Divine Reality.

All the elements of creation, earth, air, fire, and water, all the animals and trees, all the humans, are extensions, aspects, dimensions, and reflections of this Great Mystery. In other words the Divine is *within* the world, not *above* the world.

This is reflected in the well-known Lakota prayer of connection, "Mitákuye Oyás'iŋ," which translates to "All my relations" or "We are all related."

Black Elk famously said,

The first peace, which is the most important, is that which comes within the souls of people when they realize their relationship, their oneness with the universe and all its powers, and when they realize at the center of the universe dwells the Great Spirit, and that its *center is really everywhere*, it is within each one of us.

Incredibly similar to our old friend we quoted earlier, Nicholas of Cusa, remember? "Whose center, so to speak, is everywhere and whose circumference is nowhere."

This concept pulses through many of the great Indigenous spiritual beliefs, such as Gitche Manitou, as the Great Spirit is known to the Algonquin, as well as the mystical, all-encompassing power of Teotl in Aztec cosmology.

There is a beautiful quote that sums up many of these thoughts. Dictated in Onondaga by Chief John Arthur Gibson in 1912. This is a prayer revealed by the well-regarded Iroquois prophet Tekanawita, "the Great Peacemaker":

Now, therefore, we shall give thanks, that is, we shall thank the Creator of the earth, that is, he who planted all kinds of weeds and all varieties of shrubs and all kinds of trees; and springs, flowing water, such as rivers and large bodies of water, such as lakes; and the sun that keeps moving by day, and by night, the moon, and where the sky is, the stars, which no one is able to count; moreover, the way it is on earth in relation to which no one is able to tell the extent to which it is to their benefit, that is the people whom he created and who will continue to live on earth. This, then, is the reason we thank him, the one with great power, the one who is the Creator.

To a wannabe shaman, a wannabe actor/artist, and a depressed, anxious, and sometimes lost young man who had jettisoned the faith of his childhood, this made sense! The idea of Wakan Tanka worked beautifully as a "way in" to reconceptualize God—the Unknowable Essence, the All-That-Is, the Originating Mystery, the One, the Universal Mind, the Timeless Being.

This discovery had many practical implications and tangible results for me. It slowly, eventually, led me, at the height of my mental health struggles, to find a spiritual path toward greater peace, understanding, serenity, meaning, direction, and purpose.

Because, at the end of the day, it all boiled down to what did the Great Mystery *want* from me personally? What does He want from *us*, collectively? Surely there must be some kind of plan behind all this difficult, complicated beauty? Is there more at stake here than just seeking inner peace? *If* there is a Higher Power at work within, without, and beyond the forces of the natural world, what does this infinite, unknowable love/beauty/force have in store for us, individually and collectively? Surely it can't have created all of us sad and beautiful human beings and cast us on this planet like a bunch of ants in an ant farm to simply "have at it!" with a "good luck!" pat on the back and a sign-off of "Hey, enjoy all this random, useless beauty!"

There must be some kind of larger all-encompassing spiritual vision at work for us humans.

And since no network let me make a TV show about this Notorious G.O.D., I guess you'll just have to continue to explore these ideas with me on these here pages of *Soul Boom!*

CHAPTER FIVE

THE SACRED PILGRIMS

All this hurrying
soon will be over.
Only when we tarry
do we touch the holy.

—Rainer Maria Rilke

A few years back I visited Green Bay, Wisconsin, and as I emerged from its spotless, bland midwestern airport, the beefy, mustached cab driver cheerily asked, like some character from *Fargo*, "You gonna go check out Lambeau Field? You don't want to miss it. Pretty much the only thing worth seein' 'round here!" When I told him that I was attending a nearby arts festival and that I was bummed to be missing out on the renowned local football stadium, he seemed mildly disappointed. "Well, maybe you can check it out on your way back. People come from all over the world. Like a pilgrimage!" We then continued our conversation about the Packers' chances, the weather, and the varieties of local bratwurst.

But what he said got me pondering more about pilgrimages, about sacredness, and about holy spaces because, you see, my family and I had recently been on an *actual* religious pilgrimage to an actual holy site in Israel and returned a few weeks prior.

As much as I appreciate Lambeau Field and many other football stadiums I've visited, and as much as I love the transcendent rush I experience when submerging myself in the outrageous communal emotion at a Seahawks game, this other pilgrimage was prompted by my religious faith and was inspired by something I believed to be holy, mysterious, and important. After all, the dictionary definition of a pilgrimage is "a trip made to a holy place for religious reasons." Both my trip to Green Bay and the one to Israel got me thinking about what is "holy" in America in 2023 and about where we make "pilgrimages" to. Also, they got me thinking about what these old-fashioned words offer us at their deepest point of meaning and how desperately we human beings might need what the words point to.

Note to the reader: Up until this point, I know I've been all about the *big* stuff. Pandemics. God. Death. We're going to get to the other mega-doozy topic—religion—in short order. But for a few pages here, I'm going to interrupt your "big ideas" programming to wax philosophical about a simpler and subtler question: *What is sacred?* I'm going to shift gears and take a little detour by telling you a story of my travels and the profound effect they had on me. The themes and issues that I'll be laying out for you require more meditative pondering than any seeking of concrete answers. Think of the following as a kind of poetic contemplation on the sacred, the holy.

⸻

The pilgrimage I made a few years ago to the "holy place for religious reasons" was incredibly special to me because underneath the soil of the shrine I visited is buried a prophet—the interred physical remains of a holy man whom I revere far more than even Green Bay Packers legends Brett Favre or Aaron Rodgers.

The shrine is located outside of Acre or Akko, Israel, and it is called Bahji or the Shrine of Bahji (pronounced Bah-zhee), which translates to "delight" in Arabic. The name of the person who was laid to rest there is Mirza Husayn-Ali, otherwise known by His title of Baha'u'llah ("Glory of God" in Arabic). I've mentioned Him before. He was the founder of the Baha'i Faith and someone whose work, example, and mission I study, follow, and deeply admire.

Why was He buried there? Well, before Baha'u'llah passed away, He lived for many years in the small estate that is a stone's throw away from where He is now entombed. After being exiled from His native Persia in 1853 and living as a prisoner of the Ottoman Empire starting in 1863, He spent the last years of His life under house arrest there, from 1879 until 1892.

The pilgrims who visit this holy place are members of the Baha'i Faith and come to this location in northern Israel from every corner of the globe. Among the almost two hundred Baha'is visiting for our scheduled nine-day pilgrimage trip were believers from as far away as South Africa, Romania, and the Philippines. Thousands of tourists also come to visit the gardens and this particular sacred site as it is open to people of all faiths. I went with my wife, Holiday, also a Baha'i, and our teenage son, Walter, because we wanted him to experience sacredness on a visceral level that he would hopefully remember forever.

We dressed nicely, not in formalwear or anything, but we didn't want to visit this most cherished spot in something like jeans, Crocs, or cargo shorts. We arrived by bus at the visitors center with several dozen other pilgrims and prepared ourselves for the long walk from there to the central grounds and buildings.

The site of Bahji, which is several hundred acres large, is immaculately groomed, with crushed red stone pathways that flow away from the central edifice in a star-like pattern. Numerous flitting hummingbirds swoop and spin around the verdant hedges and trees. A tall, beautiful wrought iron gate frames the entrance to the outer perimeter of the shrine area, a beautiful latticework that demarcates the sacred space on the other side and helps to give the grounds a distinct, sublime feeling. The pilgrim passes through those iron gates and approaches the outside of the stone shrine with an ever-blooming attitude of respect—head bowed, hushed, reverent.

When we entered the area, we felt a change in the very air of the gardens. The scent of oranges and jasmine was profound. The air seemed to vibrate with a joyful feeling. Joyful and still all at once.

Even if you're not religious or don't consider yourself spiritual in the slightest, I can't imagine anyone approaching the grounds not having some kind of a sensation of awe or inspiration. In fact I spoke to several visitors who were not Baha'is and who acknowledged that very fact. It's in the air.

When we got to the entrance of the small stone building, the destination of our journey, we along with everyone else removed our shoes at a covered alcove outside the door that leads inside the shrine. (I'm sorry to admit this, but I was extremely grateful my socks didn't have any holes in them.) There is a small velvet box filled with prayer books in dozens of languages that folks from all over the world can use to say Baha'i prayers.

Tradition asks that you enter the simple but ornate doors with a bowed head and to always be facing the specific area inside where this great divine teacher is buried—never turning one's back toward the actual point of adoration, as that would feel slightly disrespectful. Slowly, carefully, we entered the edifice itself, which is approximately fifty feet by fifty feet and was built well over one hundred years ago, originally as a guesthouse. As we entered the main room, we saw a central alcove now roofed with glass skylights, like a greenhouse. The floors were covered in the most beautiful overlapping antique silk and wool Persian carpets that you've ever seen. Well-tended plants, ferns, and flowers decorated this central area of the inner sanctum, and the vines reached toward the ceiling and the skylights, up toward the light, allowing the space to become both a beautiful conservatory garden as well as a sacred mausoleum.

I found the room hushed and still, even when it had dozens of people inside. The muted crack of prayer beads. An occasional muffled sob. Outside, the intermittent caw of a far-off crow. A hint of sweet jasmine and incense in the air.

There were a few small rooms that branch off from the central sky-lighted one, and in every room we saw visitors in all modes of dress from their native cultures, sitting or on their knees or prostrated, always facing the burial area, which was partitioned with a translucent curtain and illumined by a small lamp—under the floor of which, Baha'u'llah was interred.

I sat on the beautiful antique silk and wool rugs and prayed. Some of the prayers I read from a Baha'i prayer book and some I recited from my heart. I said prayers for loved ones. Prayers of praise and gratitude. Prayers for help and assistance. And sometimes I would stop and just be still and silent for long, long stretches of time. And it should be noted that when I mention "said" a prayer, most of the time it was simply "feeling" a prayer—a generally beseeching kind of loving-kindness and warmth in my heart.

My mind was mostly quiet, tranquil. At times my heart was filled to bursting with emotion, joy, and exaltation. And then, at other times, I felt oddly removed. I may have wept. I can't remember. I *can* remember being very uncomfortable on the floor and adjusting my position a good deal, as my chubby middle-aged legs tend to fall asleep a lot.

I also remember thinking to myself repeatedly, kind of like a giggly teenager, "Wow! I'm in one of the most sacred places in the world. Cool!"

But mostly I was in a deeply extended place of reverence and peace among the ferns and vines and pilgrims and rugs and the aroma of holiness.

I sat in that small sacred space for what I assumed to be about an hour but could have easily been two or three. Time worked strangely in that place. It seemed to slip away and elude one's grasp for some reason. It didn't feel linear. Time felt somewhat elongated there, like molasses. It reminded me of times I had sat in a deep forest wilderness and was so transported in noticing the sounds and smells around me that I completely lost track of the clock.

Before leaving, I pressed my forehead to the threshold of the corner of the shrine, where the veil to the inner sanctum was, and said a quick, humble prayer of thanks.

When exiting the shrine, one backs away slowly, with reverence. This can be a little tricky as there are three small stairs leading into the building and walking backward down them can be a little challenging for the elderly and people like me who are prone to falling down at the most inopportune places and times. I pictured myself tumbling backward down those little stairs in front of all these reverential pilgrims like Jim Carrey from some '90s comedy and springing back up: "Alrighty then!"

Once we had respectfully backed away from the shrine a bit and turned our attention back to the surrounding gardens, I found that the world had shifted. It's like when you hit your windshield wipers and spritz the glass in front of you and all of a sudden you realize just how dirty it had been. Just like that, you can see everything outside your car with a renewed clarity.

It was like that. Only in my heart.

I saw the beautiful hedges and olive trees and birds in a new light. I felt renewed. Tranquil. Joyous. Like something unseen had shifted.

The eldest son of Baha'u'llah, 'Abdu'l-Baha (who holds a very special station in the Baha'i Faith), said of pilgrimage, "Holy places are undoubtedly centers of the outpouring of Divine grace, because on entering the illumined sites associated with martyrs and holy souls, and by observing reverence, both physical and spiritual, one's heart is moved with great tenderness."

Indeed, my heart, after just a small window of time in that precious sanctuary, was filled with a great tenderness. A tenderness that comes from repeated demonstrations and expressions of reverence as well as a prolonged contemplative silence.

The Shrine at Bahji is so sacred that for the Baha'is of the world it is the point of adoration, the Qiblih, the focus point that Baha'is turn to when they say their daily prayer. It is the point that 'Abdu'l-Baha says is the "luminous shrine," "around which circumambulate the Concourse on High," a convocation of the holiest angels in heaven. Just as many Jews focus their rites toward the Temple Wall in Jerusalem and Muslims perform their five-times-daily prayer facing the Kaaba (most holy spot) in Mecca, Baha'is from all over the world face this garden near Haifa in reverential daily devotion.

While reciting the "Short Obligatory Prayer," Baha'is both physically and metaphorically turn their hearts to this exact geographic point at some point during the day. (There's even a compass app that shows you *exactly* which direction to face.) We say a short daily prayer that Baha'is believe reveals *why* we are alive, why we were created.

Baha'u'llah writes in one sentence of this brief prayer, "I bear witness, O My God, that Thou hast created me to *know Thee* and to *worship Thee*" (italics mine). It's really that simple. It all boils down to that. Our ultimate purpose is to "know and worship" the Creator. (What that exactly means is the topic for another chapter. Or another book.) And Baha'is the world over are reminded of this purpose on a daily basis as they turn, often from tens of thousands of miles away, toward this shrine that my family and I had just visited.

In so many ways, this garden, for me, was the paragon of the sacred. So much so that in the days and weeks that followed my pilgrimage to the Baha'i Holy Lands in Israel, I kept tossing all these words and concepts around in my head. Words that we don't examine much or really think about in our daily life. Words that are almost entirely missing from everyday society and work. Words like:

- Sacred
- Pilgrimage
- Holy
- Reverence
- Divine

- Blessed
- Devotion
- Sanctity
- Devout
- Prayer
- Prostration
- Worship
- Shrine

And the word that stood out to me most was "sacred." No exploration of the spiritual journey would be complete without an examination of the sacred. It's a difficult word to define these days. What does it mean exactly? It exists somewhere on that master list of other truly difficult-to-define words, like "holy," "blessed," "divine."

In the same category as other hard-to-define words, like "frittata," "nonplussed," and "socialism."

When I asked my friends Merriam and Webster, I zeroed in on their second definition of the word as the one I'm most interested in.

I am intrigued by this definition of "sacred":

a: worthy of religious veneration: *Holy*
b: entitled to reverence and respect

What is holy? What is worthy of veneration and reverence these days? Especially in the chaos and static of the modern world? Where are our sacred shrines, worthy of a pilgrimage? Where are the devout, the devoted, the devotions among us?

These seemingly archaic, outmoded words and questions that nobody really discusses in our "unsacred" or "desacralized" contemporary society. Or that anyone thinks about in the dailiness of our lives. So as I've recently experienced the sacred in my bones and body, I thought I would try to share some of my personal feelings and reflections, and perhaps, in the doing, some meaning will gradually reveal itself.

As I laid out in the previous chapter, I had a phase in my spiritual searching where I was deeply moved and transformed by Native American ideas around spirituality. At the risk of grossly overgeneralizing, in the Native American worldview pretty much everything that exists is sacred. Especially in nature.

Black Elk once said, "Perhaps you have noticed that even in the slightest breeze you can hear the voice of the Cottonwood tree; this we understand is its prayer to the Great Spirit, for not only men, but all things and all beings pray to Him continually in different ways."

Plants and animals have spirits that are considered as real as their actual bodies. Prayers were often said over animals whose lives were taken by the hunt and whose meat and skin were used for food and survival. Nearby mountains and lakes often have a spiritual uniqueness and are ascribed with legends based on actual history. Spirits thrived everywhere and myths connected the divine world and the spirit world of one's ancestors with the natural, physical world at every turn.

These concepts were in direct contrast to the teachings of the Christian clergy when they came to the American shores. Luther Standing Bear (1868–1939), who had an incredible history, going from son of a chief to a Hollywood actor and stuntman, said of the sacredness of nature, "Only to the white man was nature a wilderness, and only to him was it 'infested' with 'wild' animals and 'savage' people. To us it was tame. Earth was bountiful and we were surrounded with the blessings of the Great Mystery."

This profound spiritual legacy of being "surrounded with the blessings of the Great Mystery" and viewing all living things as continually praying to the Great Spirit doesn't really fly these days. In fact, my life in 2023 Los Angeles is pretty much lacking in anything remotely sacred or spiritually connected. It's all iPhones, quickly devoured sandwiches, and leaf blowers. It's texts and podcasts and emails. It's pressured phone calls, calendars, and a nonstop newsfeed.

Part of the issue in 2023 America is the enormous discrepancy between what is sacred to the conservative and liberal halves of our country. In this, as in pretty much everything else, we also seem to be divided.

In a grotesquely gross generalization that certainly does not apply to everyone on the right, to a conservative, the Bible and Constitution might be considered sanctified. The traditional idea of family. As well as a church and the cross that's inside that church. An unborn baby's life is also sacred, perhaps. Jesus and how He is portrayed. The American flag. The nobility of the military. These are belief systems and viewpoints that arose from several centuries of a distinctly Amer-Christian point of view and hold true for much of the heartland of our nation.

Whereas to the more secular urban liberal (and again, this is a generalized portrayal of a belief framework), "holiness" is, at least from a religious consideration of the word, something that might at its worst be considered as "superstitious." It's a term that is often viewed as being fabricated by either a mass religious imagination or the clergy of a specific religion that has some nefarious agenda, or as some holdover from an ancient belief system.

In another gross generalization, to the contemporary agnostic of the liberal bent in urban America, "sacredness" at its best might be applied to the feeling of awe and wonder toward the universe. That science has its own beauty and sacredness to be marveled and wondered at. What should be sanctified or honored should be the dignity of one's personal, racial, sexual, or gender identity. Universal human rights are sacred, perhaps. But rarely, if ever, would the concept be applied to a spiritual teacher or a shrine, a burial site or metaphorical words in an old book. An atheist, for instance, might say that everything is equal in sanctity— a molecule, a human life, a star, a work of art, a tree.

The 9/11 memorial feels like sacred, hallowed ground that both political left and right alike could be united in a shared embrace of. We all appreciate what happened there, the sacrifices that were made, the pain of loss, the needless devastation. That, certainly, is a place worthy of a pilgrimage.

In his seminal work *The Sacred and the Profane*, the religious philosopher Mircea Eliade writes of the difference between what is holy and what is earthly or "profane." As I understand it (I *tried* to read the book, I really did), to him, a sacred space is defined by the divine meaning ascribed to it and what is profane is simply the opposite—a space or a thing that has no sacredness attached. An object or place that has, to use his phrase, no "cosmic sacrality."

Think of the individual stones of Stonehenge. Large, yes. Impressive, for sure. But sacred? Not if they are lying on a beach or in a remote valley somewhere. Not by themselves. But stand them on end and put them in a circle and correlate them to the equinox, and to this day the feeling of ancient power in the place cannot be denied. Nearby farming fields that are not ringed with impossibly placed stones would be considered profane and unhallowed in Eliade's philosophy.

His work was revolutionary at the time because the idea of the sacred has been used as a cudgel for so many centuries by the Christian Church. Sacred was *only* what was in and of "the church" or in *a* church. Everything else was profane, sinful even. Sacred equaled heaven. Blasphemy equaled hell. As Eliade's work incorporated the teachings, writings, and faith systems of other world religions and allowed for their definitions of the sacred, he opened up a whole new way of seeing the word.

Eliade's theory has a real quandary at its center, however. It implies that everything not specifically ascribed with meaning is profane. Really? Wouldn't that include all the rest of nature? What about a driveway or a bridge? An iceberg? Is a simple empty lot of land with a "for sale" sign on it profane? I think we need a new perspective and definition.

I remember a few days after coming back home, sitting in my car on a Los Angeles freeway, my phone buzzing with alerts, and how I felt a longing for those precious hours in that consecrated place. I wondered if I would ever experience anything like that again. My perspective had shifted, and my heart had been opened, but as I drove to my local coffee place or to an appointment, as I rolled calls while at a stoplight, as I dragged my garbage cans down the driveway on Tuesday evenings, I found a longing in my heart. I missed that experience of the holy that my family found in that garden in Israel.

I kept thinking to myself, Is nothing sacred? Is everything? If everything is sacred, can a 7-11 be sacred? A car wash? That area behind a strip mall, where they keep the dumpsters?

At first blush I would probably answer no. The mundane is, most likely, profane. A place created only for short-term profit, like those ever-expanding shopping areas in the exurbs, filled with chain restaurants and auto parts stores and those little speakers they hide in the bushes next to the parking spaces that pump out tired '80s hits. Places built without any thought of aesthetics or any nod to what's sacrosanct. Only an offering to the shrine of the dollar.

But we need to buy things, after all. There can't automatically and intrinsically be something unsacred about a place of business, can there?

Consider the restaurant where my wife and I had our first date: Sea-Thai in Seattle on Forty-Fifth Street. It sits in an average row of businesses on a busy arterial. It was fully created for profit, but it also holds an incredibly special place in my heart, as our relationship took root there over shrimp puffs. I imagine everyone reading this can think of a list of unextraordinary places rendered "holy" due to some memorable event that occurred there.

So is that it? Does a memory make something sacred? Was the Shrine of Baha'u'llah simply holy because it allowed us to viscerally remember his life and legacy?

Maybe it *is* worthwhile and fulfilling to take a pilgrimage to Lambeau Field, after all. I mean, there is joy there. Exaltation. History. Passion. Community. Was I being elitist and judgmental when the cab driver brought up the idea?

When I think about it from this perspective, I remember that I've had some truly religious experiences at the Greek Theatre in Los Angeles, for instance. Listening to music that transported, uplifted, and healed me. So is that then a sacred space? A shrine? Worthy of a pilgrimage?

Roughly three hundred years ago there was another pilgrim, Matsuo Basho (1644–1694), the famous poet from Japan. Some consider him the greatest author of haiku in history. In his moving, sumptuous work *The Narrow Road to the Interior* (sometimes called *The Narrow Road to the Deep North*) Basho wandered on foot hundreds of miles into various sacred temples and sites around medieval Japan in a state of spiritual and artistic contemplation. He famously said, "Real poetry is to lead a beautiful life. To live poetry is better than to write it." He also said, "The journey itself is my home." And his journey? He walked for dozens of miles every day on his poetic pilgrimage, journaling, noticing the specific details of the beauty of the natural world around him, the changes of the seasons and the sound of the breeze in the cottonwood trees. His day would end at a holy place, a crossing, a bridge, a harbor, a gravesite, a temple, or a monastery and then Basho would begin his craft. He would compose a poem, based on his travels, inspired by his personal life, wisdom, and experience, informed by his observations on the trail and in the forests, and devoted specifically to the sacred spot he was visiting on that particular day. He would then leave the poem behind him, as an offering. A gift.

For Basho, as with many Native Americans, there was no delineation between what was "holy," what was of "nature," what was "art," and what was of "religion." He wrote, "The temple bell stops but I still hear the sound coming out of the flowers." Words like that could have easily been spoken by Black Elk or Luther Standing Bear. Nature, poetry, shrines, pilgrimages, God, art, spirituality, life—it's all part of the circle of the sacred and profound in the universe of Basho.

Thich Nhat Hanh said, "In the sunlight of awareness, everything becomes sacred."

⇒◦◦⇐

So where is *my* circle of the sacred and profound? My daily challenge, our continuing challenge, is to find what is holy in our lives and recognize it. My family has a beautiful stone bench in the backyard surrounded by trees and flowers where we occasionally meditate and pray. That feels sacred to me. Perhaps it is awareness-opening meditation itself that is a gateway to the sacred, the eternal.

When I was at Bahji, in the sunlight of awareness of that holy space, that blessed trip, I felt the differences between me and others disappear. Their "otherness" melted away as we visitors joined together in this act of pilgrimage. That may be the heart of holiness itself, the melting away of the illusion of separateness.

So, dear reader, I ask you this: What makes up *your* circle of the sacred? I won't ask you for anything else (I mean, you've already bought my book!), but please take five minutes to consider, in a moment of personal reflection, these five questions for yourself:

- **What is holy to you personally?** Maybe it's a religious tome. But it doesn't have to be a thing. A garden? But it doesn't need to be a place. A family dinner, maybe?
- **Where does sacredness live?** In a poem or prayer? Sunday church services? Any group of people united in service to make the world a better place? The night sky? A remote forest or beach or mountain?
- **What should be sacred to all of humanity?** Love? Science? Families, whatever their form? Humanity—that strange family of eight billion people inhabiting the same ball of mud in outer space? Stars? Places of worship? The atmosphere?
- **What is most definitely not sacred?** Is it the profane? The mundane? Or just anyplace or anything that is filled with the worst humanity has to offer: hate, baseness, or selfish behavior? The seven deadly sins, like greed and lust and rage? Are the jabbering talking heads and outraged personalities of opinion news and social media worthy of any reverence?
- **What have we lost by not having more "sacredness" in our lives?** Our ability to pause and be still? Our sense of awe for the

things we can't explain? A connection to our souls? To nature? To each other? Would we have deeper and more meaningful thoughts, conversations, and communities if we centered our attention around and toward the holy?

My hope here is to spark only one action in your mind and heart: a moment of pause. Reflect on the questions above. Reflect on what you do or don't find sacred. Perhaps the goal is to find what you consider sublime and then slowly, ever so slowly, increase it. Increase day by day what is sacred to you. Reflect on what could be gained by finding ever more pockets of the divine in your daily life. Share your findings with someone close to you. Or, even better, someone you're *not* close to.

Going back to the cultural divide around the concept. What if it's *all* true? What if it's *all* sacred? What if it's not an either-or? Jesus taught love. That's most certainly sacred. Science teaches interconnectedness, which is (for all practical purposes) the same thing as love. Families, whatever their form, are sacred. Humanity, after all, is itself a kind of family, eight billion strong, inhabiting the same ball of mud in outer space. Stars are sacred, as are churches and trees and babies in utero. And so are human rights and the symbol of the cross and how we identify and define our individuality. What if what brought us all together, all us people in contemporary America, was a focus on the light in our lives—things that healed wounds and gave our divided, confused, distracted, and outraged world some solace and unity?

What if sacredness, rather than being relegated to a place or a thing, was a condition? A condition of holding divine light. An internal condition of communion. As when a flower turns toward the sun or an owl toward the moon. Can the sacred live in the sharp intake of breath caused by the beauty of a sunset? In the ripple of the words "I love you" said to a spouse or child or parent or friend?

The recognition of the blessed, radiant nature of each and every human being, sanctified in grace?

At the end of the day, I really don't have any answers. Maybe Basho does. I wish he were around to ask.

I picture Basho walking through our modern world in his medieval robes, demonstrating to us all how to "live poetry." Maybe that's what makes a pilgrimage at the end of the day. Living in poetry.

I imagine Basho journeying to the Shrine at Bahji, where he removes his sandals and bows his head in reverence as he picks up a prayer book. He backs out of the sacred space and, hand in hand with Baha'u'llah, walks along the freeway toward the Middle West of the United States. Captain James T. Kirk and Kwai Chang Caine join them as they walk. Together they cross the plains of the Dakotas, where they meet up with Luther Standing Bear and Black Elk and, eventually, that cab driver from the Wisconsin airport. Basho walks with all of them, these sacred pilgrims. He walks with every one of us, secular and spiritual, city folk and country folk, pilgrims all, through the streets of Green Bay to the iron gates of the legendary Lambeau Field itself. Leaving behind poetry and prayers. Making everything sacred in his wake.

CHAPTER SIX

RELIGION, SCHMELIGION

On my podcast, *Metaphysical Milkshake*, which I do with the writer, scholar, and general roustabout Reza Aslan, we ask each and every guest, "What's one eye-opening experience that everyone should have?"

I thought I'd ask myself the same question right here on these pages as I've had so many over my many ungainly years on this blue planet.

Holding my son at dawn, only minutes old, after he (and his mother!) almost died in a horrific childbirth in the hallway of a crappy Van Nuys, California, hospital.

Seeing Ingmar Bergman's mind-blowing three-and-a-half-hours-long Swedish-language production of *Hamlet* starring Peter Stormare.

Getting married as bagpipes played on the banks of a river under what was left of Mount St. Helens, my soon-to-be wife, Holiday, being rowed down the river in a raft filled with flowers.

Witnessing from a fishing boat the majestic and terrifying calving of a glacier in remote Greenland, with no one else around for hundreds of miles.

Erupting in joy along with my fellow castmates when the TV show I was on won the Emmy, mere months after it was almost canceled repeatedly. (Hint: it was *The Office*.)

Swimming next to dolphins and sea turtles with my wife and son off the coast of Hawaii.

The list goes on and on.

But my final answer?

Jerusalem. The Old City. A historical tour. Let the history and sacred beauty of this glorious and terrifying city sink in as you explore it. Hopefully with an experienced guide. Do it before you die. Please.

This is the one eye-opening experience I believe every person should have.

My wife, Holiday, and I visited many years ago and were blessed with this incredible tour guide named Bruce. He was much more than a mere tour guide. He's a nonstop monologist. Historian. Comedian. Philosopher. Immigrant to Israel from suburban Boston. Big authority on all things political and historical in the "Muddle East" (as he insisted on calling it). He opened my eyes and introduced me to a whole new way of seeing the world. *And* to some of the very best hummus, falafel, and halvah I've ever tasted.

Here's why you should take this trip.

In Jerusalem, within an area of a couple kilometers there are three of the most holy sites in the world. These sites are all centered around what is known as the Temple Mount, the Haram al-Sharif to Muslims.

It cannot be stressed enough how ancient, powerful, and revered these three locations are in the hearts of Muslims, Jews, and Christians. Millions, perhaps billions, would be willing to sacrifice their lives for these edifices. There is no greater political, social, and religious potential flashpoint for violence in the world. And when one realizes that these sacred structures are all a couple of frisbee golf throws away from one another, it is a stupefyingly enlightening revelation.

The aforementioned interconnected sites on or near the Temple Mount are as follows:

- The Wailing Wall (or Western Wall, or HaKotel, which means "wall" in Hebrew)
- The Foundation Stone, which lies inside the Dome of the Rock, a.k.a. the Al-Aqsa Mosque

- The Church of the Holy Sepulchre, which marks the location where Jesus was both crucified and, three days later, resurrected

Disclaimer: I will do my very best to describe these structures and their tremendous significance. Many *actual* historians and theologians who are much more deeply versed in Judaism, Islam, and Christianity will probably have a very different take on the importance of these sacred sites and might vehemently disagree with my feeble layman's assessment. There are a lot of passionately differing opinions on *everything* concerning the Holy Land. True story, there's even a deathly serious contention between Jews and Arabs over who *invented hummus*!

So don't judge. I'm just a stupid actor.

At the center of the Temple Mount is the Western Wall, or Wailing Wall. This is one of the most sacred spots in Judaism. You've seen it in the news and in books, magazines, and movies. Little prayers, written on tiny pieces of paper, are frequently pushed into the cracks of its edifice by throngs of yarmulke-wearing visitors. Orthodox Jews in black suits gather there, reading from the Torah. It's sacred for a whole bunch of reasons. First off, it is a place of intense prayers of gratitude and mourning and the begging of divine mercy. The "silent prayer," or Amidah, is traditionally said while facing toward the wall, no matter where a Jewish believer might be in the world.

Most importantly, it is the only existing remnant of the walls of the Second Temple, built on the foundation stones of the First Temple. You see, once upon a time, wise King Solomon built a most holy temple for the Jewish tribes, only to have it destroyed by the Babylonians a few hundred years later. That was the "First" Temple, the Temple of Solomon, created about 1000 BC. A few decades after that, following the Babylonian Captivity, when the temple was destroyed and a large portion of the population of the Jewish nation had been taken as slaves to Babylonia, the Second Temple was built. It had a lot of ups and downs, as so many ancient temples do. King Herod of biblical fame did a huge expansion of it around 20 BC, only to have the entire thing flattened by the Romans in AD 70.

Interestingly enough, as we're about to find out, this entire Temple Mount is ultimately one gigantic celebration of monotheism, but when the Romans destroyed Jerusalem, they built their new city of Aelia Capitolina right on top of it as a celebration of the god/man/caesar Hadrian, the chief Roman god Jupiter, and many other gods in their pantheon. In other words, polytheism.

But guess who's laughing now, Rome?! (Answer: God.)

The Western Wall is a segment of the wall from the period when Herod had expanded it. It is mysterious and sacred for countless reasons, religious, historical, and cultural, but notably because of its proximity to the Foundation Stone or Noble Rock, as it's referred to in Islam.

Which leads me to the next mind-blowingly sacred building, only fifty meters away, that surrounds said stone, the Dome of the Rock!

This incredible architectural achievement was built in AD 690 by the head of the Muslim faith at the time, the Caliphate, on the site where the Second Temple once stood and directly over the previously mentioned Foundation Stone.

This stone is totally rad. First off, it was, supposedly, where God created the world. So there's that. And as if that wasn't enough, it's supposedly also where He created the very first man, Adam. (In the Baha'i belief system, Adam was not the first actual human being but rather the first recorded divine messenger, prophet, or "manifestation" of God.) Cain and Abel had a picnic lunch on that rock, and— I'm not making this up—the Ark of the Covenant apparently once rested on it. It was also the very stone where Abraham, the world's first monotheist, was about to sacrifice his son (Isaac in the Hebrew Bible, Ishmael in the Muslim tradition) before God jumped in and said, "Gotcha! Just wanted to make sure you'd do anything I asked! Sucka!"

Beneath this stone is also the Cave of Souls, a place where souls await judgment on Judgment Day, according to Muslims. The space is referred to in Judaism as the Axis Mundi, the Holy of Holies, where heaven and earth converge.

I mean, a rock really doesn't get more sacred than this particular rock.

On our trip, we didn't get to see the actual stone, as the entrance to the Dome of the Rock was off-limits due to political unrest in Israel. But just being near it, one of the most profound places in all of human history, was enough to give me epic tingles. Feel free to take a moment to find an online photo of this fairly ordinary, yet monumental, flat stone around which this gorgeous, ornate, golden, rainbow-tiled mosque was built.

To Muslims, this location is the third most holy spot in the world. It is the site of the Prophet Mohammed's mystical "midnight journey" where he traveled to Jerusalem on the back of the winged steed Buraq and then ascended to the seven heavens, aided by the angel Gabriel, and met with all the previous prophets of the world's major religions (Adam, Abraham, Moses, Jesus, etc.) and received instructions from Allah about prayer.

But back to the Temple Mount. As if what I just described wasn't enough of a plethora of sacred and holy buildings, walls, rocks, and whatnot, a mere half a kilometer away sits the imposing Church of the Holy Sepulchre.

So much happened to Jesus within this awe-inspiring edifice, it's hard to keep track! Let's summarize: First, the last four stations of the cross occurred within the boundaries of the church proper. Calvary, the hill where Jesus was crucified, is right there in the corner as well. On the lower levels, there is a cave that was "discovered" by the emperor Constantine's mother, Helena, that all were sure was Jesus's original tomb. As we know from Sunday school and marquees in front of evangelical churches, Jesus, after three days, went up to heaven to be with his father. That happened in this space as well. Like I said, quite a busy site on or about the year AD 33.

Constantine ordered the giant temple to Jupiter that his Roman forefathers had built on that sacred ground to be torn down and a grand church to be built in AD 326. Within the church, the "true cross" on which Jesus was crucified was supposedly displayed for many hundreds of years.

Here's what's fascinating about this particular church: it is cooperatively shared by multiple branches of Christianity. (Remember, there are more than forty-five thousand denominations of what is often thought of as a three-headed church—Catholic, Protestant, and Eastern Orthodox.) The Church of the Holy Sepulchre is administered by the Greek Orthodox Church, the Armenian Apostolic Church (the oldest in the world), and the Roman Catholic Church, as well as, though to a lesser degree, the Coptics, Ethiopians, and Syrian Catholics. There's even a literal schedule hanging on the wall about who gets to control or be in certain parts of the church at certain times.

When I was there, the main floor of the building was shifting control from one of these towering-hat-wearing denominations to another. One group of robed priests was marching out and another marching in. They were swinging chained incense around in their smokey thuribles (yes, that's a word), as they are wont to do. Chanting and marching as they came and went, ceding and gaining authority over a small section of the real estate of the floor of the church. Suddenly, I noticed something that truly struck me. They were swinging their chained metal censures around, smoke pouring out of the holes, in a remarkably *aggressive* manner! Almost *toward* the members of the other church as they passed them. Their loud chanting was a bit hostile as well. The negative energy in the most holy church of all Christianity was palpable.

So I did what any God-fearing, tech-savvy tourist would do. I pulled out my phone and did a deep Google dive, right there under the sacred pillars and arches. What I discovered was that serious fights break out between the various factions *all the time*!

Here's a small taste from the always reliable Wikipedia:

> On a hot summer day in 2002, a Coptic monk moved his chair from its agreed spot into the shade. This was interpreted as a hostile move

by the Ethiopians and eleven were hospitalized after the resulting fracas. In another incident in 2004, during Orthodox celebrations of the Exaltation of the Holy Cross, a door to the Franciscan chapel was left open. This was taken as a sign of disrespect by the Orthodox and a fistfight broke out. Some people were arrested, but no one was seriously injured.

On Palm Sunday, in April 2008, a brawl broke out when a Greek monk was ejected from the building by a rival faction. Police were called to the scene but were also attacked by the enraged brawlers. On Sunday, 9 November 2008, a clash erupted between Armenian and Greek monks during celebrations for the Feast of the Cross.

One only has to do an online search of "monks brawling/fighting Church Holy Sepulchre" to be met with dozens of incredibly disturbing photographs of various priests going at it, UFC style, under the roof of the sacred edifice that surrounds where Jesus Christ ascended to heaven.

But as wild as that may be, by far the most interesting detail of the Church of the Holy Sepulchre is how the place is locked up at night.

As we were getting ready to leave our tour, my awesomely curious wife, Holiday, saw a little old man in a suit and tie, sitting nobly on a bench near the ancient front doors, holding an enormous key. So, of course, we had to take pictures with him. After some conversation with him and our tour guide, Bruce, we came to understand that his family, the Joudehs, Muslims all, have been holders of the key to this church for over eight hundred years, passing through the generations from father to son.

Apparently, in the year 1192, after the famous Muslim leader Salah-a-din recaptured the Holy Land from the Crusaders, he appointed a Muslim family to be the ones with ultimate access to Christianity's most holy site.

That's right. In probably the ultimate metaphor of multifaith interdependence on this volatile chunk of land, Muslims—besides having a mosque that sits on the most holy place in Judaism—hold the key to the most holy Christian location in the world. All under the jurisdiction of a country governed by the Jews![10]

And thank Allah they do because if any of the Christian clergy had ownership of it, they would probably all be clobbering each other over the head to get it, like some kind of interdenominational, silly-hat-wearing, incense-swinging *Squid Game*.

Why am I bringing all this up?

Well, yes, it's an eye-opening experience that I think every human should have. But there's more. So let me back up a little bit.

We live in a fractured world. A large portion of the population seems to live in accordance with rigid religious beliefs they have inherited from ancestors, culture, and family. Sometimes these beliefs feel like a blind, inflexible adherence to a conservative series of ancient doctrines that have not been personally explored and that have little relevance in the modern world. When I see certain Christians denouncing vaccines and condemning gays to hell, some Hindu nationalists promoting violence against women and girls, a group of Muslims praising the killing of innocent civilians as acts of holy heroism, or a community of Jews praising Elohim as they bulldoze Palestinian settlements, I frequently wish there were no religions remaining on our planet.

As do many others. I'm not alone in this. This secular portion of the world sees religion as a vestige of an ancient series of outdated, violence-inducing superstitions. This atheist or nonreligious 15 percent of the world's population (almost one billion people) adamantly believes that humanity, finally freed from its religious dogmas, will embrace the science, common sense, agreed-upon human rights, and collective ethics that will ultimately lead to the flourishing of humanity as a species.

---

10 In fact, in another odd interdenominational twist, the Jordanian monarchy, the Hashemites, has had jurisdiction over the Christian and Muslim holy sites in Jerusalem for one hundred years and views itself as the guarantor of their religious rights in the city.

Never mind that time and time again over the last century, nonreligious-based societies have failed to bring said flourishing to an even greater degree than religious attempts. The most egregious examples include Stalin in the Soviet Union, Pol Pot in Cambodia, imperial Japan, Mao's Cultural Revolution in China, and even (I'm loath to mention it) Nazi Germany. Dozens of attempts to build secular, man-made societies on a basis of nationalism, militarism, racial supremacy, and/or materialist ideals have crashed and burned and killed millions.

Now, I understand that these examples are extreme. There are *billions* of peace-loving religious folks and secular folks now and throughout history who want *nothing* to do with extremist violence. There are, obviously, *dozens* of predominantly secular/atheist cultures that, by most accounts, are working amazingly well. (Here's looking at you, Scandinavia.) And there are also many countries that are religiously balanced in culture and outlook that for the most part seem to be generally flourishing, such as Thailand, Ghana, Turkey, and a rapidly improving Colombia.

Looking at all this chaos, conflict, and confusion, it all boils down to one enormous question that burns in your mind as you witness the bizarre and beautiful happenings at the Temple Mount.

IS RELIGION EVEN WORTH IT?

As we dig into that question, we must first take a good look around at what we have—and what is effective—in terms of religion.

If you're tempted to abandon religion entirely, it's worth first asking, well, what religion is currently in place in contemporary America and, by proxy, in the majority of the Western world? What religion is actually working? How do we define religion in today's society? What do people truly worship? What is the religion we want to disband or jettison?

The scholar and historian Joseph Campbell would often speak of how we know the priorities of a culture by its tallest buildings. For centuries, it was churches and mosques whose peaks would rise above a village or town. Then it was the edifices and towers of government that stood tallest—the town halls, the presidential palaces, the official buildings of various parliaments. And, finally, over the last century, it has been the skyscrapers and headquarters of corporations that have created the staggering skylines of the world's greatest cities. These temples to capitalism tower over the government buildings and churches of the eighteenth and nineteenth centuries, signaling the ascendance of businesses, brands, and the commerce of "things and stuff" as the focal point of adoration and human accomplishment.

Is it the dazzle of the church-like spire of the Chrysler Building that America turns to in modern worship? Or what the building stands for? Success, optimism, a can-do attitude, and, of course, profit. Lots and lots of profit.

Continuing along that line of thinking, it's the figures who fill the front pages of magazines and are followed by tens of millions on social media who are "worshiped" by contemporary society. Our "gods" then would appear to be Dwayne "the Rock" Johnson, Kim Kardashian, Ronaldo, and Beyoncé. Actors, singers, sports figures, models, entrepreneurs, politicians, reality TV "stars," and those renowned for their penchant for self-promotion.

Now I'm certain that celebrities have existed in every culture that has ever been throughout the entirety of human history—artists, warriors, generals, gladiators, writers, sportsmen, politicians, as well as great and legendary beauties. We human beings *love* to obsess over the famous and infamous. Always have, always will.

But were they revered and scrutinized in the past as they are in 2023, with the same rapturous, feverish intensity? We witness through social media every red-carpet outfit, every gaff, every vacation, every romance. Every TikTok or Instagram post by contemporary celebrities is combed over, discussed, and explored ad nauseum in every possible medium. They fill our screens, our billboards, our imaginations, our mythology. And the general populace eats these stories up as swiftly as the press continues to regurgitate them.

Sports figures are our new cultural warrior-heroes—our contemporary Hercules and Odysseus. Millions can recount the stats, accomplishments, and G.O.A.T. exploits of Tom Brady, Michael Jordan, Messi, and Serena Williams. Musicians, models, and actors are our Zeus and Hera and Jupiter, their likenesses surrounding Times Square like so many towering Roman sculptures. Legions of infamous entrepreneurial icons of Silicon Valley, like WeWork's Adam Neumann, Theranos's Elizabeth Holmes, and Uber's Travis Kalanick, are showered with billions of dollars in investment, invited to appear on magazine covers, and feted like rock stars before their narcissism ultimately becomes too much to bear and they eventually crash back down to earth like some silicon Icarus.

Producer and author Gotham Chopra (Deepak's son) has an entertainment company called Religion of Sports that focuses on a main thesis of his work: in the modern world, *sports* is our religion. He posits that athletic competitions in massive arenas give the modern man everything a collective religious experience can give you: transcendence, holy moments, community, a common goal, a striving for human perfection. Awe. In his view, stadiums are contemporary society's new cathedrals, filled with passionate congregants seeking rapture.

But setting the worship of celebrity and sports aside, the fastest-growing religion is one you may not have heard of. Its followers are called the Nones. So-called because on surveys, when asked about religious affiliation, they check "none" or "none of the above." Nones are agnostics and atheists, yes, but by far the majority are self-titled "spiritual but not religious." This is a category ascribed to by well over a third of millennials and far more Gen Zers.

Sixty percent of Nones grew up in a religious family (usually Protestant). A third of Nones meditate, and again, most describe themselves as spiritual but not religious. And their ranks are growing at an outrageous rate. Since 2008, when scholars began tracking them, their membership has swelled by 60 percent. Whereas church membership has declined from 70 percent in the mid-'90s to about 45 percent in 2022.

Why are so many young Americans and Europeans identifying as "none of the above" when it comes to religion?

Certainly, there is a tremendous groundswell of an "antichurch" feeling, where young folk simply don't connect to some old-fashioned practice of "churchgoing." There are countless teachings that many twentysomethings vehemently disagree with in contemporary organized religion. Many of them have to do with sexuality—laws and moral teachings around homosexuality, abortion rights, premarital sexual relations, and traditional gender roles—laws that are frequently exhorted in more long-established church-sanctioned lifestyles. The way so many Protestants (the principal faith being abandoned in the US) have consistently aligned themselves with conservative politics is also off-putting to many who find themselves in the political center or left. Also, the strange antagonism that some branches of Protestantism have recently shown toward science, plus the emphasis on nonbelievers burning in hell, are frequently cited in surveys as top reasons that young people are leaving the faith of their parents. Many of the youth I have personally spoken to vehemently recoil from the judgmentalism and hypocrisy of so many religious institutions.

I find it fascinating that for many coastal and urban Nones, meditation is an important part of their spiritual practice. Yet so few of them formally "pray." And conversely, so many young folks from Middle America who are still practicing Christians find *prayer* to be at the center of their spiritual practice but infrequently *meditate*. In other words, half the country meditates and the other half prays, but very few participate in *both*! If prayer is defined as talking to God (beseeching, thanking, glorifying, connecting) and meditation is listening (being still and attuning to the divine vibration of the universe), there seems to be a disconnect. It would seem that the conversational back-and-forth between these two dynamics would ultimately provide the most bang for the spiritual buck, no?

As this tendency, for the most part, seems to fall along conservative and liberal lines, it once again proves that we Americans are culturally divided in almost every respect.

The other issue that seems to factor in while examining this mass exodus from organized religion is the increasing and continuing (*note: American*) emphasis put on the individual over the collective. From the outset, our nation has been founded on the idea of liberty, especially in the form of personal freedoms. "Live free or die" and "Don't tread on me" are two of our founding state mottos, after all. Liberty and the "pursuit of happiness" are two of our favorite "inalienable rights" from the Declaration of Independence. Part of the mythology of the "new world" of America is a "pull yourself up by your own bootstraps" and "self-made man" brand of rugged individualism that has increasingly led toward autonomy being synonymous with freedom.

And this seems to be foundationally at odds with so much of the collective nature of our country's founding story—when various European church groups seeking the freedom (there's that word again) to worship, assemble, and commune together in their preferred manner headed across the pond to the New England.

Over time, it seems the *community* aspect of American culture has increasingly let the populace down—churches grow less accepting; small towns and villages spread out into faceless suburbs and exurbs; government becomes ever more bloated, polarized, and distrusted; national news outlets are viewed with increasing skepticism; family-owned businesses are absorbed into faceless corporations ruled by hedge funds and multinationals that only serve the bottom line. The population has thereby been pulling away from what used to provide communal containment and ever further toward isolated and individualistic ways of interacting with the world. The collective aspects of our culture seem to have failed us, and we've lost sight of the greater good created by the institutions that previously had bound us together in the social fabric.

And this makes total sense, by the way! We have abandoned these institutions sometimes for very good reasons. But what we've left behind is perhaps the thing we need most of all: connection.

One of the fallouts of this tendency toward individualism is a very different understanding of the nature and purpose of religion itself. As our faith institutions have collectively let us down, more and more people view religion to be about a personal, internal experience rather than any kind of cooperative, shared endeavor.

William James, in his epic and influential *Varieties of Religious Experience*, pointed out this modern spiritual trend more than one hundred years ago:

> Religion . . . shall mean for us the feelings, acts, and experiences of *individual men in their solitude*, so far as they apprehend themselves to stand in relation to whatever they may consider divine.

And we must remember that many good things have transpired as organized religion has been increasingly shelved and the inner spiritual journey has been highlighted. Instead of blindly following dogmas, traditions, and empty rituals and ceremonies, many have sought truth, meaning, and beauty through a personal connection with the Divine— an organic, mystical communication that had dried out in previous decades (and centuries).

There is also a terrific case to be made for the idea of "Let there be peace in the world, and let it begin with me." It is true that peace needs to originate in the heart before it can spread to the family and then the neighborhood, town, county, state, country, and, eventually, the world. And if billions of people engaged in these personal spiritual practices, we would certainly feel a tide of healing change encircling the planet.

This is all part of a long-term cultural evolution that leads young folks toward defining themselves for the most part as "spiritual but not religious."

And yet, for all its many inspirational benefits, this path also has its pitfalls.

In my time in Los Angeles over the last twenty-some years, as I've met more and more friends in what I would call the "woo woo" yoga community, it increasingly feels like the purpose of modern spirituality is simply to "make me feel better internally." It's a form of self-care, self-help, soothing, and solace. But toward what end? Does one's spiritual endeavor simply pause when one feels a brief respite from the persistent attacks of anxiety, imbalance, and discontent?

This way of thinking can easily lead to a kind of "smorgasbord spirituality" where one picks and chooses what is best for oneself from a buffet of self-help healing options (i.e., "I like this particular yoga class and this crystal to focus on. I like this meditation app and this specific New Age author. I like this particular inspiring podcast and that particular self-help book."). In other words, picking and choosing "what works for me" in the same way that one shops for snacks at a Trader Joe's.

There is absolutely nothing wrong with tending to one's spiritual garden and seeking peace, serenity, and connection. A personal mystical and spiritual experience is crucial. As is "self-care." As the great Baha'i leader and teacher Shoghi Effendi says, "For the core of religious faith is that *mystic feeling* that unites man with God."

Personally, I pray and meditate every day in order to achieve some minimal kind of internal balance and harmony. I undertake this discipline not to make me extra wise or enlightened but simply to achieve a daily, basic functionality. In other words, my spiritual practice simply gets me to a place where I can be relatively decent and not some kind of confused, tightly wound jerk (which is where my ego, monkey mind, and family-trauma-induced internal barometer leads me).

But I don't believe the work can end there. In fact, it must not.

If the modern, more secular-minded "spiritual but not religious" person seeks only to focus on the internal aspects of the experience, this potentially moves the practitioner toward a narcissistic New Age mindset. If one's practice is simply to quell anxiety with the use of tools like meditation, inspirational quotes on Instagram, and some excerpted Buddhist-lite teachings around "being in the moment," this ultimately forms a categorical error. Anything you do purely for yourself can drift toward being self-centered and navel-gazing, which fits into our cultural penchant for narcissism and self-interest.

When I was conversing on the *Metaphysical Milkshake* podcast with Brother Phap Huu of the world-renowned Plum Village Monastery, an intimate disciple of one of this century's greatest spiritual teachers, Thich Nhat Hanh, he spoke to this false, modern version of spirituality. He said something to the effect of this: If we look at our spiritual practice in the same way we look at everything else we're doing in our daily lives (i.e., "What's in it for me?"), then we are neglecting our human family and not addressing the suffering and sadness of those around us. This is not holy, sacred, or divine. It's ultimately wrapped in the same selfishness that pervades contemporary culture.

When we think only about reducing our own internal anxiety, sadness, and dissatisfaction—and *not* about the suffering of people in Sudan or in our hometown or even in our household and family—what we miss out on is compassion for the suffering of *others*.

This line of reasoning is taking us back to the *Kung Fu* / *Star Trek* themes of Chapter 1. Over the past several decades, we have, as a culture, tended to focus on the personal transformation and not the necessary "societal transformation" element of the holy quest, the sacred path. This leads to "my life is better," but we are left with the question, Is the *world* any better?

An example of this kind of self-centered spiritual work is the recently rediscovered popularity of ayahuasca, ibogaine, and other hallucinogens. These "plant medicine" experiences have been growing in popularity over the last decade.

(Warning: unpopular opinion alert.)

This is not a new idea, kiddies. I'm old enough to remember countless folks talking about the mind/heart/soul-opening effects of LSD in the '70s. "Turn in, turn on, drop out." And how did that work out? Then in the '80s there was peyote and the Indigenous ceremonies that surrounded its usage. Then there were magic mushrooms. I went to college with many people who were essentially "microdosing" and regularly using MDMA (a.k.a. ecstasy or molly) to achieve inspiration.

These practices weren't invented recently by Silicon Valley "creatives," Joe Rogan, or spiritual adventurers traveling in the Amazon and posting about it on Instagram, Gen Zers! Over the last sixty years, countless folks have talked about hallucinogens as a shortcut to God, bliss, and spiritual enlightenment.

This is not to minimize the religious practice of hallucinogens by Indigenous peoples. True plant medicine (why is it, by the way, that ayahuasca and peyote are "plant medicines" and the coca plant and heroin poppies *aren't*?!) has been accessed as one of the many ceremonial tools toward enlightenment for thousands of years in profound religious practices by Indigenous Peoples of the Americas. However, they have been used as one small part of a ritual, in conjunction with a myriad of other disciplines, as part of a profound and ancient tapestry of cultural spiritual customs.

That's not what is happening with today's modern ayahuasca tourism.

And while there is substantial evidence that hallucinogens and other drugs, such as MDMA and ketamine, can be effectively used (with professional medical guidance) to treat extreme depression and addiction issues, to take them occasionally in an attempt to find any kind of lasting, profound, or overarching spiritual truth seems superficial. And, frankly, a bit lazy.

People who follow this path, for the most part, seem to be looking for a *shortcut*. "I'm going to the jungles of Costa Rica [or my friend's apartment in Berkeley, or an Airbnb in La Jolla] to do ayahuasca with a certified 'shaman' and have a nine-hour experience of cosmic unity, which I can talk about on Twitter, podcasts, or at parties. And then my work is done."

This is capitalist, consumerist spirituality. I can simply pay for a pre-planned forty-eight-hour experience of enlightenment and then go back to carrying on with my imbalanced work life, materialistic career goals, and chaotic personal life! It's like signing up for the instant vacation of a cruise to the Bahamas. Only in this case, it's booking a "spiritual fulfillment" vacation without any lasting devotion, practice, mission, commitment, or discipline.

Easy-peasy, lemon squeezy!

At the end of the day, in a healthy religious practice, there is a judicious balance between the two roads of *Kung Fu* and *Star Trek*. Between self-experience and community service. Between the inner quest and the outer mission. "Self-care" and self-sacrifice for the greater good.

I recently had a conversation with a brilliant writer friend of mine, and the topic drifted to religion and faith. As we spoke, I discussed various aspects of religion as a whole and why I had chosen to be a devout (albeit, flawed!) member of a specific religious faith.

It quickly became clear that religion as a source of social good was not something he had ever really considered. He thought of spirituality *only* as a means toward internal balance and not as any kind of force for community transformation and global harmony. It blew his mind as I related a few simple ideas to this effect. He was thunderstruck as I relayed to him that the core of the word "religion" originated from the Latin verb *ligare* and was devised as follows: "re-ligio" or "religati," to "fasten" or "bind together." That religion, while certainly a cause of disunity, violence, and judgmentalism, had, at other times in human history, been a force for progress, unity, and yes, even enlightenment.

Religion? Really? A positive movement for progress and enlightenment? "Impossible!" you might say. And that's certainly what our epic trip to Israel made me feel at times.

———◆———

When our tour was finished, I looked around one last time at the Temple Mount, and my heart was saddened. As I gazed over the gorgeous ancient city of Jerusalem, I could feel the disunity and mistrust between faiths. A powder keg of simmering antagonism that could lead to world war. Right here at the crux of three of the holiest sites in the world.

There in the most revered place on the planet, as we gave our hugs and goodbyes to Bruce, I was struck by the fact that sometimes peace and unity feels downright impossible. Especially here in the "muddle east."

But as I considered my trip over the following months, I came to believe that maybe there's another way. Perhaps the path to seeing the world's religions as a potential source of progress is to explore the universal truths that unite them. Common threads that could show everyone everywhere that these faiths are not, at their core, as disparate and divisive as they appear. Perhaps they are all just different paths to one cosmic truth. Oooh, that's a good idea. Let's dig into that next!

CHAPTER SEVEN

THE FABULOUS FOUNDATIONS OF FAITH

One of the most inspiring movements in human history happened during a mysterious period in our distant past. And I'm not talking about mid-'90s grunge. This particular era has fascinated me ever since college, when I took a class on the history of Christianity. It's the period between the death of Jesus and the conversion of Constantine. In other words, the first three hundred years of the Christian spiritual movement on planet Earth. We'll call it "Church 101." Before all that violent, complicated, and political "Christendom" took over.

Yes, we know about the life of Paul of Tarsus. And we know a little bit about the geographic spread of this new faith tradition thanks to the apostles. There were Gnostic gospels, rogue priests, and some weird ascetic sects of the nascent religion sprinkled about various scenic deserts. We've read stories about Christians being fed to the lions. But what was the early church *really* like? On the ground.

I'm not a Christian scholar or even a Christian, but from the little I know, I've been struck by the truly "catholic" (as in its original definition of "all-embracing") nature of the early church.

After Paul spread the gospel to the gentiles (non-Jews), and Christianity slowly moved away from being a revisionist, slightly updated version of Judaism, by and for Jews only, it rapidly spread over several decades throughout the Roman/Mediterranean world.

The idea central to the spread of the gospel in this post-apostolic phase of Christianity was that there was one God, "the Father," and that one could achieve eternal life or "salvation" by acknowledging that He had sent his son, the Christ or savior, to bring the "good news" about the building of the kingdom of God on earth. He had died for our sins, gone up to heaven, and would return again. And, most importantly, that one could show their devotion to said Christ the Savior by emulating his generous acts of service among the poor and outcast.

Around this time, multiple "cults" or small religious orders began popping up all over the place. Every city and people had their local gods, rituals, and ceremonies. People were talking about messiahs right and left. And the Roman gods were also honored, because if they weren't you'd get stabbed in the face by a centurion.

The god of the Jews (Elohim, Adonai, or Yahweh, depending) was not considered conceptually in this Roman world as the "one true God" but rather as the god of the Jewish people, in particular. One of countless gods to be worshiped, depending on geography and your tribal affiliation. Kind of like following teams in the NFL.

So when Paul called all other gods "false idols" and Yahweh or Jehovah the only true God, this was incredibly inflammatory, to say the least. The apostles taught that *all* were welcome to worship this one God, if they simply accepted His "son" as the messiah, in order to find meaning, purpose, and salvation in a blissful afterlife. This idea was quite intriguing. When the stories, teachings, and sayings of Jesus began to spread, and churches were formed all around the Mediterranean, a strange, beautiful, and utterly new thing transpired.

A world that was tribal in every way, shape, and form found itself met with a religion that accepted *all* to its membership. One simply had to be baptized in Christ. They even had church "open houses" during sections of the Sunday worship services, which were open to those simply investigating this new global spiritual movement.

So there we are, at a seminal moment in human history. For perhaps the very first time, a religious service (usually held outdoors) included a vast, diverse, and eclectic group of devotees. Picture handmade pews filled with Jewish workers, Phoenician sailors, shunned prostitutes,

African merchants, Roman citizens, Egyptian monks, former slaves, and wealthy noblemen *all* worshiping the same God.

In some ways, one might say that Christianity is the first actual "religion" in the modern sense, in that it offered a set of beliefs that folks of all backgrounds could ascribe to, as opposed to an inherited set of rituals mixed with a geographic identity and tribal inheritance. It was the first belief system one could "join," regardless of your cultural affiliation, based on the precepts laid out in the early gospels and by the nascent clergy.

So for probably the first time in the history of humanity, a religious movement was *greater* than the tribe from which it originated. And in Christ's eyes, all were equal in the church and worthy of His love. Rich. Poor. Roman. Jewish. African. No matter your history, class, or ethnicity, all people were brothers in Jesus's love. And sisters, too! Women played a significant role in the early centuries of Christianity. Especially upper-class Roman women (including Emperor Constantine's mom). It was one of the few groups (maybe the only one) of that time that had a place where women could experience equality under God.

A big tent, indeed.

And as if that weren't enough, *Charity! Alms! Service!*

Early Christians were known for sacrificing their own comfort, time, and money to help the less fortunate of *other* tribes, races, classes, and peoples. *WTF!?* Why on earth would members of this crazy (formerly) Jewish cult spend their time, energy, and resources *helping* others outside of their own family, village, or tribe? They would even bring food, aid, and succor to poor folks who worshiped idols! All this in honor and emulation of this miraculous day-laborer Jesus guy who hailed from some Podunk dump called Nazareth over in Galilee.

The early church was astoundingly revolutionary. This was a new, civilization-wide idea: all are welcome, and altruism to all. The ripples of this idea are felt to this day, all stemming from the Mediterranean world on or about the year 100. Altruism. Belonging. Unity in diversity.

Service to something greater than our mere tribal identities. All springing from, you guessed it, a *religion*!

Christians often get a bad rap in the press and online. But any time
you're involved in a cause that involves a large, diverse group of people,
think of the Christians. Anytime you are at a gathering where there is
an urge toward something greater, something transcendent, think of
early Christianity. Anytime you're working side by side with others in
service to the less fortunate, remember the founders of the church in
those early centuries.

There are examples of this kind of cultural evolution from other religious movements as well.

Early Buddhism had great similarities to the Christian movement.
Throughout the Hindu world, acolytes were spreading the teachings of
the Buddha on the root causes of and solutions for suffering among
many other spiritual tools for profound personal enrichment. They
focused on a set of transcendent doctrines that were for *everyone*, not
just for worshipers of a certain Hindu god or of a specific race, class,
tribe, or geographic area. It was a faith practice that de-emphasized
gods and rituals and re-emphasized the path to personal spiritual
enlightenment. Enlightenment for *all*—including women, who were
allowed to become acolytes by Siddhartha Gautama and his early followers. And, most importantly, this was a philosophical movement that
was open to *every caste*! Rich or poor, touchable or untouchable, all were
welcome to receive the profound teachings of the Buddha and participate in gatherings and devotions.

In Islam, a bunch of disparate, warring polytheistic tribes on the
Arabian Peninsula, united under the banner of Mohammed and the
Quran, had within a century created an awe-inspiring civilization that
spread from Morocco to India. This worldwide flourishing Muslim culture with profound spiritual roots created algebra and soap and coffee
and chemistry and rugs and surgical instruments and countless other
inventions used today. They instigated a flourishing of arts that eventually trickled over and inspired the Renaissance in Europe and scientific

advancements that the world had never before witnessed and are still used to this day. (Hello, algorithms!) In the golden age of Islam, all were welcome, regardless of tribe or background. United by the simple phrase, "There is no God but Allah, and Mohammed is His prophet!" And this was an empire founded on tolerance of members of other religions. The Quran states, "Do not abuse those whom they worship besides Allah" (6:109). And the Imam Ali was quoted as saying, "Know that people are of two types: they are either your brothers in religion or your equals in creation" (Nahjul Balagha, Sermon 53).

Not only that, but one of the five pillars of Islam is charitable giving, called zakat, putting it in a similar category as Christianity with baked-in altruism in its genes.

It can be challenging and somewhat misleading to categorize the various religious and spiritual movements that have appeared every five hundred to a thousand years or so under one vast umbrella of "worldwide religious movements." At first glance, it feels like Buddhism is nothing at all like Islam, and Judaism couldn't be more divergent from Hinduism. Many faiths are monotheistic, some are polytheistic, and some are divinely agnostic. The karmic religions of the East, for the most part, feel completely and utterly different from the Abrahamic faiths in most every way. Some believe in a form of reincarnation. Others have a central authority (like a pope). Some are as decentralized as one can possibly imagine. Christianity has forty-five thousand various denominations around the globe. Islam has, essentially, two main sects. (Two that, like Catholics and Protestants of centuries past, often have zero qualms killing each other in their prophet's name.)

So when trying to reframe "religion" as a worldwide social movement and a source of progress in the gradual but necessary evolution and maturation of humanity, we need to shift our perspective to a twenty-thousand-foot view. For the purpose of this discussion, let's float up into the atmosphere and take a peep down on the foundational reality of these many historic faiths. Not their many differences, which are often discussed, but their commonalities. These major religions of planet Earth share much of the same spiritual DNA when examined *macro*scopically, sociologically, evolutionarily. And as different as they may appear, the world's major faith traditions are philosophically bound together in many ways. French sociologist Émile Durkheim was the first to examine religions from this broad perspective. He defined "religion" as a "unified system of beliefs and practices relative to sacred things." There's that "sacred" word again.

Perhaps these disparate religions are all different pathways leading somehow to the same ultimate truth? In what specific ways do they "bind together" or "re-ligio" their adherents? Can we boil all the great religious movements that hold over six billion of us humans in their membership down to let's say ten essential universal truths that they all hold in common? True, some of these bleed over into one another and there is tremendous overlap, but nevertheless I'm going to give it a try.

Here's my stab at these universal commonalities:

1. A higher power
2. Life after death
3. The power of prayer
4. Transcendence
5. Community
6. A moral compass
7. The force of love
8. Increased compassion
9. Service to the poor
10. A strong sense of purpose[11]

---

11 Disclaimer: An obvious commonality among all the world's major religions is the organization around the message of a "central figure"—the larger-than-life, divine teacher, such as Buddha, Krishna, Moses, Christ, Mohammad, or Baha'u'llah, who was revered and who sacrificed His life for his respective messages of inner

———◆◆◆———

1. A HIGHER POWER

Whatever you call it, God in some way, shape, or form exists in every religious faith. He comes by many names, but all the world's major religions identify a divine force that is or was or permeates all things. I covered this pretty extensively in Chapter 4, and I don't want to take up any more space or time waxing on about the Notorious G.O.D.

But I'd like to use this literary real estate to address one specific point in the context of this master list: Buddhism and God.

Many point to Buddhism as an example of a religious movement without a central concept of a higher power, but this isn't entirely true. Yes, Buddhists do not "worship" any supreme being, but in seeking bliss, nirvana, and enlightenment, there is an inherent spiritual force guiding that process. Siddhartha Gautama, a.k.a. the Buddha, proclaims in Udana 8:3 of the Khuddaka Nikaya, "There is an Unborn, an Unoriginated, an Unmade, an Uncompounded; were there not, O mendicants, there would be no escape from the world of the born, the originated, the made, and the compounded."

This, in my opinion, is another way to describe God without all that pesky Judeo-Christian anthropomorphism. In the Buddhist universe-view as I see it, this force is the spiritual juice that makes the salvation of nirvana possible. Which is very much in line with Christian philosopher Paul Tillich's definition of God as "the Ground of all Being" and with Baha'u'llah's view of God as "an Unknowable Essence."

---

peace and world love. You know, the OG influencers of planetary spiritual transformation. But the existence of a central figure won't be one of the ten truths we explore. For one, over the centuries, many of these great individuals have become, sadly, divisive figures. And my goal is to focus on the core teachings that emerged through the revelations of these great figures, not the presence of the figure itself.

So there it is—the first (somewhat obvious) unifying principle of all religions—a belief in something or someone bigger than creation, who is beyond all comprehension.

And the benefit of this in a religious context? Humility. To think of the Divine Source is to feel rightfully small in an expansive universe. A reminder that, despite what our self-obsessed society tells us, the band Kansas was 100 percent right when they sang, "All we are is dust in the wind."

2. LIFE AFTER DEATH

Every religion has some form of ideology that includes life after this physical life, something I discussed in depth in Chapter 3. But I want to touch on the foundational nature of this concept and how it relates to the roots of religion itself.

Remember, the very first proof of humanity's spiritual impulse are burial sites where our ancestors from the Upper Paleolithic era (from about forty thousand to fifty thousand years ago until about ten thousand years ago) were buried alongside grave goods they might require for their journey forward into the afterlife. A sword, a map, food, a pet dog. And in the case of King Tut, actual chariots!

While the mythologies from various faiths might differ greatly as to what "the end" is (Heaven, Happy Hunting Grounds, Nirvana, Zion, Valhalla), all faiths point to the central idea that the end of the physical life is not the end of our journey. That the material world is not the only world.

Zoroastrianism, which is more than three thousand years old and is the incredibly rich foundational source of so many religious and mythological beliefs in both the West and the East, was the first to posit the existence of a fravashi, or what we would call a soul. The soul, created by the greatest god, Ahura Mazda, is immortal and has its resurrection at the time of what is called "the Great Renewal." After one dies, the soul is judged immediately. We essentially pass over a bridge, and the good will ascend to the House of Songs that is paradise, with angels watching over them, and those who have lived evil lives will be directed to the House of Lies that is hell.

The Hindu tradition of reincarnation is, I believe, frequently misunderstood. As far as I, a total non-Hindu, understand it, there is a cycle of life and rebirth on the physical plane, called samsara, and this cycle continues until one achieves enlightenment, after which there is something called moksha, and the soul is released to be with the Supreme Being. In other words, reincarnation does not go on forever. The ultimate goal and end point of reincarnation is a blissful reunion and merging into the oneness of the divine planes of existence.

Likewise, in the Buddhist tradition, eventually you step off the wheel of samsara (the cycles of birth, suffering, and death) and "enter" nirvana. Of course, nirvana is not a three-dimensional space; it is a spiritual realm of selflessness, or "no-self-ness."

In every faith tradition, the idea of a nonmaterial world after this world, one that is a totally blissful reunion with the cosmic universe, is positioned as the end goal. Again, this frames our work and growth here on earth, as this plane is seen as but a way-stop, albeit a crucial one, on the path to far greater spiritual realms and experiences.

3. POWER OF PRAYER

All religions have some version of prayer, of supplication to and communion with the Divine. Whether mystical, personal, communal, or ceremonial, prayer seeks a dialogue with the Profound Mystery that both surrounds and surpasses all of us. Perhaps it is having a personal conversation with Jesus, performing dawn devotionals, or lighting incense or candles. Maybe it's chanting, counting prayer beads, group singing, shouting praise, or invoking hymns. Or it might be ecstatic dancing, ringing bells, cleansing ablutions, bowing in a certain direction, or a circumambulation. Whatever form it takes, devotional prayer is among the oldest acts of humans on the planet. And among the most sacred.

The Jewish siddur (prayer book) offers many beautiful prayers. The Modeh Ani is recited upon awakening each morning before leaving one's bed: "I give thanks before you, King living and eternal, for You have returned within me my soul with compassion; abundant is Your faithfulness!"

A Hindu prayer begins, "My soul listen unto me! Love thy Lord as the lotus loves water."

Daily obligatory prayers or salat are recited five times a day by Muslims as they bow in humility toward Mecca. "Glory and praise be to You, O Allah. Blessed be Your name and exalted be Your majesty, there is none worthy of worship except You."

Although Buddhism doesn't necessarily subscribe to a creator god, Buddhists nonetheless supplicate to the majesty of the universe with such beautiful prayers as the Metta Prayer and the Golden Chain Prayer.

One of my most favorite offerings comes from the Navajo (Diné) people:

In beauty happily I walk.
With beauty before me I walk.
With beauty behind me I walk.
With beauty below me I walk.
With beauty above me I walk.
With beauty all around me I walk.

Indeed, prayer is a core aspect of every religion; it is central to any spiritual journey. As the brilliant Anne Lamott says in her classic book about prayer, *Help Thanks Wow: The Three Essential Prayers*, "So prayer is our sometimes real selves trying to communicate with the Real, with Truth, with the Light. . . . And in this light, we can see beyond our modest receptors, to what is way beyond us, and deep inside." And, "Prayer means that, in some unique way, we believe we're invited into a relationship with someone who hears us when we speak in silence."

Lamott pretty much covers it: *Help*, prayers of supplication and the begging of assistance for the infinite travails of life. *Thanks*, prayers of gratitude. And *Wow*, prayers of awe and wonder.

Meister Eckhart, the medieval Catholic mystic, echoes this idea: "If the only prayer you ever say in your entire life is thank you, it will be enough."

Personally, I start every day with this mystical outreach of "Help, thanks, wow!" And my life is all the richer for it.

But the best prayers—and the reason I think prayer is such a powerful tool for change—rise above words and chants and transform into tangible acts of love and service.

One of my spiritual idols, Oprah Winfrey, says, "As far back as I can recall, my prayer has been the same: 'Use me, God. Show me how to take who I am, who I want to be, and what I can do, and use it for a purpose greater than myself.'"

And continuing this idea of prayers as action items, 'Abdu'l-Baha, the wise Baha'i leader, memorably said, "Therefore strive that your actions day by day may become beautiful prayers."

4. TRANSCENDENCE

> There are more things in heaven and Earth, Horatio,
> Than are dreamt of in your philosophy.
> —*William Shakespeare (Hamlet)*

On the macro level, religion has helped (or some might say it's even *caused*) humanity to transcend being mere organic, animalistic bio-robots whose behavior is shaped by the rewards and punishments of our environments. Instead, through some core ideals of religious practice, humans have been able to rise above the demands of their genes and evolutionary programming to put community ahead of their selfish interests. All faith traditions urge us toward this type of transcendence.

Buddhism encourages meditation to realize that we can not only rise above self but also come to the realization that we had no "self" to begin with. Islam, especially through its Sufi form, urges reaching the state of *fana*, a transcendental selflessness.

In the Hindu holy text, the Bhagavad Gita, transcendence is described as a level of spiritual attainment in which one is no longer under the control of materialistic or animalistic desires.

When scholars of the positive psychology movement Christopher Peterson and Martin Seligman searched the major holy books and philosophical texts of humanity for universal virtues, one of the six they identified was transcendence. (The other five are wisdom, courage, love, temperance, and justice.) Those psychologists consider the basic human trait of transcendence to include the character strengths of spirituality (or sense of purpose), appreciation of beauty, gratitude, humor, and hope.

Remember Plato's famous allegory of the cave? Human beings are chained to chairs facing a stone wall, unable to turn around. Behind them there glows a great light from a fire and an even greater reality that exists outside the mouth of the cave. Between the fire and the backs of the people in their chairs are other folks carrying miscellaneous objects, dancing, and using shadow puppets. The chained humans watch the flickering shadows dancing on the stone wall (like a *movie*!), convinced that *that* is reality, when, in fact, there is *far* greater truth, beauty, and *actual* life just outside of the reach of our perception.

This idea that there are realms of mystery, truth, and glory just beyond our vision, that we are intimately connected to these realms, and that it is part of our journey to eventually partake of them—is inherent in some way, shape, or form to all the religions of the past.

In most all faith traditions, we are not just our bodies, minds, or feelings. Reality is not just "stuff." There are realms, invisible to the eye, to be perceived only by spiritual means. And part of our sojourn in this glorious, infuriating land of mud is a longing for the transcendence radiating from the light outside the mouth of the cave.

This is a profound idea that can unify humans around the idea that there is more to life than the sometimes tedious day-to-day pursuit of pleasure, status, comfort, and the obtaining of stuff.

5. COMMUNITY

What is a community? According to *Merriam-Webster*, it is a "unified body of individuals." The definition continues: "people with common interests living within a particular area."

People with common interests? Explains why early communities were simply extended family in a cave. But eventually, that definition gradually evolved to local village to tribe to city to general geographic area to nation to people/race.

And then there's "religion," a way to bind folks together in some never-before-seen ways. It was no longer what village or family or even "people" you hailed from. It was what you *believed*. Social cohesion was created by the rituals, worship, and ceremonies adherents collectively engaged in, plus a shared set of ethics and a common sacred mythology. What bound us was no longer solely based on genetics, familial affiliations, or ancestry.

Religious communities allow the communal love to go far deeper than the familial. Or rather, it extends the concept of family to fit a larger vision. It binds us and bonds us while giving perspective through life's most difficult transitions, including marriage, birth, and death. It allows a witnessing of a common divine spark within diverse believers, creating a commonality on a transcendental level.

But more important than these factors, there is a set of behavioral consistencies that emerge from a group of people focused on the same collective mindset. A common purpose, mission, and sense of meaning that creates inner peace and social stability. Evolutionary biologists have even suggested that religion was naturally selected because it was so successful in building communities in which everyone cared for each other, thus increasing the survival rate of adherents.

Picture, if you will, colorful Hindu festivals filled with joyful celebration; Buddhist monks deep in the stillness of contemplation; the
ecstatic whirling dervishes of the Sufi tradition; raucous, praise-filled
Baptist choirs lifting the entire congregation; sacred Indigenous American sweat lodges (or sun dances); Muslim pilgrims encircling the Kaaba
in glorious submission; Jews sitting shiva after a death, being lovingly
visited (with food!) by countless members of the local temple. The Sikh
concept of *langar*, which creates a vibrant communal table open to folks
of every caste and societal class at every Sikh temple—a practice that
expands to encompass feeding the poor and destitute.

This is how community feels. How it works. What it provides. And,
to a large extent, what is increasingly missing from our fractured, postmodern lives.

Today, we often find community not in a town hall or a church but
rather online. Church membership in the United States has plum-
meted, and instead of filling pulpits, we now log on to screens to find
"our village." On Reddit message boards, for instance, there are subred-
dit communities for whatever interest or passion you might have, be it
squeaky-toy collectors, Alabama socialists, or foot fetishists. These odd
assemblages *feel* like community due to sharing similar interests, but the
intimate bonding, trust, and camaraderie can frequently be lacking.

New York Times political and cultural commentator David Brooks,
in his recent (magnificent) book *The Second Mountain: The Quest for a
Moral Life*, says of this shift to online community,

> Living online often means living in a state of diversion. When you're
> living in diversion you're not actually deeply interested in things;
> you're just bored at a more frenetic pace. . . . Such is life in the dizzi-
> ness of [online] freedom. Nobody quite knows where they stand with
> one another. Everybody is pretty sure that other people are doing life
> better. . . . When a whole society is built around self-preoccupation,
> its members become separated from one another, divided and alien-
> ated. And this is what has happened to us.

Again, it is completely understandable that modern man has jettisoned organized religion, but have we thrown the baby of community out with the proverbial bathwater of faith? Also, does that sentence even make sense?

6. A MORAL COMPASS

Nobody likes morals. Yuck. No one wants to be told about what's right and wrong. Especially these days. We in the modern Western world want to be free to do what we want, where we want, when we want. And we certainly don't want any judgmental church lady, ancient dusty book, or moralistic cleric lecturing us on what is good or bad, right or wrong.

That being said, morality and ethics are everywhere and inescapable.

You simply *don't* go into a Starbucks and just grab any drink off the counter.

You don't cut someone off and slip into the parking space that they've been inching toward.

And this is for my son, Walter, if you're reading this: you don't grab someone's remote and change the channel while they're in the middle of watching their show!

What seems to be happening in contemporary society is that universal morals—ideas about what is essentially right and wrong—are being continually downgraded and degraded for ever-shifting socially constructed ethics and mores.

Here is an example that I hope illustrates what I'm describing.

In politics, there used to be a measure of civility that arose from a greater historical sense of basic human decency. There are basic time-honored precepts that one should be kind and respectful and never call people names. (I mean, didn't our moms and kindergarten teachers tell us not to?) But now we find that the political parties in America, both of which claim to be inspired by Christian values, find it perfectly OK to label political enemies with insults and crass nicknames. Every day we see politicians excoriate each other—taunt, mock, and name-call other "public servants." And not only has this become acceptable, it is lauded as a show of strength and real leadership.

In other words, what historically was seen as grotesque bullying is now commonplace. This behavior has moved from the "never do this; it's not right" column to the "this is now awesome" column because social ethics have trumped basic universal rights and wrongs. In this scenario the ends justify the means. Civility be damned. As long as the right team wins, it doesn't matter how immorally, divisively, and cruelly a candidate or campaign behaves.

This lack of civility in public life has been largely fueled by the increasing use of the internet and social media. People are bullying, mean, and derisive in ways they would *never* be in real life. We see racism, sexism, and general cruelty being expressed on the web in ever-increasing volumes.

From the vantage of a spiritual framework, the fundamental reason one does not mock, bully, and call other people names is because (besides it being unkind) it is not good for the development of the soul, nor is it in emulation of the great spiritual teachers and leaders (Jesus, the Buddha, Mohammed). Such behavior does not bring us closer to the divine will and is not in alignment with the great cosmic creative spirit of the universe.

What faith communities throughout history have provided their adherents is the idea that there is a higher sense of right and wrong, a list of shared values, that comes from a timeless vision, from an ancient soul-place, a horizon of what is just and acceptable. From the Divine Source even.

When universal moral frameworks accede to acceptable current societal ethics, to quote William Butler Yeats, "The center cannot hold."

Pulitzer Prize–winning historian Barbara Tuchman, author of the amazing *The March of Folly: From Troy to Vietnam*, once said, "Have nations ever declined from a loss of moral sense rather than from physical reasons of the pressure of barbarians? I think that they have."

Now, there is a much more complicated and nuanced conversation to be had about morality and ethics, far too complex for us to get into here. And I certainly don't mean to imply that society's "moral decay"—frequently shouted from pulpits, the mouths of reactionary pundits, and the political campaigns of the world—means any kind of return to the "good old days" of slavery, sexism, colonialism, and patriarchy. But there is a balance between ethics and morality on one side and individual rights, freedoms, and choice on the other that seems crucial to societal development, and we humans haven't quite figured out that give-and-take yet.

Perhaps there are clues to be found as we keep unearthing ancient wisdom from deep in our historical bedrock. We can still listen to our conscience and access our modern ethical rationality, but ultimately religious morality is not just church ladies, "thou shalts," and Sharia law. It can provide the universal scales upon which to weigh the promptings of our hearts and the occasional faultiness of our reasoning.

7. THE FORCE OF LOVE

The strongest spiritual practices begin with one quality—love. Unconditional love for self, for our human brothers and sisters, for God.

Let's see what some of the greatest mystics and poets of all time have to say about it.

> This is my commandment, That ye love one another, as I have loved you.
>
> —*Jesus*

> This is love: to fly toward a secret sky, to cause a hundred veils to fall each moment. First to let go of life. Finally, to take a step without feet.
>
> —*Rumi*

What we love we shall grow to resemble.

—Bernard of Clairvaux

Love is the only reality. . . . It is the ultimate truth that lies at the heart of creation.

—Rabindranath Tagore

Love is all you need.

—The Beatles

That pretty much sums it up.

The Indigenous Arctic natives are said to have dozens of words for snow. It is said that in Sanskrit, there are ninety-six words for love. But in contemporary American English, anything that is vaguely associated with a warm feeling is given the moniker "love." It can be romantic in nature, friendly feelings, common affection, or even in place of the word "like." It's a generalized umbrella feeling that covers all positive relations. I love my car. I love my dog. I love Sunday mornings. I love my wife, my infant son. I love waterskiing. I love pumpkin spice lattes. I love humanity.

That's pretty messed up. Especially for a culture that prides itself on the majesty, history, flexibility, and poetry of its great language. English has more words than any language in the history of humanity, but we really dropped the ball on words for love.

(It should be noted that in Klingon there are zero words for love. Only *qamuSHa*, which directly translates to "unhate." I *qamuSHa* you. I "unhate" you. Just FYI.)

Search the holy texts and you'll find some far more interesting words that orbit the concept of love.

In the Hebrew scriptures, God's nature again and again is described with the word *hesed*. The word comes from an idea of bowing one's head to another and roughly translates to "steadfast love," "covenant love," "mercy," and, especially, "loving-kindness." We are blessed and grateful because God's love for us is chock-full of *hesed*.

The ancient Greeks and early Christians used the transcendent concept of agape. It is the highest form of love, which embraces love of God for humanity and love of humanity for God. It's also a universal love that incorporates a love of nature and finds its greatest expression in selfless service to others. And the more you explore it, this concept of agape folds ever outward in waves increasing in scope. Martin Luther King Jr. poignantly relates, "Agape means recognition of the fact that all life is interrelated."

Throughout every religious tradition on the planet, there is an awe-inspiring, all-encompassing, mystical emphasis on love surpassing its more common understanding as a warm feeling of connection felt in the chest. Instead, love is described as a primal force that pulses throughout the universe. And every historical spiritual path encourages us to lift our gaze and open our consciousness to ever greater conceptions of what this love might be. To go beyond the love between spouses or for our children to the idea that love is (at risk of going full-blown hippie on you) a cosmic power, an energy that binds us all together just like it binds together (as its metaphorical physical twin, gravity) the planets, the stars, the atoms, the majesty of the universe. As light is both particle and wave, so too is love.

In the Baha'i teachings, 'Abdu'l-Baha calls it "a most great law, a unique power, a magnetic force!"

He continues:

Love is the light that guideth in darkness, the living link that uniteth God with man, that assureth the progress of every illumined soul. Love is the most great law that ruleth this mighty and heavenly cycle, the unique power that bindeth together the divers elements of this material world, the supreme magnetic force that directeth the movements of the spheres in the celestial realms. Love revealeth with unfailing and limitless power the mysteries latent in the universe. Love is the spirit of life unto the adorned body of mankind.

If one thing unites all religions, all faiths, it is the universality of the law of love.

And as with my point about prayer, we are called to move our concept of love from beyond a mere feeling in the chest to *action*! Because isn't that what it's ultimately about? If you love your relations, your country, your planet, you *do* something to help, nurture, and support them, right?

Mother Teresa sums this up with, "Love cannot remain by itself—it has no meaning. Love has to be put into action and that action is service."

8. INCREASED COMPASSION

The yin to the yang of love is the Golden Rule, a simple yet profound teaching found in every religious tradition in the world.

Let's look at a few:

AFRICAN TRADITION

One who is going to take a pointed stick to pinch a baby bird should first try it on himself to feel how it hurts.

—*Yoruba proverb*

BAHA'I FAITH

Lay not on any soul a load that you would not wish to be laid upon you, and desire not for anyone the things you would not desire for yourself.

—*Baha'u'llah*

BUDDHISM

Treat not others in ways that you yourself would find hurtful.

—*The Buddha*

CHRISTIANITY

In everything, do to others as you would have them do to you; for this is the law and the prophets.

—*Jesus*

CONFUCIANISM

One word which sums up the basis of all good conduct . . . loving-kindness. Do not do to others what you do not want done to yourself.

—*Confucius*

HINDUISM

This is the sum of duty: do not do to others what would cause pain if done to you.

—*The Mahabharata*

ISLAM

Not one of you truly believes until you wish for others what you wish for yourself.

—*Muhammad*

JAINISM

One should treat all creatures in the world as one would like to be treated.

—*Mahavira, Sutrakritanga 1.11.33*

JUDAISM

What is hateful to you, do not do to your neighbor. This is the whole Torah; all the rest is commentary. Go and learn it.

—*Rabbi Hillel, the Talmud*

SIKHISM

If thou desirest thy Beloved, then hurt thou not anyone's heart.

—*Guru Arjan Dev Ji 259, Guru Granth Sahib*

TAOISM

Regard your neighbor's gain as your own gain and your neighbor's loss as your own loss.

—*Lao-tzu*

ZOROASTRIANISM

Do not do unto others whatever is injurious to yourself.

—*Zoroaster*

To me, the fact that the phrasings of this essential spiritual law are so similar over countless centuries indicates the deepest foundational oneness of all faiths.

In fact, in the past I've done a public exercise where I've written all the versions of the Golden Rule on slips of paper *without their source* and had participants try to guess which faith the phrases come from. No one can ever discern whether that version of the Golden Rule comes from a two-hundred-year-old or twenty-five-hundred-year-old religion.

At its core, the Golden Rule is about one universal concept: *compassion*. Deeply consider, the great spiritual traditions implore, how your actions might affect another person. Put yourself in their shoes. Exercise empathy. Use your heart's imagination and consider their feelings in the same way we innately consider our own. Put this into action. Make it spiritual law. Not only will your life be better for it, but the world will be a better place as well.

9. SERVICE TO THE POOR

Which brings us to one of the truest forms of love and compassion we can show—a principle that every religious faith on planet Earth has built into its bones: service to the less fortunate.

Poverty was, and still is, one of the most crucial and pressing issues on the planet. In the year 1800, more than 80 percent of the world lived below the extreme poverty line. Today, that number is less than 10 percent. Tremendous progress, yes, but still an unacceptable number in the hundreds of millions.

In some of the earliest writings in human history, which happen to be early religious texts, there was a clarion call to help the less fortunate. In early Hindu tradition, there is the concept of *daana*, which is benevolent giving to others without expecting anything in return. This idea is found in some of the earliest texts on the planet, the Vedas, a central text of Hinduism. The Rig Veda from approximately 2000 BC states, "Let the rich satisfy the poor implorer, and bend his eye upon a longer pathway, riches come now to one, now to another, and like the wheels of chariots are ever rolling."

From the get-go, faith traditions have trumpeted the centrality of the altruistic impulse. As a spiritual practice, in Buddhism, generosity is the first of six "perfections."

The Buddha says, "What is the accomplishment in generosity? A noble disciple dwells at home, with a heart free from the stain of stinginess, open-handed, pure-handed, delighting in relinquishment, one devoted to charity, one who delights in sharing and giving. This is called accomplishment in generosity."

Nearly every faith tradition supports tithing, the setting aside of a certain portion of funds for the support of the impoverished as well as the clergy.

In the Jewish faith, setting aside a portion of your income for the poor, called tzedakah, is considered a mitzvah, or good deed, done from a sense of religious duty.

The great Indian poet Rabindranath Tagore pretty much sums it all up with the famous refrain,

I slept and dreamt that life was joy.
I awoke and saw that life was service.
I acted and behold, service was joy.

Indeed, in many spiritual traditions, the idea of the virtue of generosity is highlighted as a remedy for, and in opposition to, the inherent human vices of selfishness and self-centeredness. A desperately needed quality for both personal transformation and societal progress.

10. AND (FINALLY), A STRONG SENSE OF PURPOSE!

We are all here on earth to help others; what on earth the others are here for I don't know.

—*W. H. Auden*

Having a spark of consciousness in this mysterious, difficult, and gorgeous universe fills us with questions: Who are we? What makes the sun and the stars move? How can I feel happier? What happens when we die? What does it all mean? The mythologies of religious writings and traditions offer us potential answers to these timeless, persistent inquiries.

In fact, I believe it's a key reason why many world faiths thrive and, occasionally, work. Religion provides solace, if not always answers, to many, if not most, of life's biggest possible questions. And when those questions are addressed with wisdom, we begin to get clarity. Most every spiritual path provides its followers with that most vital, most juicy ingredient of all: *the meaning of life*! And its corresponding sense of purpose and direction.

Buddhists strive to live in the moment, free of attachment, following the eightfold path toward enlightenment and bliss. Muslims live in "submission" to Allah and His will, study His word in the Holy Quran, and follow the five pillars of Islam. Christians find deep meaning in enacting the Lord's two greatest commandments: (1) "You shall love the Lord your God with all your heart, with all your soul, and with all your mind." (This is the first and great commandment.) And its corollary, (2) "You shall love your neighbor as yourself."

Hindus find meaning and purpose in life through *dharma* (ethically fulfilling personal duties that lead to service of all creation and God), through *artha* (striving for material and spiritual wealth, success, and prosperity), through *kama* (enjoying the practical activities of life in moderation and in pursuit of one's dharmic destiny), and finally, through *moksha* (enlightenment or awakening).

Having a sense of meaning in your difficult, complicated life is a big prize. But what kind of meaning are we talking about? The big-picture purpose, like, "What is the purpose of life itself?" (The outer, more *Star Trek* path.) Or the micro-picture purpose, as in "What is *my* purpose in life?" (The internal *Kung Fu* path.)

Fortunately, religion offers enlightenment around both sets of purpose-filled questions.

The big-picture purpose question is answered by integrating many of the universals of religion found in this chapter: build a loving, compassionate community guided by justice (right and wrong), seeking to transcend its humble monkey-mind beginnings to reach for the stars. And it's not just about occasionally giving a couple bucks to the poor but collectively putting prayer, love, and compassion into *action* so that poverty itself is no longer allowed to exist.

Conversely, turning toward the inner path of our own individual purpose, we are called on to nurture our God-given talents, develop our divine attributes (kindness, love, honesty, compassion, etc.), and find tranquility and unity while in service to the aforementioned big-picture purpose.

In a nutshell, religions give us both a personal reason to exist as well as a greater, loftier collective goal. In a world where we are suffocating in a pandemic of despair, loneliness, and anxiety, discovering meaning, focus, purpose, and direction is what we need more than ever in this exceptionally chaotic time.

———————

So there you have it. My take on the ten foundational principles exemplified and encompassed by most of the world's religious traditions. The rich, raw, meaty stuff that comprises the building blocks we need to both construct a vibrant human community and become better, more enlightened human beings.

As I related in Chapter 2, one of the biggest pandemics sweeping the world as I write this has very little to do with COVID-19 and much more to do with the mental health decline infesting the psyches of young people.

It bears repeating: the numbers are astounding. For the first time in history, the attorney general of the United States issued an advisory on the youth mental health crisis in 2021. To quote one tiny section of the report, "Between 2007 and 2018, suicide rates among youth ages 10–24 in the U.S. increased by 57%."

And from a 2022 article in the *New York Times* on the teen mental health crisis, "In 2019, 13 percent of adolescents reported having a major depressive episode, a 60 percent increase from 2007."

The statistics continue to pile up unabated.

In his wonderful book *Plays Well with Others: The Surprising Science Behind Why Everything You Know About Relationships Is (Mostly) Wrong*, author Eric Barker cites a study looking at the brain scans of lonely people. The scans showed that those who feel lonely search their environment for threats *twice* as often as nonlonely people. Humans are quite skilled at sweeping our surroundings for perceived dangers—it's how we survived for millennia. It's what kept us alive. The shake of a bush, the crunch of a twig—these could easily be a lion or bear seeking to eat us. And if lonely people are living their daily lives scanning for bush shaking and twig crunching at twice the normal rate, then their anxiety skyrockets. And the greater the anxiety, the deeper the loneliness. Which creates more anxiety. And round and round the cycle goes.

What are some of the most powerful tools in relieving this anxiety and disconnection?

I believe they can be found in some of the universals of religious wisdom mentioned here—shared purpose, connection to the transcendent, and the building of community. It's the support and bonds of these loving communities that relieve both loneliness and its close companion, anxiety.

Those concepts, along with prayer, love, and increased compassion, help decrease loneliness, and provide serenity and well-being. They also help generate that most precious of resources in today's world: *hope*. In other words, perhaps this mental health epidemic could be allayed by what we might have lost by the jettisoning of all things "religion."

So which religion, right? That's the question you've all been thinking. *But which one, Rainn?* And maybe none of the existing religions can work—they're perhaps too mired in stigma, historical failings, bureaucracy, and bad PR.

Hey, here's an idea! Why don't we build our own damn religion? One that can change the world for the better and give us a fresh start!

Possible? Let's see.

CHAPTER EIGHT

HEY, KIDS, LET'S BUILD THE PERFECT RELIGION!

Seriously!? *Another* chapter on religion!? You're killing me with this, Wilson! I thought you said early on that we didn't need religion, that we need spirituality and the tools that come with it but not necessarily the "R" word. Didn't you say that the fastest-growing belief system was "spiritual but not religious"? I'm sick of all this religion talk. (Vomit sounds. Vomit emoji. Indicates vomit by sticking finger in mouth.)

I feel your pain, precious reader. Let me explain.

Modern society, particularly in the last twenty to thirty years, has frequently dismissed religion outright and banished it to the purview of the dim-witted, old-fashioned, and superstitious. As we explored in the previous two chapters, much of this is very much the fault of the religions themselves. At least what humanity has built up around (and taken away from) the essentially beautiful core messages of the initial prophets/founders.

It's no wonder, then, that in the Western world we are seeing a mass exodus from organized religion, especially among younger generations, who see religion as backward and hate-filled.

Part of the issue, it seems to me, is evolution. We humans see almost everything as naturally, albeit fitfully, evolving and moving forward. There might be occasional setbacks and some natural ebb and flow, but we see technology, social justice, government, economics, and overall social enlightenment continually progressing, growing, and transforming us over the course of time.

Not so much with faith movements. Humans don't perceive religion as something that has progressed, grown, and transformed over the centuries. For the most part, we view it as static, musty, unchanging, and unchangeable. Gems of ancient truth held in a kind of irrelevant, historical amber.

Today's youngest generations increasingly don't believe religion suits the needs of where humanity is currently headed and where its greatest issues lie. They see it as the problem, not the solution. As something that's holding us back, not propelling us forward. And I completely understand.

Yet here we are, surrounded by all those deadly global pandemics on all sides, unable to effectively solve any of them, and we continue to be crippled by declining mental health and increased anxiety. *Something is clearly not working.* Perhaps there is more to be gleaned and withdrawn from religion. Perhaps we can "take what we like and leave the rest" as they say in the twelve-step programs.

According to the Pew Research Center, the gap between happiness in Christian versus nonreligious communities is steep. Some 36 percent of Christians in the United States consider themselves "very happy" compared to only 25 percent of unaffiliated respondents. Study after study shows that people who belong to a strong religious community often cite higher levels of personal contentment and inner peace. They live longer and are also more civically engaged. They are less depressed and less anxious. They give more to charity and, get this, smile and laugh more. So it becomes clear from the science that something about religion clearly *is* working.

Dr. Lisa Miller, professor of psychology and the founder of Columbia University's Spirituality, Mind, Body Institute (SMBI), writes of this in great detail in her excellent work *The Awakened Brain*. She discovered through rigorous scientific study and brain scans that not only are we hardwired for spiritual development but also that having a spiritual and religious practice and belief system greatly helps reduce depression and increase resilience, especially for teens. This mindset "awakens" our brains to the possibilities that the universe is reaching out to us and that we can foster deeper connections with others and with nature.

Yet it seems highly unlikely that today's millennial and Gen Z adults are going to be lining up any time soon to enroll as Muslims or Methodists or Sikhs, so this leaves us with no other choice than to (drumroll and trumpet flare, please!) . . .

BUILD A SUPER-COOL NEW RELIGION!

Erich Fromm, a godfather of early psychology who posited that (contrary to Freud) man's main drives were for freedom and belonging, wrote an opus called *The Sane Society* in 1955. In it he also explores many of the themes we're discussing here, such as mental health, finding one's path, and the perils of a materialistic society. He also has a brilliant summation of the need for a new religion in the modern age:

> A new religion will develop which corresponds to the development of the human race. The most important feature of such a religion will be its universalistic character, corresponding to the unification of mankind which is taking place in this epoch; it would embrace the humanistic teachings common to all the great religions of the East and of the West; its doctrines would not contradict the rational insight of mankind today, and its emphasis would be on the practice of life, rather than on doctrinal beliefs.
>
> Such a religion would create new rituals and artistic forms of expression, conducive to the spirit of reverence towards life and the solidarity of man. Religion can, of course, not be invented. It will come into existence with *the appearance of a new great teacher*, just as they have appeared in previous centuries when the time was ripe.

Now, this prediction very clearly states that such a religion will "not be invented" and that we will need another teacher to launch such a world-sweeping, modern movement. "New great teachers" we don't have in this little bookish endeavor. I'm certainly not one. I shudder at the thought of being any kind of actor-guru, dispersing wisdom in a kaftan from my Instagram feed alongside jokes about farts and robots and dachshunds. I mean, I can barely get through the average day without some mini anxiety attack or crisis of self-doubt. Plus, I'm just too weird and deeply flawed. And besides, no one wants to follow a religion run by some unemployed actor!

So without any great teacher at the center, let's start this endeavor off with a great underlying story.

MYTHOLOGY

It's crucial that this new religion we are assembling, like those from the past, be grounded in a profound, sweeping mythology that is rich with parable and metaphor.

Consider how universally lauded the fictional mythology of *Star Wars* is.

A young, floppy-haired blond dude on an alien desert planet discovers a message hidden inside a random droid. This, in turn, leads him to discover an enormous battle between good and evil going on and that he has an innate connection to a secret congregation of mystical warriors with access to a mysterious power called "the Force." A power stronger than anything created by mere technology. And *then* he discovers a connection between him and his sister, a literal princess; his father, a *dark lord*; and his own *internal* battle between good and evil! I mean, come on! How great is that?

If you're a film history buff, you know that George Lucas formulated his epic tale in consultation with author Joseph Campbell, a professor of comparative mythology. His celebrated outline of the core story points to the archetypal story of *The Hero with a Thousand Faces*. This symbolic structure is part of what makes the *Star Wars* epic so powerful.

In the surprise sociology best-seller *Sapiens: A Brief History of Human-kind*, author Yuval Noah Harari offers a panoramic history of humanity in the context of a species transforming itself and being transformed as it evolves on a planet in space. It details some of the key turning points of our fragile and adaptive race as we progress technologically, agriculturally, and socially. This mythological/sociological perspective is incredibly valuable—the book highlights the sweeping reverberations of one species on a planet and makes the journey of our genus feel epic in scope.

Both Joseph Campbell and Yuval Noah Harari connect dots in memorable (albeit disparate) ways, both specifically and metaphorically, about who we are, how we got here, and where we might be going.

Fundamentally, I believe the new faith we fabricate will require some more powerful voices and thinkers than me to articulate the need for this movement in a greater mythological sense—to tell the story of where we are headed in our spiritual evolution *and* revolution. We don't need a movie or graphic novel filled with monsters and lasers and good versus evil, but we do need a compelling narrative that reveals how humanity can and will evolve at the grassroots from a fractured, warlike past toward a united, peaceful future.

But back to the task at hand. Inventing a new religion. We have here some collective ideas that have been mulled over, sifted through, and codified for your perusing pleasure. (Yes, I'll admit, many of the key points of this imaginary faith are remarkably similar to those of *my* faith, the Baha'i Faith. I'm not stealing; I'm only borrowing! I mean, why not? It's got a great and inspiring foundation!)

We have been concocting a religion for you, dear reader, to actively *investigate* and make a conscious *choice* to become a member of, which is a complete departure from how most people join a faith. In most cases, a person *inherits* the faith community of their parents and surrounding community. People throughout the world rarely, if ever, "convert" these days. If your parents, family, and village are Catholics in Sicily, well then, by gum, you're a Catholic! You're not out investigating Tibetan Buddhism or going to an informational Sufi gathering. If your village in rural Pakistan is Muslim, well then, so are you! You're not seeking out a study group on the Bhagavad Gita or going to a local Quaker prayer circle.

So let's get to work. We are going to attempt to create out of whole cloth, right here on these very pages, a religion that could potentially help us to progress spiritually in a revolutionary new fashion. To help humanity mature and collectively make increasingly moral, compassionate choices. To help youth deal with the epic mental health struggles and other pandemics that surround us. To help individuals find peace, hope, and meaning in their hectic, disconnected modern lives. To make the world a better place.

Fasten your spiritual seat belts!

First things first: we need a name.

As we need an enormous *explosion* of spirituality to move toward this new reality (and putting the unfortunate "boomer" connotation aside), I'm going to go with SoulBoom, the Religion™. Apologies if this comes off as narcissistic or self-promotional, but it's my book and I get to do as I like. So kiss my holy ghost.

Now, what does SoulBoom™ believe? Look like? Practice? Stand for?

Let's start by assuming that SoulBoom has all the universal markers of any of the world's great religions. Those ten fundamentals we explored in the last chapter. To recap:

1. **A Higher Power.** SoulBoom officially believes in a Big Guy/Gal/Force/God/Creator thingy. A force that has our best interests in mind. A creative, cosmic source, closer to the concepts of art, love, and beauty than any kind of judgmental Sky-Daddy. Enough said.

2. **Life After Death.** There is no concept of hell as a specific location or place of eternal hellfire and damnation in SoulBoom. Remember our Higher Power is not childish, vindictive, or mean, so why would He banish people to infinite torment? He's not Voldemort!

Does that mean hell doesn't exist? Not exactly. I've been in "hell" before. When I was living with addiction, despair, anxiety, and a few brushes with suicidal ideation, I was miserable, lost, overly medicated, and confused. I was in a literal and figurative hell. So in SoulBoom, hell is simply distance from the source of divine joy. Distance from light, from love, from belonging. Hell is being lost in self and pain and isolation. But it's not some destination for the damned and the nonbeliever.

3. **Power of Prayer.** We are a faith with a spiritual "practice" at its center. A discipline. One that is challenging. Rigorous. Not namby-pamby. But at the same time, rewarding, refreshing, life-affirming! We are not reinventing the wheel here—we know what works! Prayer and meditation. Both. Together. That great mystical back-and-forth conversation with the vibration of the universe.

4. **Transcendence.** SoulBoom practices will incorporate the findings of modern positive psychology and the current mindfulness movement, alongside the ancient wisdom of the Vedas, Lao-tzu, and the Pali canon of Buddhism—spiritual tools to hold our ego in check and keep the satellite dish of our hearts pointed in the right direction. Up. Only then will we find deep surrender to the creative source and nurture the spark of that primal longing to connect to something greater than ourselves. The Great Mystery.

5. **Community.** At SoulBoom, our diverse community will embrace inclusion at every level—more on that in a little bit. Most importantly, however, our community will have a singular focus on empowering, training, and investing in children and youth. Our goal here is social revolution via spiritual transformation. Century after century, it has been youth who sparked the greatest revolutions in the world: the Arab Spring, the Velvet Revolution, the Greensboro lunch counter sit-ins, the Tiananmen Square protests. All the way up to Black Lives Matter and

the young women and students leading an uprising against oppression in Iran. The SoulBoom community will embrace and center around these young spiritual rebels.

6. **A Moral Compass.** Like it or not, we at SoulBoom are all in favor of figuring out what's right and wrong. We would *love* to have a belief system that allowed followers to simply "do what feels right." But a core moral code that doesn't bend with the ups and downs of social trends is crucial. Here's how ours will differ, though. We will establish a SoulBoom council of wise folks who peruse the divinely inspired universal moral codes that have been passed down for eons from both the Eastern (karmic) and Western (Abrahamic) faith traditions to decide, through long, loving, and frank consultation, the collective moral parameters for Soul-Boomers. Your personal relationship with this new SoulBoom moral code will ultimately be between you, your conscience, and the Creative Cosmic Force (a.k.a. G.O.D.). That is, you won't get kicked out for failing to follow the guidelines.

7. **The Force of Love.** We at SoulBoom headquarters are all about the biggest possible L-O-V-E. (Warning: this is going to get all sorts of corny.) Everything boils down to love. We mean everything. Light is love. Friends are love. Trees and birds and the ocean are love. Language is love. Time is love. Laughter is love. The type of love that is a beautiful and hilarious series of high fives with the universe. We believe in love as a universal law like gravity and that our love for everyone should radiate out like sunlight. Rumi said it best: "Love is the bridge between you and everything."

8. **Increased Compassion.** In the original *Star Trek*, Dr. McCoy says, "Compassion: that's the one thing no machine ever had. Maybe it's the one thing that keeps men ahead of them." A profound focus on compassion, the energy source that keeps us on the right track, will be at the core of SoulBoom because it is the essence of our humanity. Without the ability to empathize and

deeply feel for others, especially those most unlike ourselves, we will never be able to harness the power of spiritual tools in pursuit of a healthier, more harmonious world.

9. **Service to the Poor.** Here at SoulBoom, we don't like the word "charity." It implies the worst kind of service to the needy—pity for "those poor, *poor* people" who don't have stuff, so we patronizingly hand out sandwiches and juice boxes and knapsacks to the "have-nots" and do nothing to change the imbalanced, unjust systems that led to this poverty mess in the first place. Nothing against soup kitchens, but foundationally, the solutions to poverty must go beyond a meal and temporary housing. Therefore, our new faith will ask all its followers to work in substantive ways to prioritize and empower the disenfranchised— providing mental health services, access to addiction services, community centers, job skills, education, and opportunity. And yes, juice boxes and sandwiches when appropriate.

10. **Strong Sense of Purpose.** Like most faith traditions, SoulBoom will offer both personal meaning and a larger collective purpose for this here life. Both the *Kung Fu*–esque individual answers we seek and the *Star Trek*–like big-picture stuff. Our purpose will be inspired by the words of Albert Einstein: "The religion of the future will be a cosmic religion. It should transcend a personal God and avoid dogmas and theology. Covering both the natural and the spiritual, it should be based on a religious sense arising from the experience of all things, natural and spiritual, as a meaningful unity."

There you have it. The SoulBoom take on religion's fundamental verities. These elements alone are beefy enough for any upstart belief system, but for our ultimate goal of making SoulBoom as relevant to the present moment as possible, I offer up an *additional* ten principles. The goal of these next ten qualities is to show how this new faith community will embrace the ideals needed to remake and progress our modern world.

11. **No clerics.** What would you think about a religion with no clergy? We here at SoulBoom are all for it.

One of the miracles of the Twelve-Step Recovery Program at AA is the lack of leadership roles. The inmates are running the asylum! Elected servant-leaders run the meetings for limited terms while following the adage "principles above personalities."

As expertly quoted in the Twelve Traditions of the AA Big Book, "For our group purpose, there is but one ultimate authority—a loving God as He may express Himself in our *group conscience.* Our leaders are but trusted servants; they do not govern."

What if modern religion was like that? (Or politics, for that matter!) Leaders as trusted servants. We no longer need people with funny hats (whose only historical "expertise" was knowing how to read when most of the population didn't) to interpret the holy writings for us. What if no member of this faith had more power or authority than any other member? What if, like at an AA meeting, there were regular, democratic elections, where a rotating staff of elected folks helped to serve the needs of the community . . . and nothing else?

When I ponder the unconscionable acts committed by so many of the world's clergy, the violence encouraged by many clerics against those not of their faith, it feels like we all need a break. Therefore, at SoulBoom, we hereby designate all laypeople with the responsibility of growing and running this grassroots spiritual movement! A faith where everyone's interpretation of the holy writings is valid and worthy of consideration and consultation.

And we can *collectively* oversee the kitchen chores at our meeting hall, the fundraiser planning, and the scheduling of park cleanup volunteers.

12. **Diversity plus harmony.** Goes without saying (though we already kind of said it in describing the SoulBoom community) that this is a faith open to all. All are embraced, included, and welcomed with loving, open arms and a spirit of light.

All races. All classes. All genders. All sexual orientations. All identities. All creeds. All languages. All cultures.

Sound too idealistic? It is . . . and it isn't. In truth, diversity is how our world naturally thrives. Consider agriculture. What we've learned after hundreds of years of commercial agricultural practice is that a *lack* of crop diversity depletes and drains our precious topsoil of all its essential nutrients. Crops become harder to grow. Yields decline. The earth itself becomes less fertile. I mean, you saw all that corn dying in *Interstellar*, right?

The solution? Regenerative agriculture, an emerging farming practice that seeks to plant a variety of crops and plants in a single field—some for harvest, others simply to provide green matter to the soil. The results? Dramatic improvements in soil biodiversity that reverses the damaging, draining effects of single-crop planting.

SoulBoom is our field, and the diversity of our community is what will strengthen and reverse the damage our current divisions are causing.

This central garden image from the Baha'i writings encapsulates this idea quite beautifully:

How unpleasing to the eye if all the flowers and plants, the leaves and blossoms, the fruits, the branches and the trees of that garden were all of the same shape and colour! Diversity of hues, form and shape, enricheth and adorneth the garden, and heighteneth the effect thereof. In like manner, when diverse shades of thought, temperament, and character are brought together under the power and influence of one central agency, the beauty and glory of human perfection will be revealed and made manifest.

—'Abdu'l-Baha

One more thing. While our fundamental POV on all this diversity is that it is to be honored, savored, and celebrated, diversity should not come at the expense of recognizing our inherent commonalities, the qualities that unite us. Today, so much of society is laser-focused on self-identification—these are my pronouns, my ethnicity, my background, how I affiliate. Which is crucial when there has been a long, dismissive, and often violent history of oppression against nondominant groups. But simultaneously, we are also members of one human species who all love, play, create, grieve, and seek belonging. We are all spiritual beings having a human experience. Our inherent and shared humanity, our divine souls, our inherent goodness—these are the things we should see *first* when we look at our fellow SoulBoomers.

13. **Centrality of the divine feminine.** To quote one of the world's great philosophers, Ariana Grande, "When all is said and done / You'll believe God is a woman."

The journey of many of the world's oldest spiritual practices has been to move from a reverence for the matriarchal/feminine to a rejection of the mother/earth/womb mythology. Indeed, modern religion embraces the stricter, more controlling patriarchal father.

When God Was a Woman is a seminal book written in 1976 by the historian Merlin Stone. In her research about Paleolithic societies, she writes, "Development of the religion of the female deity in this area was intertwined with the earliest beginnings of religion so far discovered anywhere on earth." She states that their goddesses were "creator and law-maker of the universe, prophetess, provider of human destinies, inventor, healer, hunter, and valiant leader in battle."

Then, around 1500 BC, the tide turned away from worship of the female deity and became patriarchal. Priest, king, and eventually

Father/God took the place of the divine feminine, often in ways that obliterated the previous mythologies. And historians tell us that the role, rights, and status of women declined greatly over this time period as well.

Well, we at SoulBoom want to course correct this backward-ass way of thinking. We need to *re*honor the woman/divine feminine in our construction of the faith of the future.

We are not naive. We know this will take an incredible amount of work. The patriarchal narrative of our culture is so deeply engrained in our psyches that it will likely take decades to undo. In *Cassandra Speaks: When Women Are the Storytellers, the Human Story Changes*, author Elizabeth Lesser asks the question, What if women had been our storytellers? What story would Eve have told about picking the apple? Why is Pandora blamed for opening the box? Lesser reframes these stories from the perspective of the woman as the central narrator. And reading them is a dramatic and drastic departure from the stories we know—one that challenges the core of how you see the world.

So for this ideal to work, we propose starting with something tangible—women's rights in the modern world. In our fabricated faith, women will be, without exception, accorded every single right, honor, and benefit that men have. More, perhaps. The voices of women and girls should be given priority in public discourse. They should get equal pay and greater protections under the law, and their role as mothers should be sanctified. Plus, if resources are limited, women should be the first to be offered access to education, opportunity, and advancement.

We're with you, Ariana.

14. **Cooperation between science and faith.** If there's one thing that differentiates SoulBoom from the majority of mystical faiths of the past, it is a core belief in the essential harmony between science and religion.

Our universe is not singular; it is unified. A unified field of physical and spiritual forces that shape and determine our lives. Science is often seen as logical and objective and spirituality as "airy-fairy" and subjective. However, it's time to rectify once and for all this false dichotomy. As Louis Pasteur said, "A little science takes you away from God but more of it takes you to Him." Both are methods of examining and interacting with the same reality.

We understand the physical world, its laws, operations, and mysteries through the lens of science. Science is both a database of knowledge *and* a system of learning about natural laws by using repeatable experiments that reveal factual truth about those systems.

We at SoulBoom would argue the same is true of the spiritual world. Spiritual guidance from the world's great faith traditions and from Indigenous belief systems allow us to understand the "why" that exists beyond the "how" of science. If science leads us to create an atomic bomb, religion shows us that peace is the ultimate goal. If technology helped create tremendous advances in transportation, energy, and construction, a wise, moral imperative tells us that the resulting CO_2 in the atmosphere will be devastating to our species and thousands of others and must be limited for the good of our descendents.

Humanity is clamoring for a unity between these two forces like never before in its history, as the stakes simply could not be higher.

15. **Profound connection to the natural world.** I've written a bit, mostly in general terms, about Indigenous spirituality and how, throughout the world, native cultures have a deep connection to the cycles, beauty, and mystery of nature.

Think of the power and mystery in the last words of Chief Crowfoot, quoted in 1890: "What is life? It is the flash of a firefly in the night. It is the breath of a buffalo in the wintertime. It is the little shadow which runs across the grass and loses itself in the sunset."

We have so much to learn from that poetic gem. We humans have drastically lost touch with our living, sacred connection to nature in this modern world. Our lack of direct access to and interaction with our pulsing, living earth is, I believe, directly responsible for how disconnected we have become from the real threat of man-made climate change.

Neuroscientist Dr. Rachel Hopman of Northeastern University has studied the neurological changes that happen to humans who have regular exposure to the outdoors. Among the benefits are improved neural functioning, enhanced cognition, and reduced stress and anxiety. In fact, time in nature lights up the same parts of the brain as regular meditation.

Hopman has gone so far as to propose a formula for time in nature to maximize these benefits. Her "nature pyramid," like the food pyramid we all learned in elementary school, follows a 20-5-3 rule. It goes like this.

To maximize the neurological benefits of nature, humans must spend

- *twenty minutes, three times a week* outside doing something like a light stroll in a neighborhood park;
- *five hours per month* in semiwild nature like a forested state park; and
- *three days once a year* off the grid (the top of the pyramid!)— camping, renting a cabin, being on a boat in the ocean— surrounded only by wild animals and zero cell reception.

At SoulBoom, we believe in prioritizing access to and deep time in nature as part of our faith's inherent practices. Instead of gathering inside of soul-sucking buildings, let's sit together and pray by a stream. Instead of putting Sunday school students under harsh fluorescent lighting, let's allow them free rein of a park for several hours of the day. Choir practice at the beach! Mandatory nature hikes! Let's remind our souls of the vastness and fragility of this beautiful planet—the only one we have—on a daily basis. And watch as our individual stressors and anxieties are healed as well.

16. **Centrality of justice.** Today, the phrase "social justice" has become, oddly enough, controversial. Same with "environmentalism" and "women's rights." The manipulative forces of political and corporate interests have framed the pursuit of justice and equity as something with a partisan agenda attached to it.

And yet in Isaiah 1:17, it says, "Learn to do right; seek justice. Defend the oppressed. Take up the cause of the fatherless; plead the case of the widow."

I mean, if that's not a clarion call for social justice from the heart of the Bible-thumping Bible, I don't know what is!

In fact, there are *dozens* of quotes on justice and equity from the Bible that are as relevant today as when they were written:

I John 3:17–18—"But if anyone has the world's goods and sees his brother in need, yet closes his heart against him, how does God's love abide in him? Little children, let us not love in word or talk but in deed and in truth."

If humans dug deep into the clarion call of the book of John, we would fight like hell to *not allow* injustice to exist anywhere.

At SoulBoom we believe justice is a precursor to lasting peace. And without peace, there can't be unity among humankind. Justice first, and the rest will fall into place.

17. **A life of service.** We've already talked about service to the poor as one of the ten fundamentals. But we want SoulBoom to take the underlying concept of service and expand and apply it to every space of our lives.

Is it possible to build a faith where every believer wants their life, family, and career to be centered around doing good for others? Being "other-centered" instead of "self-centered"? How do we inspire people to ask themselves every day in their marriage, in their friendships, in their workplace, How can I be of service today? And even harder: How can we find ways to show kindness and service toward people we dislike or have little in common with?

Because of my Baha'i identity, I have many Iranian friends. There is a common trope (and many shared jokes) among these immigrant families that their children are anxiously encouraged by their parents to be doctors, lawyers, and engineers. No wonder, as they are practical jobs that can easily land you an immediate and substantial income as well as great prestige.

My dear immigrant friend Mr. Mogharabi, father of four adult Mogharabi girls (one of whom, Shabnam, cofounded SoulPancake with me), told me that the only advice he ever offered his daughters about their careers was "to find a way to be of the most service to the most people." That single goal will bring you not only the most fulfillment in your work but the most happiness as well. Now one daughter works for the Environmental Protection Agency doing communication to protect local air and water, one works for Verizon to implement technology at underserved schools, one is an elementary schoolteacher, and dear Shabnam makes uplifting video content for millions of young folk.

This is backed up by a 2007 study from *The Journals of Gerontology* that found that seniors in their seventies who reported feeling "frequently useful" to friends, family, or neighbors were, seven years later, 64 percent less likely to be dead and had better health outcomes than those who responded they "never" felt useful.

Spiritual wisdom aligns with this:

Generosity and kind words,
Conduct for others' welfare,
Impartiality in all things;
These are suitable everywhere.

These kind dispositions hold the world together,
Like the linchpin of a moving chariot.

—*The Buddha*

And from two of humanity's greatest thought leaders:

Life's most persistent and urgent question is, "What are you
doing for others?"

—*Martin Luther King Jr.*

The best way to find yourself is to lose yourself in the service of
others.

—*Mahatma Gandhi*

Those are some pretty powerful words, all told. I love that
dance between "finding yourself" and "losing yourself" in service that Gandhi speaks of. A little different from many of the
modes of finding oneself that are used in modern America. These
quotes provide a profound shift in perspective from three of
humanity's greatest souls who put service to *all*—friends and
enemies alike—at the center of their life's work. That's what it
will truly mean to be a SoulBoomer.

18. **Practical spiritual tools.** I once gave a TEDx talk on spiritual
life hacks.

You know how the internet is full of memes, Instagram
accounts, and viral videos featuring "life hacks" to make your life
better? Things like: use the sticky edge of a Post-It note to clean

the dust between the keys of your keyboard! Or: freeze grapes and put them in your white wine glass to chill your delicious wine beverage without diluting it!

Simple. Easy. Practical.

And when you hear these life hacks, you go, "That's brilliant! Why didn't I think of that before!?"

Well, I believe that SoulBoom needs to be filled chock-a-block with spiritual teachings in that same vein: bite-sized pearls of wisdom and guidance from all the ancient prophets, thinkers, and philosophers that are practical, applicable, and make everyone's life better in tangible ways.

One of my favorites is from 'Abdu'l-Baha. He said, "If a man has ten good qualities and one bad one, to *look at the ten and forget the one*; and if a man has ten bad qualities and one good one, to *look at the one and forget the ten*" (italics mine).

This is the kind of spiritual life hack that resonates for me.

We are all surrounded every day by super challenging, annoying, and difficult people. At the store. At school. At *The Office*. It can be one of our greatest tests in life!

So how do we deal with these folks? Well, I try to harness the words of 'Abdu'l-Baha. If I'm with someone who has ten amazing qualities but *one super annoying one*—perhaps, for instance, they are kind, lovely, and compassionate *but* they constantly interrupt—why do I consistently focus so much on the bad? Why do I let the nonstop interrupting rankle me so much even if I really like the person overall and can see their many other positive qualities? This is a pattern that I can correct with a simple shift of focus on a daily basis.

The converse is even more challenging. We all know someone who is rude, selfish, unkind, toxic. We do our best to avoid people like this. But what if we tried instead to consciously find *one good quality* about that person? For instance, what if they are a total jerk in every way but have great hygiene and always smell like freshly baked chocolate chip cookies? When I'm able to consciously focus on the good quality of a person, not only is my day better but my relationship with that person improves. And eventually, other good qualities are revealed to me that I might not have taken the time to see previously.

In other words, focus on the cookies. And *don't* focus on the negative.

Gandhi backs up this whole enterprise with his characteristic humility: "I look only to the good qualities of men. Not being faultless myself, I won't presume to probe into the faults of others."

The above is a practical, spiritually minded tool that increases my quality of life. It's something I can use every single day in my interactions with workmates, challenging family members, and neighbors. And it's an example of how SoulBoom teachings need to be grounded in the real world and have a "meat and potatoes" focus on increasing well-being and quality of life.

19. **Emphasis on music and arts.** Every social revolution has the arts front and center. Often driven by the energy and idealism of youth and young adults. One simply cannot imagine the civil rights movement, or the Vietnam war protests, or Black Lives Matter without the arts and youth. Hand in hand.

And of all the art forms, there is simply no substitute for the joyful, passionate energy generated by music. Music transcends language, space, and time. It imprints itself on our brains and hearts. It's why seniors with dementia often can't remember something as simple as their own name but will sing all the lyrics to a favorite song after hearing just a few notes.

Think of a roster of incredibly powerful songs that have helped fuel movements old and new: "War" by Edwin Starr, "Ohio" by Crosby, Stills, Nash and Young, "Freedom" by Beyoncé, and "This Is America" by Childish Gambino. Anything by Bob Marley. "The Times They Are a-Changin'."

The arts even saved the whales. True story.

In the '60s, whale numbers were dwindling, with more than fifty thousand whales being slaughtered around the world every year. The ecology movement had only recently been launched, and environmentalists, try as they might, couldn't get the public to pay attention to the imminent destruction of our largest, most beautiful species. No one cared.

Meanwhile, a nerdy whale scientist named Roger Payne listened to a military sonar recording of humpback whales "singing" and became obsessed. He made more recordings and started spreading them around fanatically. After he gave singer Judy Collins a copy, she used the sounds on her album *Whales and Nightingales*. Payne then released an entire album of these recordings called *Songs of the Humpback Whale*. This album went on to become the best-selling nature album of all time. *National Geographic* even sent out ten million flexi-disc pressings of excerpts of the album to subscribers.

Greenpeace piggybacked off the album's success to start its famous "Save the Whales" campaign, and it started to blast whale songs from giant speakers at whaling ships while they were butchering the gorgeous, endangered creatures.

Over the course of the '70s, public opinion around whales shifted, in large part due to people hearing these plaintive, beautifully human songs. Soon after, the International Whaling Commission put an effective ban on whaling. Humpback whale populations increased from less than one thousand to nearly eighty thousand currently.

All because of an album. Because some young artists, environmentalists, and activists harnessed the power of art to create change.

So how will our spiritual movement of SoulBoom tap into the energy of revolutionary change at a grassroots level? By incorporating arts (especially music) into its foundation and empowering youth to use those arts for personal and societal transformation.

20. **Humility.** And last but certainly not least, the SoulBoom faith admits that it doesn't know the best way to do anything.

We don't have any absolute answers. We're in a humble posture of learning. We provide but a few markers, guideposts, and clues along the winding path of the spiritual game of life.

A morsel of meaning. A soupçon of serenity. A kernel of the eternal. And plenty of questions along the way.

As Richard Rohr, the wise Franciscan priest and philosopher, said, "Healthy religion is always humble about its own holiness and knowledge. It knows that it does not know. Anybody who really knows also knows that they don't know at all."

Unlike most other faiths, we can't guarantee to know the way to certain salvation. We believe people who don't follow the SoulBoom path are just as likely to find some kind of spiritual enlightenment as we are. We would never judge anyone else for the choices they make, the God they worship or don't worship, the practices or rituals they undertake, or the confusion and struggles they might have along the way. Bless us every one.

With that, we at SoulBoom submit that we would love to learn from and collaborate with each and every one of you and each and every one of your religious faiths and spiritual practices!

You can write us at Hello@SoulBoom.com with all your learnings, experiences, and wisdom.

And just because, I offer one additional ideal:

BONUS #21. Potlucks! There will be no SoulBoom without potlucks. The bonds between the two are indissoluble. One of the greatest Native American contributions to world culture of all time. So, SoulBoomers all, bring on your grandma's recipe for baked ziti as well as that damp tossed salad from a bag. And don't forget to take your serving bowl back home with you!

———◦⊰◦———

There you have it, folks. The outline for a new religion that just might meet some of the needs of folks in the modern world.

And we made it ourselves. Right here on page 191 of *Soul Boom!*

We covered the ten fundamentals of religion from the SoulBoom POV as well as my ten (actually eleven!) SoulBoom-specific religious concepts in the most cursory of ways, but it's a start! We would probably need another thirty-nine years to flesh things out and make our nascent religious movement a bit more substantial.

But, dear reader, I blithely fabricate a religion on these here pages to prove a point. Although SoulBoom the Religion will never exist, there are some universal, foundational truths that religion addresses and that humanity is longing for: purpose, community, devotion, transcendence, and service.

Do you need an actual religion in your life in order to be connected to some of these spiritual ideas? Of course not.

But as humanity has thrown the *good* of spirituality out with the *bad* of religion, I think it's time we look at all the ingredients that comprise the spiritual bedrock of an organized faith with fresh eyes. Hopefully this is the start of a much larger conversation.

One thing I've been pondering is whether our mythical SoulBoom movement might need to have a presence in Jerusalem. Since real estate on the Temple Mount is somewhat limited, perhaps we could rent a nearby Airbnb? A big space, a big tent, so to speak, where all are welcome. No clergy. A completely volunteer crew of diverse young folks. A handy-dandy booth that points people to dozens of nearby service opportunities. Maybe Bruce the tour guide is at the door handing out lemonade and halvah.

Star Wars and *Star Trek* are on a constant, harmonious loop on some big-screen TVs. Whale songs and Bob Marley are playing in the background. Local Muslims and Jews are playing Ping-Pong and chess together in perfect harmony. Nature walks on the hour, perhaps. Basho haiku reading nights.

A big sign over the front door with the word "HOPE!" on it.

And, of course, nonstop potlucks.

CHAPTER NINE

THE BROKEN BLUE MARBLE

> We are watching the birth, more than the death, of a world.
> —*Father Pierre Teilhard de Chardin*

One of the most seminal and transformative events in human history was the taking of a photograph. And it happened almost by accident.

The famous photo is called "The Blue Marble," and it was taken by one of the astronauts of *Apollo 17*. It was snapped in December 1972, during NASA's last manned lunar landing. One of the three astronauts, spontaneously inspired by all that beauty, pointed a Hasselblad camera out the window and snatched the first image of the entirety of Earth, illumined completely by sunlight, surrounded by the dark, starlit immensity of space.

It was the first photograph that showed us our true home. All was revealed. We are floating in outer space on a beautiful round, cloudy, vibrant miracle, alone in the black vastness.

I remember seeing this iconic photograph when I was a child and resonating with the power it held. It's the most reproduced photograph of all time, and like the whale songs, it was a necessary, beautiful testament to something important and essential. It launched movements. Environmentalists, educators, and peace activists would time and time again showcase "The Blue Marble" as part of their mission, their vision.

Wars seem obsolete when gazing at the image. Pollution seems like a grotesque crime. It sparked countless conversations, and that single image urged us toward world unity in a way that little had done previously.

I've alluded to this before, but in the '60s and '70s, world peace seemed possible, doable, buildable. We mock them now, but beauty contestants used to wish for "world peace" when receiving their trophies. And they sincerely meant it! Students in the '70s would write reports on world peace. Hippies would have probing conversations about it. Politicians would talk about it with a straight face. The threat of the A-bomb hung over our heads, and humanity longed for a way out of all those deadly wars of the twentieth century, and WORLD PEACE was on the banner at the finish line. And throughout all this, "The Blue Marble" hung in every classroom as a testament to the possibility of peace and love on our beautiful little home.

Unfortunately, somewhere over the course of the next twenty years, that lofty goal, urged on by a single photograph, faded away into a jaded haze of cynicism and a core belief that humans will always be at war in some way, shape, or form. Get used to it, buddy. We have come to collectively believe that world peace was a pipe dream, only idealized by the naive, the foolish, and the childish. It is pretty universally thought that countries will *always* be armed to the teeth and deadlocked in a series of cold wars with proxy battles around the globe. Humans will be humans, after all, and our warlike nature will never change—at least that's what the pragmatists, Marxists, and postmodern moral relativists continue to trumpet.

As for me, what is evoked by that picture of a planet hanging in the immensity of outer space? Well, and this may seem off-topic, but here's what that photograph makes me think of today: *aliens*!

Recently, the American government released previously classified intelligence about the staggering amount of unidentified aerial phenomena (UAPs, the new term for UFOs) that have been recorded, documented, and verified over the last fifty years. And it is astonishing.

An incredible number of sober, conservative, eggheaded, career-military pilots and scientists have now come forward, on the record, to describe their interactions with UAPs. The sheer volume of credible photos and videos of these flying objects makes denying them now as ludicrous as believing in them was perceived to be forty years ago!

It is eminently clear that all those wackos who were talking about space aliens back in the day weren't the tinfoil hat nutjobs we all thought they were. *They were right!*

So many questions arise. Are the ships operated by alien species? Or are they *future humans*, time-traveling back to observe ourselves in our own distant past? Are they some kind of threat? Galactic scientists? Interdimensional explorers?

Here's what I imagine is going on. And I can truly think of no other plausible possibility:

Aliens are watching us, observing us. Many different species, which explains all the different styles of ships—triangles, disks, and cigar-shaped vessels. Starships from many different and diverse planets and even galaxies. These aliens are actively viewing a fumbling, crazy, lovable, and reprehensible species, potentially on the verge of wiping itself out.

So let's put ourselves in their alien shoes (tentacles?) for a few pages.

What do we imagine the aliens are discussing at an alien council meeting at their base on the dark side of the moon? I mean, they must be communicating with each other, right? Probably in a fashion not entirely dissimilar to the way Mork (played by the legendary Robin Williams) would talk to Orson about humans at the end of every episode of yet another great '70s television show, *Mork and Mindy*. How might they be processing what they are seeing on planet Earth? What would that conversation sound like?

As a matter of fact, in one of my many unsuccessful offbeat entertainment pitches, I once proposed a weekly part-scripted/part-improvised podcast about aliens observing human customs, politics, behavior, and society overall. These comedic characters would also end up becoming *huge* consumers of human media, film, and TV and use them as ongoing reference points.

So bear with me while I indulge that idea here on these pages. For your reading pleasure, I commence with some possible dialogue between two of these alien observers that we'll call Scoobash and %*&^11+[12]:

SCOOBASH: Any update from your recent aerial flybys and media monitoring on planet Earth, %*&^11+?

%*&^11+: Yes. We have triple confirmed that humans have full awareness of the imminent and catastrophic dangers of climate change due to heat-trapping gases that they are emitting from a variety of sources. There are articles in all the major newspapers. Documentary films and television specials as well as research papers from top scientists provide undeniable, verified data. Discussions about the issue are happening in the halls of their immature government gatherings. Occasionally, a little Swedish girl attends these gatherings and yells at the officials, "*How dare you!*"

SCOOBASH: And well she should! If they know about the disastrous repercussions of unchecked CO_2, nitrous oxide, and methane emissions, as well as rampant deforestation, why are they doing nothing to stop it? I mean, they must also know that they are at the point of no return.

%*&^11+: Well, they *are* bringing their own shopping bags to the supermarkets.

SCOOBASH: What?!

%*&^11+: You know, because of the plastic . . . Never mind.

SCOOBASH: Again—what?!

%*&^11+: I believe humanity's lack of response to the climate crisis is explained within the pages of that book I sent you, *The Lorax*.

---

12 Pronounced Percentasteriskampersandcaretelevenplus, or Percy for short.

Scoobash: *Loved!*

%*&^II+: Classic, right? Just metaphorically substitute Truffula trees for the Earth's environment in toto. For decades a vocal, well-funded minority denied climate change was even happening and funded a massive disinformation campaign. Now that that phase is over, the new tactic is downplaying the damaging effects of climate change and extreme weather events. Many of this coterie chalk up all the "disaster talk" to alarmist Chicken Little–ish doomsaying. But bottom line? They complain about the expense of doing anything about it as implementing green technology, reducing CO_2, and transitioning to alternative energy sources comes with a hefty price tag.

Scoobash: First question, what does "Chicken Little" refer to?

%*&^II+: Long story. I'll send over the mediocre animated film starring the voices of Zach Braff and Steve Zahn from 2005.

Scoobash: *Ooooh*, good casting! Also—*the expense*?! Does this species understand the billions in overall expense that catastrophic flooding, extreme storms, persistent droughts, and plant and animal extinction will have? That this completely solvable problem will wreak havoc on world economies over the coming decades?! And that *time is of the essence*!?

%*&^II+: Yup.

Scoobash: I'm confused.

%*&^II+: Well, this species is not very good at setting aside their immediate wants and needs for the long-term good. They have no collective vision for the future of their species or their planet.

Scoobash: What about *Star Trek*!?

%*&^II+: Great show. Every version of it! Not a huge *Voyager* guy, but it has its supporters.

Scoobash: OK, but wait. Didn't humankind *just* face one of their worst viruses in history, pull together, create and distribute a vaccine in record time, and save untold lives? Wouldn't *that* example unite people?

%*&^II+: *Ehhh* . . . no. Because of partisan factionalism, no one thinks it's a triumph of collective action in the face of global disaster.

SCOOBASH: Wow. I . . . kind of can't wrap my head around all these contradictions.

%*&^II+: Neither can humanity! In fact, much of the world is still governed by authoritarian states that only seem interested in aggressive nationalism and militarism and invasions of neighbors. And the other half, the "democratic" half, is locked in corruption, ennui, and selfish, materialistic pursuits. They do have a collective council called the United Nations, but it's ineffectual and bureaucratic. It's in a cool-looking building, though.

SCOOBASH: Wait. They're *still* at war or threatening and/or planning for war? They've lost *108 million* of their kind to armed conflict over the last hundred years or so!

%*&^II+: I suppose I would refer you to the sequential illustrations I sent of the bald-headed boy-child who is repeatedly tricked by a glowering, assertive female into attempting to kick a football.

SCOOBASH: OK, war and climate catastrophe aside, what else have you been observing for all these solar years? Give me the lowdown.

%*&^II+: Well, a haircut called the mullet just came into fashion again for like the third time. Oh, and here's a fun fact! There are eight people on the planet who have as much wealth as half of the planet's population.

SCOOBASH: Wait, *what*? Can you repeat that?

%*&^II+: Yes. Eight male humans in the last quarter of their lifespans are worth 426 billion United States dollars. That's as much as four billion of the poorest human beings on the planet.

Scoobash: I'm sorry, I just don't understand. I'm flummoxed. Why would this be allowed? Why don't they give away their money to the poorer people? Why don't the governments intervene? Why don't the four billion people just rise up and storm the houses of those eight male humans?

%*&^ii+: Woah, Scoob—let's not get placed on a watchlist here, OK? It's just that many humans don't believe in any economic action that might be seen as potentially limiting "job creators" and "entrepreneurs." But there's a bit more to it . . . Politics. Plus, racism.

Scoobash: What's racism?

%*&^ii+: Humans have different-colored pigments in their skin and have self-sorted into "races," socially constructed groups whose creation and abuse has ultimately caused no end of oppression, injustice, and disunity. Did you read that "Star-bellied Sneetches" book I sent you?"

Scoobash: *So good!*

%*&^ii+: Well, it's basically that.

Scoobash: Tell me, %*&^ii+. Why should we not just leave these lunatics to their own devices? Or simply blow up their planet for them?

%*&^ii+: Scoobash, don't say that! That would break all seventeen of my hearts! These human beings, flawed as they are, are capable of such good, such beauty. In addition to the work of their most famous doctor, Seuss, the artistry of their various populations is staggering. They've produced masterworks of music, literature, and architecture from every corner of the globe. I mean, perhaps not Orlando, but—

Scoobash: OK, fine. Stick with it. Maybe they'll get their fecal matter together one of these days. Also, I'm enjoying this *Game of Thrones* dragon prequel far more than I thought I would . . .

%*&^11+: I know, the former Time Lord and Prince Philip, now playing that rakish Targaryen, is fantastic!

Scoobash: I mean, it's not *Star Trek: The Next Generation* good.

%*&^11+: Nothing is, Scooby. Nothing is . . .

And so on. You get the idea.

I find the idea of looking at humanity through an alien lens to be infinitely refreshing. If one pictures a more advanced lifeform monitoring our news and media, as well as watching our cultural activities, growth, and conflict on the planet, it opens up a whole new way of visualizing our preposterously misguided and backward ways.

Here's an example of one of them: Political ad spending in the United States for midterm elections in 2022 was almost $8 *billion*. This is for all those idiotic, mean-spirited ads shouting at you (that you never pay any attention to) on television, radio, and digital platforms (Facebook, Google, etc.). And this was during a *midterm* year! And this is just in one country! Just *think* about what we could do for education, health care, or the environment in the United States with *allll* that money! But we don't discuss this. Ever. It's a big, fat sacred cow. It's *free speech!* And *personal expression. It's democracy at work!* This amount keeps growing exponentially every election cycle and will continue to expand, ad infinitum and ad absurdum.

There are thousands of other examples like this.

For instance, in a similar but larger vein, *global advertising itself* in 2022 reached $781 billion. That's TV, radio, billboards, online, and print across the globe. Ads: the lifeblood of capitalist enterprise! The entire *reason* that my old network television show *The Office* was created: to showcase advertisements for Ford trucks and Dr. Scholls insoles and Snapple during the act breaks! We will provide you with twenty-two minutes of entertainment, and you will, hopefully, watch eight minutes of tastefully placed ads that don't disrupt the flow of your entertainment-seeking escapism.

But think about it. With that nearly trillion dollars, we could *fix* world hunger. Climate change. Education. If we, all eight billion of us, collectively decided to not advertise "stuff" or "things" or "products" or "goods" or "services" for *only one year*!

I know it's a teensy bit more complicated than that, and of course one might argue that the trillion dollars in advertising helps drive the economic engine of many more *trillions* of dollars. Jobs included. But surely, naivete aside, if some ad dollars were somehow redirected for philanthropic purposes, somehow, the world economy would percolate along just fine, don't you think?

The point is, our global priorities seem epically misguided and upside down, and there are countless examples of the absurd choices we humans make on the largest of scales. To combine two uncombinable metaphors, so many times it feels like we're frogs in the boiling water rearranging the deck chairs on the *Titanic*. So many of our systems, our ways of doing things, are broken, outdated, nonsensical, unsustainable, and destructive that sometimes it takes an alien perspective to highlight our collective folly.

But are we truly living in folly? Some might disagree with that assessment.

There is a school of contemporary writers called the "new optimists," which includes Steven Pinker, Hans Rosling, Matt Ridley, and many others. This best-selling tribe of feted intellectuals, writers, and TED talkers has one central point to make:

"The world has made spectacular progress in every single measure of human well-being and . . . almost no one knows about it," says Pinker.

"Every day we're bludgeoned by news of how bad everything is . . . yet we've made more progress over the last one hundred years than in the first one hundred thousand," says Gregg Easterbrook.

And even Bill Gates is in on it. He says, in a book blurb for Ridley, "There have been constant predictions of a bleak future throughout human history, but they haven't come true. Our lives have improved dramatically—in terms of lifespan, nutrition, literacy, wealth, and other measures. Too often this overwhelming success has been ignored in favor of dire predictions."

And by many measures these secular-liberal-capitalist-lovin' writers are right. There are, in fact, far, far fewer people living below the poverty line. In fact, extreme poverty has fallen from 90 percent to 10 percent in a century or so. Global life expectancy has dramatically increased, from twenty-nine to seventy-one years, and infant mortality has dropped from 30 percent to 3 percent over the last one hundred years.

Barack Obama once said, "If you had to choose a moment in history to be born . . . you'd choose now."

And technologically, advances continue to make our quality of life better and better. Think of all the progress made even in the last decade! GPS and touchscreen glass on every phone. Blockchain. 3D printing. Alexa and other smart home technology. And what about all these nifty food delivery apps? Zoom! Crowdfunding websites! Self-parking cars! Cloud-based streaming music and video! Instant Pots!

In so many ways, the new optimists are dead-on. And the goal of their work is, ultimately, to give us *hope*. Because if we can't *see* that progress is possible, that humanity *can* make things better, then why even bother to try and fix the myriad of other problems we face?

And yet, as I've posited in the preceding chapters, at the *exact same time*, here we are with many of those same problems getting colossally worse, not better. In this moment, unlike any other time in history, humanity seems on the verge of destroying itself in about seventeen different ways. The stakes have never been higher, and—data aside—the world just *feels* on the brink of collapse.

So which is it? Are things getting better? Or are things falling apart?

For many young people that I speak to at colleges, these are very difficult dichotomies to process and make sense of.

For instance, despite all the controversy around these movements, the Black Lives Matter and #MeToo tidal waves that swept across the national conversation over the last several years have brought much-needed awareness and (slight) changes to two of the pandemics I described earlier: racism and sexism. Have they fixed the issues? Not even close. *But* these were necessary youth-based movements of great power and passion, and I can't imagine we will ever go back to the previous, more deluded way of looking at these vital issues.

Progress, not perfection.

Conversely, things also seem pretty darn horrific. On the political home front, our democracy seems on the verge of collapse. Meanwhile, increasing extreme weather events kill ever more people around the world, and the disastrous effects of climate change continue to pile up.

So that's bad.

The list goes on and on. Revolutionary progress in some areas, and never-before-seen destructive setbacks and global threats in others.

So what do we put our focus on? The bad or the good? How do we hold both of these world-warping, contradictory forces in our mind at the same time?

Embedded in the teachings of the Baha'i Faith, there is a key concept that helps me make sense of what exactly is happening in the world right now—how the disparate and conflicting energies of our time are at work in the transformation of human society on a global level. It's relatively simple but astonishingly revelatory. The concept explains that at any time, there are two parallel powers working on the world at once: the forces of integration and the forces of *dis*integration.

In other words, both destruction and evolution are happening *at the exact same time*! And believe it or not, they are *both* urgent and necessary.

The leader of the Baha'i Faith in the early and mid-twentieth century, Shoghi Effendi, described this phenomenon perfectly, all the way back in 1938:

A twofold process, however, can be distinguished, each tending . . . to bring to a climax the forces that are transforming the face of our planet. The first is essentially an *integrating process*, while the second is fundamentally *disruptive*. The former, as it steadily evolves, unfolds a System which may well serve as a pattern for that world polity [commonwealth] towards which a *strangely-disordered world* is continually advancing; while the latter, as it's disintegrating influence deepens, tends to tear down, with increasing violence, the antiquated barriers that seek to block humanity's progress towards its destined goal. [emphasis mine]

From this perspective, we are headed toward global unity one way or another. Unity of humanity. Unity of class, creeds, nations, and cultures. That's the only way forward. It's the only conceivable final result. Remember, we all live on a blue marble floating in space. Whether we almost destroy ourselves along the way or not is up to us, but the ultimate outcome is a human species inhabiting a planet together in harmony. (Even if there are only 147 of us left.) Much like humanity in *Star Trek*, we are sometimes gradually, sometimes pell-mell and chaotically, headed toward the creation of a global society that is just, balanced, wise, and compassionate.

Antiglobalist fearmongers can doomsay all they want, but the eventual movement toward a unified human family, sharing the resources of our fragile planet and taking mutual care of each other, is what we need to strive for, as naive and utopian as that may sound in these jaded times.

But before we get into all that "changing the world" stuff, there's one phrase from that previous quote by Shoghi Effendi that really pops out: "*strangely-disordered world*." And to me, those three words really sum up what a spiritual revolution is all about.

Our world *is* strangely disordered. So much about *how* we do things, as our alien friends earlier demonstrated, is upside down, backward, and inside out. And things have to change if we want to achieve the mental, physical, and spiritual wellness we long for on a personal and a global level.

One thing I'm struck by when I read the news is how "strangely disordered," how broken, *ALL* the modern organizational structures are. I mean, what field of endeavor or area of business, society, or government is *not* broken? Name an existing system, large or small, and chances are it's essentially out of whack at a fundamental level.

I'm going to spend the next few pages briefly describing some systems that are gravely, strangely out of balance, most specifically in the United States. Obviously, I don't have the time, room, or expertise to go into detail in these pages. I'm simply trying to set the scene to make a much larger point.

Which means . . . yes, things will get a little dark, but we'll get to some uplifting solutions before too long. Promise!

Some "strange disorders," in no particular order:

If you talk to a doctor, nurse, or a public health official, they will tell you in endless detail all the ways our health care system in the United States is fractured, unfair, dysfunctional, and unjust. And don't get anyone started on the complete lack of any kind of *mental* health care policy in our country.

Direct evidence of this systemwide dysfunction can be seen in the opioid epidemic, which continues to ravage the country and has taken half a million lives in the last twenty years. This is due in large part to our broken, corrupt health care system being so directly enmeshed with the broken, corrupt pharmaceutical industry or "Big Pharma"—the five large global companies that essentially control the entire pharmacological ecosystem.

Moving on.

If you speak to any teacher or school administrator, you will hear the same thing about education. Underprioritized. Overcrowded. Dysfunctional. Political corruption and union battles. A rapidly degrading system that is funded based on local property tax values, so the poorest neighborhoods are continually left behind.

And one can't bring up schools without mentioning the epidemic of school shootings.

Gun ownership and reasonable firearms regulation is another broken system in our country. We have more than 120 guns for every 100 people in the United States, and yet it's harder for a teenager to get a driver's license than an AR15. While most Americans want common-sense gun registration laws enacted, nothing changes as mass shootings continue unabated. The debate has become entrenched and deadlocked, driven by partisanship and funding from a massive gun lobby . . . all while children continue to get gunned down in classrooms.

The criminal justice and prison system is another area that has grotesque systemic imbalances and racist policies that haven't been altered in a hundred years. Mass incarceration of blacks and Latinos. A bail system that criminalizes being poor.

And what about the foster care system?

Immigration policies?

Unaffordable and unsubsidized daycare and childcare?

The housing crisis and the unhoused population?

Modern university education, staggering tuition and student loans, and the bizarrely insular world of American academia?

All struggling with brokenness in one form or another.

And don't get me started on modern news media, corralling viewers with incessant fearmongering and endless shouting matches. Opinion journalism is regularly gussied up as factual news, while the whole "for-profit" enterprise is entirely funded by one emotion: *outrage*. Outrage fuels an ever-incensed viewership, brand loyalty, and click-throughs on websites.

Think about all the things off-kilter about agriculture that allows massive government subsidies for gigantic corporate farms that "mono-farm" single crops (usually corn and soybeans), saturating them with fertilizers and pesticides that cause health issues and deplete the soil. Two companies, Cargill and COFCO, own 40 percent of the global commercial seeds. A huge amount of increasingly precious water is systematically wasted.

Meanwhile, in "food deserts," junk food is cheaper and more available to the low-income consumer than fruits and vegetables, which fuels diabetes and the obesity epidemic, which in turn overwhelms the health care system. And we're right back where we started.

Now on to my field: show business. A swamp rife with bloated, toxic personalities and the relentless pursuit of who's hot and who's not. Star fu%@ers, all. Youth obsessed. Millions wasted on vanity projects and outrageous salaries. Ineffectual management of networks and studios by inexperienced, arrogant executives who are driven by fear, anxiety, and bloated egos that drive the creation of countless hours of mediocre content.

But maybe I'm a bit biased.

Chances are there are another few thousand fields of endeavor that for those who work in them are just as flawed, dysfunctional, and fractured. Fields as divergent as, oh, I don't know . . . regional table tennis competitions, international freight shipping, medieval archaeology, and the traveling circus.

Now let's turn our attention to the government. Ugh. The worst, right? I mean, where do you start?

Gerrymandering. Super PACs and campaign finance. National debt. Unchecked military spending ($800 billion in 2021). Social security. Pork-barrel politics. Waste. Bureaucracy.

I'm going to bypass all these issues and go right to the mother of all brokenness in our government: the *partisan politics* of the two-party system.

Hundreds of books have been written on the history of political parties in America, their ups and downs, when they actually worked, *if* they ever actually worked, and the devolvement into the current morass of the last half century. Not my area of expertise in the slightest. But it's important to shine a light on this particular apparatus for a moment because it is a barometer and bellwether of most everything that is out of balance with modern society.

Basically, I believe the toxicity of partisanship is one of the greatest threats to our way of life, the future of our nation, and perhaps the fate of the world. The reason it is so particularly pernicious today is because the diseased roots of this adverserialist system go back over two hundred years.

Don't believe me? Many of our beloved founding fathers are with me on this.

> There is nothing which I dread so much as a division of the republic into two great parties, each arranged under its leader, and concerting measures in opposition to each other. This, in my humble apprehension, is to be dreaded as the greatest political evil under our Constitution.
>
> —*President John Adams*

I heard a podcast recently about soccer/*futbol* hooliganism in Argentina. There are these gangs of obsessive club fans called *barras bravas* who are responsible for hundreds of deaths and thousands of violent acts and injuries. Politics and soccer are so enmeshed in Argentina that politicians run for office with the support of their local club gangs, who are also involved in what essentially boils down to organized crime. The *barras bravas* provide muscle for the politicians and receive favors in return. They are in charge of parking and concessions and frequently sell drugs as part of their business model. They also actually help control who plays for the club and who manages the teams.

The violence has been so bad, in fact, that in Buenos Aires only hometown fans can go to games at the home stadiums. Visiting fans were just getting beat up and killed too much to attend games in opposing stadiums.

(Imagine what our friends Scoobash and %*&^ıı+ would have to say about the *barras bravas*. I'll let you compose that dialogue yourself.)

All this over a game where you kick a ball around. "The beautiful game."

Why do I bring this up? Well, because to me, it reminded me on a core level of how partisan politics works. The loyalty, which can verge on violent fanaticism, for one's political party affiliation often seems as random as the fandom loyalty for a soccer team.[13]

America has two *gigantic* gang-backed, flush-with-cash soccer clubs, called the Republican and Democratic parties, and we have pledged our loyalty to our teams, come hell or high water. It doesn't matter if a candidate from either party is grossly unfit for office or riddled with hypocrisy. We vote for them based on our affiliation.

What about actual policy, you might ask? Don't people vote for policy?

Yes and no. While there are some substantial political differences between the two parties, the opinions of actual voters are often more alike than we probably realize.

Members of both parties, when you sift through the data and polling, are remarkably in agreement on countless items: fixing immigration laws, reducing health care costs, reducing greenhouse gases, and having automotive fuel-efficiency regulations. Raising the minimum wage, reasonable gun regulation, reforming campaign financing, nuclear arms control, a balanced federal budget, and counteracting gerrymandering. These are all shared priorities.

Members of both parties adore the working class, farmers, nurses, and construction workers and distrust the monied elite. Both generally distrust the government *and* large corporations.

So with all this agreement, why is there so much discord? Of course, there are many policies and issues that the political right and left disagree on. While members of both parties might agree on the *what*— that immigration needs to be reformed, for example—the *how* of such a reform couldn't be more divergent.

---

13 Note: I'm focusing very specifically on the United States in this little exploration. But the problems of partisan politics, polarization, and corruption are global ones, with the effects being seen in "democratic" governments everywhere, from the United Kingdom to India to Brazil.

But do we ever hear about the areas of shared alignment on so many of these issues? Never. Instead, it's disagreements and deadlocks. The image that's drummed up by politicians, the media, and the parties themselves is that the "other side" are monsters threatening the American way of life.

Call me old-fashioned, but I thought our political system was supposed to be about finding *public servants* to transparently, fairly, and selflessly enact the policy positions that benefit the most people. Unfortunately, it's not. It's about getting and holding power. Getting 51 percent of the votes. It's about winning, not governing. It's about victory instead of sharing, uniting, and healing. And it's often about money.

On both the left and right, you'll hear solutions offered for this massive problem of broken politics. *If* some political condition can be met, *then* things will get substantially better and turn a corner. Things like:

- We need another Obama/Reagan/Kennedy. (Insert the dynamic, charismatic president of your choice.)
- We need our party to win a supermajority in Congress.
- We need to go back to the good old days of polite political cooperation.
- We need less woke policing.
- We need less unjust gerrymandering.
- We need a third party.
- We need to undo the Electoral College.
- We need to get rid of the filibuster.
- We need campaign finance reform.
- We need more Supreme Court justices.

But even if we did make several (or all!) of these changes, the system would find some other way to eat itself from the inside out. Like so many of the previous broken systems we examined, the entire way we elect public officials needs to be completely reimagined. It can't be fixed with Band-Aids.

Here's the crux of the matter: *people so rarely think that partisanship itself is broken, only that the opposing party is broken.*

Picture partisan politics as a house being held up by two giant support beams. Both have termites, black mold, and water damage. No amount of repairing windows or appliances or floorboards or shingles will make the rot underneath go away. And if you add a third (or fourth or fifth) beam, the rot will only spread, and we'll find ourselves in the same situation.

Why? Because the entire foundation is constructed on a faulty, unsustainable premise. This imaginary house we're discussing, the partisan political system, is based on the proposition that winning, no matter what, is the ultimate goal. *And* that these win-at-all-costs goals are best achieved by competition, contest, one-upmanship, power, control, backstabbing, bluster, rivalry, domination, aggression, contention, and, most importantly, money. Lots and lots and lots of money.

We need an altogether new foundation. A solid and balanced one. One held up by cooperation, unity, humility, and selfless service. A foundation where the goal is the maximum good for all, especially those who have been traditionally left out. Building that foundation is where the real work lies.

I know, I know. Naive. Unrealistic. Unobtainable. (Insert collective eyeroll here.)

"How do we get there, idiot?" you might be asking at this juncture.

Well, that's kind of the point of this book. And besides, it's about time we got to the whole revolution part, isn't it?

Yes, it most certainly is. And remember—the reason I paint so bleak a picture is to remind us all of how high the stakes are. What we're up against. And if we're going to have a rebellion, even a spiritual one, don't we need to understand what it is that we're rebelling against?

Remember, we're collectively hitching our wagons to the unifying forces of integration and witnessing, confronting, and overcoming those dastardly forces of disintegration.

Before we get to the revolution itself, let's recap our journey thus far and set us up for the final chapter.

We talked about (well, I talked about) how we're on a spiritual journey on both an individual and a collective level, part *Kung Fu* and part *Star Trek*. How our personal path is crucial, but we must also consider a larger soul-vision for our planet, our species: humanity's transition out of its raging adolescence and toward its inevitable maturity.

We did a fairly extensive tour of a lot of the obstacles that lie before us. I described these issues as problems so all-encompassing that they really should be thought of as pandemics. In this chapter, I companioned those pandemics with a glimpse into the many broken systems around us. Systems built on old assumptions and unsustainable conflict, greed, opposition, and self-interest.

Waxing mystical for a few chapters, we delved into some of the deepest possible human topics and their spiritual reverberations, like death, atheism, religion, consciousness, the sacred, and the grandaddy of all grandaddies, God.

We explored the idea that "men die miserably every day" for *lack* of what is found in the holy writings of the great spiritual traditions. I proposed that many of the spiritual themes and practices that we take for granted may require a deeper examination and redefinition. Words like "God," "religion," "faith," "soul," "sacred," and "pilgrimage." I even strove to bring us back to some occasional kernels of Indigenous wisdom to put things into perspective.

I spent several chapters excavating the idea of "religion" because, for all the destruction they have perpetrated on our planet, I believe faiths serve a purpose. So much of what religion can provide is what we're going to need in order to affect a true paradigm shift.

We even got to create a super-cool *new* religion, SoulBoom™, based on those foundational concepts and some other groundbreaking ideas for a grassroots religious movement!

Why did we cover all this? Because all these big spiritual ideas that make up the majority of this book are often waylaid by folks' general distaste for religion itself. We've thrown the spiritual baby out with the religious bathwater and in doing so have lost access to a treasure trove of wisdom and perspective that might truly aid our maturation.

I believe that only by recognizing that we are, in fact, spiritual beings having a collective human experience will we be open to the kinds of soul-level transformations we're going to need to make—the spiritual revolution that this book promises. A revolution that is urgent and necessary in the healing of our beautiful but broken blue marble. And remember, the ultimate aim of this endeavor is my grand attempt to advance a conversation about the importance of the divine dimension of existence and how it can influence our lives and our futures, collectively and individually.

So there you have it. The pot has been stirred. Discussions had. Questions raised. Perspectives shifted. Countless opinions blathered on about by the author. Topics both profound and mundane have been sifted through. And to continue the cooking metaphor, hopefully enough spiritual ingredients have been added to the SoulBoom stew for us to open our hearts, minds, and tastebuds to what is next.

Because it's time for a spiritual revolution.

CHAPTER TEN

THE SEVEN PILLARS OF A SPIRITUAL REVOLUTION

> We can't solve problems by using the same kind of thinking we used
> when we created them.
>
> —*Albert Einstein*

When I was a teenager, I had to buy my own car, and as I had no money, if I wanted it to run, I had to learn how to fix it. I was nineteen and working full time driving a delivery truck for Ballard Marine Supply and Hardware and attending the University of Washington on the side, and I bought an old Volvo for $400. It was a dilapidated piece of junk. But thankfully, it was a *hardy* piece of junk. I affectionately called this car "The Newt," after the burning of the witch scene from *Monty Python and the Holy Grail*. The Newt's claim to fame was that I could pull the stick shift up and out of the transmission while driving, which would create a large hole that you could peer down into and see the pavement whooshing along about a foot and a half underneath the car floor. Occasionally, I would take a girl out on a date and, while driving, pull the shifter lever thingy out and let out a panicked scream as if I had lost control of the car before sticking it back in again. This never went over terribly well, but I continued doing it because it made me laugh and, unfortunately, that's just the kind of person I am.

Over the course of my year with the Newt, I personally changed the starter and the muffler and the brakes and calipers and the battery and the tires and routinely changed my own oil and filters. I got to know and annoy the guys at the local auto parts shop as I would pepper them with questions. I would love to say that all this effort and sweat set me up with a valuable set of life skills, but mostly it was just a colossal pain in the ass. I did learn something quite interesting about cars over that long, impoverished year, however.

A car, at its simplest, is a metal contraption with an internal combustion engine that transports passengers on four wheels. At its most complex, it's a series of interconnected systems all working together to power a moving vehicle. The number of structures that need to work in harmony are various and many. Besides its body and drive train, every car has an electrical system, a transmission, a fuel system, an ignition, and an exhaust system. And when something is not working, you look under the hood or crawl underneath or, if you have a real-life automotive garage, you put it up on the lift and take a look in order to try and determine *which* of these systems is not functioning correctly.

We can do the same kind of examination for the web of integrated systems that allow human society to operate.

Continuing with this terrible analogy, if we put the *car of humanity* up on a lift and take a look around at what's not working, what would we diagnose? Instead of transmission and brakes, we examine health care and education. Instead of exhaust and air conditioning, we shine our headlamps onto international trade, human rights, or agriculture. Is it one or two systems that are out of whack, or is something more pervasive going on?

As we discussed in the previous chapter, it seems that practically every single societal structure has some serious irregularities and design flaws, and most importantly, the systems don't work together in harmony the way they're supposed to.

Before I give my personal SoulBoom diagnosis of what's wrong with the car of humanity (ugh, I truly hate this analogy), let's take a long look forward to where we want to go.

HEY, KIDS, LET'S BUILD THE PERFECT WORLD

Earlier in the book we assembled some elements for a new, awesome religion. How about we do the same, John Lennon style, to "imagine" the perfect world!?

Harkening back to "The Blue Marble" and all those sappy Miss America contestants from the '70s, what would the ingredients be to build this harmonious world? What is the SoulBoom vision for a peaceful, just, and united planet filled with a kind and fulfilled population?

Well, guess what? *We already know what the answer is going to be!* I really don't need to take up much space in these pages to explore it. It's quite basic really. The vision of what the aforementioned "kingdom of God on Earth" looks like is like *Star Trek* but instead of zipping around space we're dwelling peacefully on our home planet, Earth.

Everyone gets along.

As hippy-dippy as that may sound, it's really that simple.

In a nutshell, there's no more war. Armaments are just enough to defend a nation from attack. When there are disagreements, the various countries of the world come together to work out their conflicts with the greater good in mind. The differences between our cultures will be celebrated so that unity shines through a diversity of humanity.

There will probably always be some degree of rich and poor, but the extremes will not be so . . . well . . . extreme. There will be enough food, enough challenging employment, enough clean water, and enough cheap, renewable energy to keep our population both content and motivated. The arts and sciences will thrive and be incorporated into all facets of our various cultures. Education will be eminently available without any ideology or agenda except knowledge and enlightenment, with some tangible job training thrown in. Health care will be accessible and thorough and treat every patient with dignity.

Like our Indigenous ancestors, we will cherish our planet, honor its resources and beauty, and seek to live sustainably for the generations that follow.

Most importantly, in emulation of Jesus Christ, we will all love our neighbors as ourselves. We will live in service to one another, with kindness and care for the downtrodden and a deep respect for one another.

You get the idea. Like I said, regardless of political view or religious belief, we can all visualize this utopian future quite easily.

But—and this is the trillion-dollar question—*how do we get there!?* Do we achieve this lofty goal by making modest reforms, tweaks, and adjustments to existing organizations and ways of doing things?

Well, let's go back to my stupid car analogy. (Maybe, before this book ends, I can find a better one!) What do I see when I look under the hood of humanity? I see a series of systems, as we've previously explored, that have been faultily, unsustainably engineered. Design tweaks, legislation, and more checks and balances won't repair the essential brokenness. That would be the equivalent of using duct tape, Band-Aids, and chewing gum to try to jury-rig a solution to a much larger issue.

It comes down to this: The many and various adversarial systems that run our world are driven by and founded on some of the *worst qualities of our species*: aggression, self-interest, greed, disunity, hunger for power and self-aggrandizement. Ego. One-upmanship. Business, sports, and government actually all essentially run on this same fuel of combative competition. So to continue the preposterous automotive metaphor, we're headed for a breakdown.

We have a spiritual imbalance, a spiritual disease. And the answer, rather than being political, economic, or legislative, is primarily spiritual as well.

A spiritual solution for an essentially spiritual problem.

Of course, we need to acknowledge that in part we have an innate adversarial nature and that it's an aspect of our species, our history, and our *Homo sapiens* reality. But we don't need to be victims of those baser impulses. We don't have to build our society on them and their dynamics.

We need to transition from basing our systems on the worst qualities of humanity to basing them on the best of humanity. And what is that, exactly? What is this rumored "best of humanity"? I'll tell you. It's the essential spiritual qualities illumined by the deep reservoir of religious teachings that go back to the dawn of time. Ancient wisdom combined with divine attributes and positive character traits: selflessness, kindness, compassion, humility, honesty, and generosity. And dozens of other virtues as well. As crazily simplistic as it may sound, it all boils down to working together in cooperation rather than opposing each other in competition and conflict.

The essence of this work is summed up by one of my all-time most cherished quotes by everyone's favorite philosopher/architect/futurist, Buckminster Fuller:

> You never change things by fighting the existing reality. To change something, build a new model that makes the existing model obsolete.

A new model that makes the existing model obsolete? Easier said than done, right?

Unfortunately, I, a mere actor, do not have the skill set to present on these few remaining pages an action plan that is thorough and expansive enough to inspire all of humanity to reorganize itself around spiritual principles. For that I apologize. I do, however, wish to leave you with a series of key concepts and action items that I believe will be crucial in igniting a transformation. "Seven Pillars," if you will, on which to potentially build this movement, or to at least give us a head start. It's an eclectic group of ideas that is, like the rest of the book, here to shake things up a little and inspire a deeper conversation. They are:

1. Create a new mythology.
2. Celebrate joy and fight cynicism.

3. Destroy adversarial systems.

4. Build something new; don't just protest.

5. Systematize grassroots movements.

6. Invest in virtues education.

7. Harness radical compassion.

Let's start with the most important one:

WRITE A NEW MYTHOLOGY OF HUMANITY

Everything begins with a story. A story is the most powerful of art forms because it shapes how we think about the world. Remember, "history" has the word "story" embedded right in it.

As someone working in film, television, and theater, I've been privileged to be a part of telling dozens and dozens of amazing stories. I've witnessed their power and importance to the human heart. I've seen stories change lives.

For over a hundred years, we've heard and retold the legend of the *Homo sapiens*—how we evolved from living in caves to living in towns and then cities and then nation-states. We hunted, killed, and conquered. We've heard about how our species was propagated by survival of the fittest, and in this dog-eat-dog world, the most aggressive and technologically advanced nations and peoples prospered, while others were enslaved, oppressed, and left behind. We're taught over and over again at school that every human undertaking is based on a quest for power. It is epoch after epoch of wars. In fact, my son, Walter, took a preposterously stupid AP world history class that was almost entirely made up of memorizing the dates and locations of various wars and who won them. Because, as our children are insidiously brainwashed, "history was written by the victors," and "to the victor go the spoils."

Well, that's one way of looking at it.

But what if we started telling an altogether different story? What if we rewrote the legend of the *Homo sapiens*?

I once had a discussion in which a fascinating question was posed: What was humankind's biggest idea ever? What's the grandest concept we've ever come up with as a species? One of the propositions that arose was that *money*, and all its powers, complexities, and dynamics, was humankind's biggest idea to date. Sadly, I tend to agree.

Think about all the various facets of commerce and capitalism and how deep their tendrils have been woven throughout the whole of human society and history over the ages. It affects every single thing we do and has a deep, complicated, and dark history as well. Madman and philosopher Slavoj Zizek has said that it is easier to imagine the end of the world than it is the end of capitalism, and I kind of agree with him.

You have a thing and I want that thing and I pay you a sand dollar or a shiny rock or a shell or (eventually) a coin for said thing. I stockpile my shells or coins and leave them to my children. The more of this money I accrue, the more social capital, clout, and dominion I and my tribe can amass. Money becomes connected to ownership and empire. We eventually create moneylenders or banks that stockpile stacks of these currencies and lend it with interest, generating even more. Serfs have to pay off debt to landowners. Wealthy merchants fund sailing expeditions across oceans to bring back goods as an investment. Gold equals power. Labor gets compensated by wages in the industrial age. Money buys armies. Arms. Companies. Land. Homes. Prestige. Then there are stocks and bonds and Treasury notes. Then credit cards. Student loans. Budgets and deficits on a household and governmental scale. Subprime mortgages and global financial crises. The crypto gold rush.

On many levels the history of humanity can be boiled down to a history of money. In fact, the first known writing was a four-thousand-year-old tablet recording of what? A song? A myth? A fable? A funny story? No. Money. A recording in cuneiform of the wages of some Mesopotamian workers.

I don't mean to indict capitalism. Many could cogently argue that *all* of the progress that humanity has made to this point has been due to the exchange of goods and services, and money has been and still is the most convenient way to oil the wheels of commerce that leads to humanity's social and material evolution. They would posit that the epic list of improvements to quality of life and lifespan over the centuries couldn't have happened without some kind of currency or marketplace.

But at times it sure seems like the entire definition of humanity and its journey forward is about the getting and owning of things. Consumerism and materialism. The taking of things away from other people who have things. We end up with a culture that mirrors the famous quote by John D. Rockefeller, who, when asked by a reporter, "How much money is enough?" responded, "Just a little more."

How much is enough, and can I make a little bit more? That pretty much sums us up.

To quote the esteemed philosopher David Lee Roth, "Money can't buy happiness, but it can buy a yacht that sails right next to it."

Surely at this juncture in human progress we can find a bigger, grander, more all-encompassing idea than commerce. And maybe our new mythology can also rise above the dark, dystopian visions of the future that our children have been raised on through countless books and movies. A story about humans overcoming their differences, prejudices, and pettiness to create something global and beautiful, perhaps? Where is our big imagination now, at this most crucial of crossroads?

Here's an example. I remember in school being shown pictures of tall trees and short trees and how "survival of the fittest" applied to a forest. The tall trees "win," I was told repeatedly. The weak trees "lose" and die, we were taught. The tall trees get all of that precious sunlight and grow the deepest root systems while weaker plants struggle but eventually don't make it. Natural selection in the woods.

In her nature masterpiece *Finding the Mother Tree*, Suzanne Simard disproves this theory and instead shows a kind of collective altruism from tree to tree. She documents with science, personal history, and exquisite emotional sensitivity how the interconnected ecosystem of trees operates. Before *Avatar*, she was pioneering research into this interplay and interdependence she calls the "Woodwide Web."

Simard discovered that trees and plants communicate and share information and resources like a vast green brain: "The network in the soil is a neural network and the chemicals that move through it are the same as our neural transmitters." No longer trees as solitary creations, seeking their own self-sufficiency, but repeated examples of mossy, loamy interdependence on a grand scale.

Dr. Simard revolutionized how we think about nature itself. In addition to helping inspire the "Tree of Souls" imagery in James Cameron's *Avatar* and the central character of the Pulitzer Prize–winning *The Overstory* by Richard Powers, Dr. Simard has single-handedly changed how botanists and ecologists and tree-ologists theorize about how a forest works.

All this by rewriting a story. A story of Darwinian "survival of the fittest" transformed into a tale of cooperation, connection, and mutual support. With mushrooms and root systems.

Can we not apply that same vision to our rich history of human cooperation and interdependence? And can we not look forward while holding that vision as a goal?

Archbishop Desmond Tutu once said, "The atomized homogeneous groups that existed in the past are no longer the truth of our world. We must recognize that we are part of one group, one family—the human family. Our survival as a planet depends on it. *We are part of one family, and we are fundamentally good.*"

Humanity is one family, and we are inherently good. Now that's a story for us to get behind.

This is the first pillar of our spiritual revolution: the creation of a new mythology for humanity during its transformation into a lovingly united global community, based on a foundation of spiritual principles instead of adversarial ones. We will not obtain this story from any current world leader, politician, or internet personality, but rather think of it as something we all visualize, create, and *hope* for collectively.

Hope. There's an idea. This new mythology, this new story, this new *big idea* needs to have something in it that is unabashedly hopeful!

I'll give it a stab here. It may not be right, but it's a start.

The *new* legend of the *Homo sapiens*: When humans lived in caves and villages, community was everything. We sought safety, warmth, love, and family in the collective. We communed with nature, understood it, feared it, lived in harmony with it. Over the years, we aimed high and dreamed big, invented world-changing ideas and concepts, worked together to eradicate diseases, came together to try to solve problems and fight evil. Sadly, along the way, we also lost sight of our inherently sacred and spiritual selves. We found ourselves at a crossroads. Humankind had a choice: keep doing what we've always done or hit restart. We took a bold and revolutionary path of hopefulness, relying on the idea that the human spirit is inherently good, to build a new world based on heart-centered wisdom. We left behind our selfish, aggressive ways and came together as one family. And the result? Humanity achieved peace and unity and found, dare we say it . . . *joy*.

What do you think of my new mythic story? Or do you like the old one better?

Speaking of joy. This brings me to my next foundation for a spiritual revolution.

FOSTER JOY AND SQUASH CYNICISM

"Hope" is the thing with feathers -
That perches in the soul -
And sings the tune without the words -
And never stops - at all -

—*Emily Dickinson*

I studied acting for a time with the great theater director and philosopher André Gregory. He was the subject of the amazing art film *My Dinner with André*.

He would have tea occasionally with his students, and as I was finishing a cup with him one day and getting ready to leave his beautiful West Village apartment, I turned to him and said something to the effect of, "Mr. Gregory, sometimes I just feel so bitter. So hopeless about the future. It's so hard to not be cynical."

I'll never forget what happened next. He *grabbed* me by the wrist, pulled me closer, looked into my eyes with a ferocious intensity, and said, "Don't do it! Don't give in to cynicism. If you do, they'll have won. They *want* you to be cynical because then nothing will ever change. You *must* keep hope alive. Keep going. Promise me you won't give in!"

I nodded, a bit overwhelmed, and stepped out onto the cobblestone street, seeing the world in an ever so slightly different way. I'll never forget that interaction for as long as I live.

And as I write this, I realize that not only was André Gregory spot-on, but there was most probably a pandemic I left off my list in Chapter 2: cynicism.

We're all so cynical, so bitter, so pessimistic these days. Myself included. I struggle every day to "not give in." And the more cynical we get, the more nothing gets done because, well, "what's the point!?"

This particular pandemic is insidious because we don't realize we're suffering from it. Especially the youth. To what extent is this wet blanket of hopelessness contributing to the deadly, overwhelming mental health epidemic they are suffering from?

David Brooks in *The Second Mountain* says, brilliantly, "Our society has become a conspiracy against joy. It has put too much emphasis on the individuating part of our consciousness—individual reason—and too little emphasis on the bonding parts of our consciousness, the heart and soul."

I think Mr. Brooks and Mr. Gregory are on to something with this idea of a conspiracy against joy. The forces that control and shape our world (and no, I'm not talking about some conspiracy about a cabal of the super wealthy, smoking cigars in boardrooms or in Davos, Switzerland) want things to stay the same so that they can continue to profit from the world staying exactly the way it is. How could we ever "build a new model that makes the old model obsolete" if we believe in our heart of hearts that things will never change, that they will always stay in the same messed-up mode?

So what is the remedy? I propose that the opposite of cynicism isn't optimism. The opposite of cynicism is *joy*!

Why? Well, optimism has a kind of inherent clueless "look on the bright side" sheen to it. And recent research in the field of positive psychology tells us that there is such a thing as "toxic positivity," where one can feel externally pressured to "be positive" at all times in a way that is insensitive to the difficulties that might surround a person. By urging people in a blanket way to always keep a positive mindset, we disregard the complexity and darkness of being human. This generalized positive attitude of "optimism," frequently propagated on social media, flattens out any authentic experience and can cause shame in someone who is struggling to process superficial platitudes like "keep your head up" and "turn that frown upside down."

Joy, however, inherently acknowledges sorrow. It doesn't disregard the hard stuff. Joy knows that negativity is a part of life as well. Joy says that life is hard but there is a place you can go, a tool you can use. Joy is a force. A choice. Something that can be harnessed. A decision to be made.

Even if one is "not feeling it" in one's heart, one can spread joy to others. 'Abdu'l-Baha gives us one of my all-time favorite quotes about joy: "Joy gives us wings! In times of joy our strength is more vital, our intellect keener, and our understanding less clouded. We seem better able to cope with the world and to find our sphere of usefulness."

In other words, joy is a superpower! It gives us strength, clarity, and resilience, and it helps us find our path, especially in helping others.

I completely identify with what 'Abdu'l-Baha is saying. As someone who has struggled with depression and anxiety my entire life, I find truth in his observation: those occasions when I feel more joyful, I'm more focused, productive, and open to new experiences, and my mind and heart work in far greater harmony.

Now, this is not a chapter on *how* to find joy. There are plenty of those works out there. (In fact, Archbishop Desmond Tutu and the Dalai Lama have an inspiring treatise called *The Book of Joy*!)

There are also about three gazillion books on happiness—how to find it, achieve it, and hold on to it. I don't have the space to explore this topic here, I'm afraid. But I will add another tremendous quote attributed to 'Abdu'l-Baha: "If you are so angry, so depressed and so sore that your spirit cannot find deliverance and peace even in prayer, then quickly go and give some pleasure to someone lowly or sorrowful, or to a guilty or innocent sufferer! Sacrifice yourself, your talent, your time, your rest to another, to one who has to bear a heavier load than you."

I just love the message contained in this profoundly spiritual and utterly practical teaching. Essentially, if you're feeling down, give happiness and comfort to someone who has it worse than you do! The spreading of joy, in other words, has a positive impact on one's own emotional state.

This is what is referred to as "prosocial" behavior, and its efficacy has been backed up by innumerable studies in the field of positive psychology. Those who engage in altruistic behaviors have a greater sense of well-being than those who don't. Yet another example of where science and spirituality coalesce.

Joy is a depleted resource these days. As is hope, the thing with feathers. In a world with so much discord and disunity, how do we nurture them?

The international governing council of the Baha'i Faith (the Universal House of Justice) underlined a terrific way for all of us to move forward in a letter they wrote in 2020.

They challenged Baha'is and others around the world to "discover that precious point of unity where contrasting perspectives overlap and around which contending peoples can coalesce."

This idea is both important and inspiring. Finding a precious point of unity as a path to finding hope.

I remember speaking with the brilliant climate activist Callum Grieves, who works with Greta Thunberg as well as other youth activists, and he told me essentially the same thing. He was speaking about his work on climate change and told me of the "clean air" initiatives he had worked on. He said that people's opinions about climate change may differ in countless ways depending on their political point of view, but something like "clean air" is something that folks on all sides of the political spectrum can get behind. It doesn't matter if you think that climate change is some kind of liberal hoax or the greatest possible threat to our future, *everyone* wants cleaner air for their children and grandchildren. It's the "precious point of unity" at the center of the climate conversation. And guess what? Cleaner air means less CO_2 and other emissions that cause climate change. So win-win all around!

The author Alexandra Rowland made quite a splash a few years ago when she introduced a concept for an entirely new genre of fiction. In response to the unwaveringly dark works of fantasies like *Game of Thrones* and the hundreds of despairing dystopian novels, films, and TV shows churned out each year, which are sometimes referred to as "grimdark," she coined the term for the opposite: "hopepunk." Works of fiction in which a vulnerable and human protagonist fights against an unjust system and seeks to bring meaning, balance, and, yes, *hope* to the world.

She is quoted as saying, "Hopepunk says that genuinely and sincerely caring about something, anything, requires bravery and strength. Hopepunk isn't ever about submission or acceptance: It's about standing up and fighting for what you believe in. It's about standing up for other people. It's about *demanding* a better, kinder world, and truly believing that we can get there if we care about each other as hard as we possibly can, with every drop of power in our little hearts."

Although hopepunk's manifesto was built around the field of imaginary and speculative fiction, I envision the message and moniker spreading to ever-wider pastures as we collectively demand a better, kinder world. As we don't shrug and retreat under the toxic wet blanket of pessimism and hopelessness.

Sign me up! Let's weave hopepunk into the altogether new myth and story of our species.

And the better, kinder world that she speaks of is only possible if we rethink all those broken systems and start replacing them one by one.

REINVENT ADVERSARIAL SYSTEMS

Over a decade ago, when crypto currencies (Bitcoin and several hundred others) and blockchain were first launched, there were hundreds of articles and blog posts written about how these new peer-to-peer digital currencies, not dependent on any banks or central governments, would change how money is used and would eventually transform the world for the better. Treatises were written about how crypto and blockchain would end poverty, revolutionize finance, and democratize banking tools.

Although we've only been collectively exploring this crypto world for a little over ten years, and there may still be some transformative benefit yet to be found, it currently seems to most to not be delivering on its promise. In fact, what started as an encouraging premise, for those who work in its sphere, has given way to the reality that the world of crypto is just as corrupt as other financial systems, if not more so.

Why? Because this brilliant new concept that reinvents financial infrastructure is ultimately driven by the same greed that drives the old-school systems. Instead of a coterie of banking and Wall Street elites raking in money from transactions, it's a somewhat larger and different coterie of "crypto bros" profiting at other people's expense.

And there is no incentive to stabilize crypto currencies, because the volatility itself leads to the variety of "pump and dump" get-rich schemes that flood and define the crypto marketplace. One friend who worked in the field described it as a "junkier stock market where the value of the currencies has zero correlation to performance." The "market mania" of crypto is driven purely by self-interest and not by any purported altruistic intentions to transform the economic system.

The core of this system was built on the same old foundation of competition, self-interest, and greed. It is both a symptom of a deeper spiritual malady as well as something that exacerbates this imbalance.

I'll provide an altogether different example that I believe best highlights what the opposite looks like.

In her book *High Conflict: Why We Get Trapped and How We Get Out*, *New York Times* best-selling author and *Wall Street Journal* and *Time* journalist Amanda Ripley investigates a seemingly modern but most likely timeless and universal human issue: when conflict gradually morphs into something larger and more toxic than the original disagreement itself. Her work tracks people who were able to get out of the loop of blame and outrage and move into *healthy* conflict from which they are able to grow and evolve. Partisan politics and the divides it creates is one of her central topics.

In her book, she actually uses the Baha'i Faith as an example and examines how it organizes and conceptualizes its elections. She says, "Baha'i elections are to politics what mediation is to the legal system: a different game altogether—one designed to exploit the human capacity for cooperation, rather than competition."

In the Baha'i Faith there are no clergy, so the entire administrative system is made up of elected common folk who are in service to a larger idea. On the local level, every year a community, town, or city will elect nine members to serve on what is called the Local Spiritual Assembly. Every year, Baha'is at the district level elect delegates to vote for a governing body for their respective country, called the National Spiritual Assembly. There are currently around two hundred of these national governing councils. Every five years the members of the national assemblies gather in Haifa, Israel, for the election of what is called the Universal House of Justice, a governing body that oversees the guidance of the entire Baha'i world.

Ripley describes the process like this: "Every spring, everyone in each of the seventeen thousand Baha'i locations gathers together to elect leaders. It's very close to a pure democracy, operating in 233 countries and territories. Here's the twist: everything about these elections is designed to reduce the odds of high conflict. . . . People are not allowed to campaign for a position or even discuss who might be the best person to serve. They can only discuss which *qualities* are most needed."

These elections are undertaken in a completely unique fashion. There is no campaigning or electioneering. There are no nominations for potential positions or any kind of parties or coalitions to be formed either. Baha'is vote by secret ballot and are encouraged to choose those who are of "unquestioned loyalty, of selfless devotion, of a well-trained mind, of recognized ability and mature experience," as Shoghi Effendi once wrote.

Not only that, but the voting process is also undertaken in prayerful silence and meditation. According to Shoghi Effendi, "The elector . . . is called upon to vote for none but those whom prayer and reflection have inspired him to uphold."

When you go to a Baha'i election, it is astonishingly different from any other you've ever witnessed in your life. A roomful of silent, prayerful people in deep contemplation about who in their community shows the greatest faithfulness, sincerity, and competence. Voting is done in silent-ballot fashion, and the tellers take great care to make sure no one's vote is known by others. No one makes position speeches. There are no fundraising emails. No yard signs. No canvasing or jockeying for position and favor. No debates, promises made, or gifts given to potential voters.

In fact, if someone were to behave in a way that sought to draw attention to themselves so that they might seem worthy of a position, this probably would be perceived by the community as conceited and antithetical to the spirit of enlightened service.

Ripley says, "The Baha'is try to select people who do not crave attention and power. . . . This is the opposite of traditional elections, of course, which self-select for people who yearn for recognition."

(She is essentially describing Socrates's proposal that a society should elect *unwilling* leaders because anyone who *seeks* a position of leadership is actually unfit for that position. The best ruler, according to Socrates, has no interest whatsoever in leading but sees it ultimately as an obligatory service position.)

It is important to note that Baha'is who are elected to these various assemblies hold no special station above anyone else in the religion. Their opinions are not held with any greater esteem. They fulfill their duty as representatives only when in consultation with other members of the body to which they were elected and outside of the meeting have no authority or additional status.

I've seen incredibly powerful videos capturing the diverse members of various National Spiritual Assemblies arriving from all over the world to assemble at the Baha'i World Center in Israel, where they prayerfully vote for the Universal House of Justice. The delegates, wearing their native dress, silently but joyfully stride up to the stage in a convention hall as the countries are called on in alphabetical order. The sight gives me the spiritual tingles. Humanity at its very best. More than a thousand radiant and humble servants dropping envelopes into a wooden box in an atmosphere of hushed reverence to elect the body of nine believers who will guide the affairs of the Baha'i world.

Ripley sums up her discussion about the Baha'i election process by saying, "If social scientists designed a religion, it would look like this."

Compare that sublime vision to the reality of contemporary elections throughout the world, especially in the United States. Outraged yelling, bragging, and name-calling. Months of hypocritical, vain posturing, while countless millions of dollars are spent—only to have nothing change.

Let's envision how this process could work in the world at large. Let's imagine the small town of Pancake Flats, Colorado, which has a city council. The council members are getting fed up with divisive politics everywhere, even in their own little town. They decide that for the next election they will all resign their positions and pass a city code to disallow any campaigning or partisanship. They ask the populace to come together to the high school stadium on election night and instruct them that they can vote for any person over eighteen years old who lives within the city limits. They then ask community members to contemplatively consider all the people they have ever met and to ask themselves, "Who are the wise, upstanding human beings I know in Pancake Flats who passionately care about fairness for everyone?"

After an allotted time of reflective silence right there at the stadium, all registered voters, silent-ballot style, vote for the best group of people they know. Now, many, many people will receive only a handful of votes, but eventually a majority or plurality will emerge. Some of the elected will be totally bummed out because they are busy businesspeople, or busy librarians, or busy plumbers or what have you, but they realize they have been *summoned* to this very important role in their cherished community. And because they are the best of citizens, they are willing to sacrifice their personal business and comfort for the good of the whole and choose to serve the town of Pancake Flats, Socrates style.

This is a small, feeble example of what it would take to enact the same method of electing a democratic leadership as the Baha'is do in the "real world." Would this scenario even be possible? Would a number of gradual steps need to be taken before we could hold an election like this? Or would humanity need to be significantly more mature before something like it could ever be undertaken?

Those are difficult questions to answer, but these examples stand as a total reinvention of a system that is grossly out of balance. If we are to undertake a spiritual revolution, we will need reconceptions of this sort across all manner of previously competitive systems.

Making these changes will require incredibly hard work and sacrifices all around. And in order to do it, we will need to shift our efforts away from protesting what is currently broken and toward building new models that make the old ones obsolete.

DON'T JUST PROTEST, BUILD SOMETHING!

Humanity is incredibly effective at one thing: war. We are so very good at it. We kick ass at killing. We could destroy our world hundreds of times over with our nuclear arms stockpiles. Our global military expenditures (well over $2 *trillion*) and our arsenal of weapons of destruction are horrifically awe-inspiring. We can wipe each other out in all manner of violent and painful ways.

We even use war analogies and rhetoric for most everything we do. The marketplace is a battle. Politics is a war fought in battleground states. Sports are combat. We have a "war" on drugs. We "battle" diseases. We walk through metaphorical minefields at work. We "drop a bombshell." We "come under fire" for something we've said. We "make a killing" in a business deal. Hell, Pat Benatar even sang that "love is a battlefield." We fight, win out, fire salvos, lob grenades, arm ourselves, and fend off invaders at every turn.

This all-pervasive language influences our attitudes toward how we do most everything. Even if we're attempting to achieve something positive—like protesting injustice. Because we live in a culture of oppositional protest. Protest for the greater good paired with aggressive antagonism—a combination that is inherently contradictory and ultimately self-defeating.

Part of the problem with our culture of overzealous competition (and I'm tipping my hat throughout this section to someone who says all this far more effectively than me—Dr. Michael Karlberg and his magnificent book, *Beyond the Culture of Contest*) is that a culture based on contest easily lends itself to a culture of *protest*.

When some grave injustice happens—a killing of an innocent black man by the police, a mass shooting, or an unpopular law is passed—we rise to battle via *protest*. And many times this is for a good, important, and just reason.

Online, however, not so much. Someone posts an innocent opinion, and a flurry of aggressive comments appear, trying to tear it down. The voices that present as the angriest are given the most credence. People cry out in outrage, many times out of fury and pain, but also in order to *feel* like they've done something or made some sort of difference.

Complicated social issues that would require an overwhelming amount of extraordinarily difficult work to attempt to remedy are often

reduced to simplistic sayings that fit in a hashtag or meme or on a protest sign. Think "Defund the Police" and "Abolish ICE" on the left, or
"Build That Wall!" on the right, or "My Body, My Choice," which has
become a rallying cry for both, depending on whether you're referring
to abortion rights or vaccines.

Catchy, yes. Viral, definitely. Effective in creating real change?
Maybe not so much.

After some of these flare-ups in our ADHD-like twenty-four-hour
news cycle, a corporation releases a statement, an elected representative
speaks out, there's a general hubbub, a couple of Twitter apologies,
and then we go back to doing everything the exact same way. Before
long the whole sequence repeats itself as we move on to the next perceived injustice and ensuing outcry.

(Lest we forget, oftentimes the forces of disintegration, acting as
forces of control, *want* the populace to have a certain measure of protest
as a release valve. They allow the populace to blow off a certain amount
of steam and anger, knowing that things will just settle down and go
back to the way they have always been.)

This culture of protest is an inadequate response to the kind and
number of problems that currently face us. And often power plays, factionalism, and infighting—in other words, *the self-same qualities that
are being protested against*—take over these opposition groups and ren-
der what they are protesting moot. In fact, history shows time and time
again when protest turns to rebellion, once those who used to be in
opposition take power, they simply transform into the oppressors.

I have personal experience with this. I lived three years of my childhood in Nicaragua. Soon after we left, the communist revolution, led
by the Sandinistas fighting against the dictator Somoza and his cronies,
polarized the world and sparked the Iran Contra scandal and a
US-funded Nicaraguan civil war that devastated the population.

However, the exact same things the Somoza regime was accused of
were enacted by the new communist-leaning government to an even
greater degree: cronyism, corruption, shutting down a free press, and

arresting the political opposition. Over and over again, those who rebel use the same battle-themed toolkit they once opposed and end up creating the exact same system.

As I consulted with Dr. Derik Smith from Claremont McKenna College about these ideas, he mentioned something important.

There is much talk in social justice circles about "decolonization," the important work of undoing colonialism and its many ills. Ills that the colonizers of Nicaragua, including the United States *and* the United Fruit Company, inflicted on this innocent country. But what decolonization does *not* mean is switching the colonizers and their methods with the colonized so that they merely exchange places. It's about replacing the entire power dynamic of colonialism itself. Getting rid of the adversarial "us versus them." Good versus bad. Those who are subjugating (superior) holding sway over those who are subjugated (inferior). Othering.

Decolonization means finding a new way to coexist, collaborate, and create community, freed once and for all from the grotesque power hierarchies that colonialism creates. If we don't rectify this essential dynamic, we'll find the same thing happening time and time again, just as it did in Nicaragua.

Here's the bottom line: *It is* far *easier to protest something than it is to create something new.* Especially something like a new model that makes the old one obsolete. Because it's long, hard, difficult work!

It is far easier to send out an angry tweet about climate change than to collaborate with an environmental organization. It's simpler to write an angry email about women's rights than to educate and empower adolescent girls regarding the underlying issues. It's easier to go to a march for a couple hours than to research a problem, assemble a like-minded team, and work for an actual solution. It's easier to yell than to educate, to tear down than to assemble, to blame than to consult.

Because you don't fight the darkness with more darkness. You fight it by turning on a light.

Obviously, I'm not suggesting we collectively ignore injustice and stop protesting altogether. We must lift up our voices and shout when something is wrong, unsustainable, and unfair! And it goes without saying that there have been many effective long-term demonstrations combined with social action over the past decades that have significantly shifted policy and public attitudes. From #MeToo to the protests over the public murder of George Floyd. (Even #FreeBritney and #Oscars-SoWhite were effective in a smaller fashion.) Some campaigns have mobilized millions, led to substantive legal revisions, and demonstrated that protest can sometimes lead to tangible results. However, protests are largely ineffective in the long term unless they are used as a tool to *construct* something. That's where *true* activism lies.

And in the vein of taking my own advice to write a new mythology based on hope, I want to remind you, dear reader, that examples of activism turned action are everywhere if you look for them. These heroic builders do not have one hundred million Instagram followers. They don't have paparazzi following them every day. Cable news channels rarely feature them. They just do the work, quietly, for the greater good.

I'm looking beyond the Greta Thunbergs of the world. To people like Boyan Slat, who started the Ocean Cleanup Project at the age of eighteen and between 2014 and 2022 has developed tech that works with ocean currents to remove plastic from the Pacific Ocean—more than one hundred thousand kilograms of plastic between August 2021 and July 2022. Or Ron Finley, who was in his early thirties when he started guerrilla gardening to provide residents with access to fruits and vegetables in LA's food deserts. There's Ghetto Gastro, started by three friends in their twenties trying to provide healthy, vegan, non-GMO foods to poor neighborhoods in New York City. Or Cristina Jiminez, who was twenty-four when she started United We Dream to advocate for the dreamer immigrants who, like herself, came to the US when they were kids; she has spent more than a decade working to push DACA through Congress.

These are the builders. The doers. The people who strive to unearth the deeper root causes of imbalances and create community movements to systematically address injustices. What is wrong with our society that these people aren't household names but people who do unboxing videos or silly dances on social media are?! These should be our cultural heroes; they should be on billboards and have statues in town squares. Forget the models, reality stars, and influencers, *these* are the folks whose every move should be emulated and adored.

And where and how did these local heroes create this change? At the grassroots!

IT'S GRASSROOTS, BABY

When we created the digital media company SoulPancake, our team learned a great deal along the way—building our company from a staff of four to a staff of forty, growing from zero videos to more than seven thousand pieces of content, evolving from an unknown brand to an award-winning, profitable production company with an audience of millions and over a billion video views. (Sorry to brag, but it was pretty darn cool!)

But we also had our fair share of challenges and learnings. We took the audience interactions on our YouTube and social media channels very seriously, monitoring comments and watching our fans and their behaviors. One time we noticed a very interesting thing happen. A young man, obviously white and from Middle America, posted a comment on a video featuring black participants, writing something along the lines of, "I grew up poor and in a trailer park. Everyone calls me white trash. Real question: How do I have privilege and the people in this video don't?"

This being the internet, people were extremely gentle and understanding, guiding him toward a more nuanced perception of the issues with great sensitivity and tact.

Just kidding!

People jumped all over him. Many comments shouted, "RACIST!!!" Others said, "You ARE THE PROBLEM." Others wrote multiple-paragraph diatribes about the history of white supremacy and his unknowing complicity in it. He tried to explain himself and his comment, but to no avail. "Racist!" they shouted.

In our moderation attempts, we asked people to be polite and respectful and to not "hit below the belt." It didn't work. He was lectured, shamed, blamed, and shunned.

Then we noticed something quite interesting. Another group of people approached him in the comments section. White men, it became clear. And *actual* white supremacists, not confused, lost kids like he was. They gently responded and interacted with him in the comments section. "See?" they would say. "These people don't understand you. They think anyone who's white is evil. *They* are the problem, not you. There are lots of people in the world who totally get what you mean . . . check out these other sites and videos." They used gentle and inviting language. They expertly guided this young, impressionable fellow to racist websites, alt-right newsletters, and anonymous social communities. They welcomed him with understanding, drawing on the resentment he was feeling about the venom he had received online and planting the seeds for him to become a fellow white supremacist.

And just like that, his comments became more and more volatile and violent until he was gone from the SoulPancake community. We watched this play out in front of our eyes. It was astonishing.

And this was our takeaway: *the other side is extremely well organized.*

(The "other side"? Am I being adversarial? Probably just a little. My bad.)

To sum it all up: in order for the forces of progress, hope, and unity to combat the forces (another war analogy!) of *disintegration*, we would need to be as organized and systematic as they are!

Loretta J. Ross, a black feminist professor at Smith College, is combating "cancel culture" by offering classes such as "Calling In the Calling-Out Culture."

In the *New York Times*, she talked about how being called out on social media falls into a few categories: "presumption of guilt (without facts or nuance getting in the way); essentialism (when criticism of bad behavior becomes criticism of a bad person); pseudo-intellectualism (proclaiming one's moral high ground); unforgivability (no apology is good enough); and, of course, contamination, or guilt by association."

Can you imagine if the ignorant young man on SoulPancake had been "called in" instead of being publicly shamed? Because that's exactly what the overtly racist faction did. They called him in, all right . . . to a racist way of life.

People *need* a movement. To be a part of something bigger than themselves, larger than their own small self-interests. To feel like they belong. Collectively, we want something to fight for.

Unfortunately, we often think of social movements and progressive initiatives as best undertaken in small, impromptu groups. As something that just arises at a flashpoint, almost out of thin air. People mistakenly see big sweeping campaigns for social change as having come together randomly or by accident. We often feel that "grassroots" community work should be inspired but disorganized and that a systematic approach should be avoided at all costs.

This could not be further from the truth. The most effective "grassroots" campaigns require orderly, organized, systematic, and thoughtful planning. Many ingredients need to be in place in order for the populace to rise up and for public opinion to shift.

Let's take the civil rights movement as an example. It was anything but disorganized, impromptu, or piecemeal. When I was taught about the movement in school, this is what I learned: a bunch of sit-ins, strikes, marches, and activations sprang up out of an angry response to grave systemic injustice. Sounds good, right? The problem is that is not how it went down. I'm certainly no expert, but I do know from reading a bit about Martin Luther King Jr. and the Southern Christian Leadership Conference that the movement was anything *but* ad hoc, reactive, or improvised. It was systematic, well thought out, and expertly choreographed to achieve maximum impact on both the legislative side and on the totality of American public opinion.

Rosa Parks was not some random "tired seamstress"; she was an activist (secretary of the local NAACP) who came from a powerful line of activists in her family and community. Her courageous act of resistance was born out of a long history. A bus boycott had been planned well before her brave act of defiance, and after the catalyst of her arrest, the well-organized Montgomery Improvement Association sprang into action under the new leadership of Dr. King.

As an example of their organization, when black taxi drivers were penalized for aiding protesters by giving rides to black folk, a citywide carpool system was set up, with three hundred drivers giving rides to black residents. When eighty boycott leaders were charged with conspiracy, many arrested and fined, including Dr. King (whose home was also bombed), the movement continued forward with new leaders who rose up to take the reins as needed. And then, victoriously, about a year later, the Supreme Court finally ruled that bus segregation was unconstitutional.

The larger movement then had the momentum it needed to continue for the next decade or more to tackle crucial systemic changes to laws and attitudes concerning the rights of black citizens. But always systematically!

The nonviolent social protest work of Gandhi was studied like a science and put into practice alongside the Christian ethics of most of the organizers. King once said, "Christ showed us the way, and Gandhi in India showed it could work."

Throughout the movement, there were countless (and I'd imagine quite difficult) strategy sessions on how the work would ultimately lead not only to greater justice but also to an awakening of public consciousness around the issues at hand. "Schools" were set up to provide nonviolence training for the imminent torment that marchers and protesters were going to have to endure: the spitting, the beatings, the hoses, the jail time, the ugly threats, and even the dogs. Throughout, there was continuous disciplined action behind the scenes.

Black newspapers provided context and information about what was at stake for readers across the nation. Black intellectuals used the newspapers to disseminate a system of thought and to inform citizens about the movement's ultimate goals. Because if you don't know what your ultimate vision is, it's impossible to persevere through the drudgery and difficulty of the many steps that need to be taken along the path.

Churches provided activists with food, shelter, space for organizing, and emotional and spiritual support, as they had been doing for their communities for decades.

All in all, a well-oiled machine, filled with conflicts and disagreements, yes, but with a foundation of consultation and a unity of vision to transform the lives of millions and influence justice all around the world. A movement that was created with systematic action and highly focused organization, *not* an impromptu rising up of various pockets of resistance.

My point in all of this, going back to our racially clueless friend at SoulPancake, is that the side of injustice, of division, of *dis*integration is ready, organized, and waiting. The other side already has a movement in place, and THEY. ARE. ORGANIZED! They are systematic. They have hierarchies, blueprints, and action plans.

We should as well.

Soul work is tough work, real work. It requires great thought and careful planning. Spiritual revolution is difficult stuff that is formed in the trenches (yet another war analogy!). Everyone is needed, and all are participants. No one is going to do it for you. This is *not* a top-down enterprise. We all have a role to play. We are all protagonists for social change, not passive followers waiting for some leader to initiate action. We need to build community at the grassroots. Start small. Gather your friends and neighbors; log on to Next Door, Facebook, or Meetup.org; and find a common issue in your area that needs addressing. Create a community with a common cause that might, perhaps, build toward a movement. A community that "calls in," spreads joy, highlights service, and begins to launch a whole new story.

Remember what Mother Teresa once said: "Not all of us can do great things, but we can do small things with great love."

Love. It's the queen of all virtues.

VIRTUOUS EDUCATION

Here are some of the things I learned in school: how to be an effective crossing guard; how to make a paper snowflake; how to write in cursive; how to find a book using the Dewey decimal system; how to square dance; how to make finger puppets, dioramas, and pretty much anything from paper mâché; how to recite the state capitals, lists of presidents, and obscure facts about Washington state history; and—believe it or not, because this was the 1970s—how to properly dive under your desk in case of a nuclear attack.

Here's how many of those I put into use in any kind of regular way: the nuclear desk one.

Other than that? Mostly useless.

Now, I understand that education is a complicated thing. Many assigned tasks—learning the periodic table or trigonometry, for instance—that we may not use very much in our daily lives have tremendous value because the act of learning them does wonders for the growth of our rapidly developing brains.

But perhaps, just perhaps, we are doing some essential things completely wrong when it comes to education. Because when you ask people what they *wish* they had been taught in school, the lists are illuminating.

Here are a few topics that top various lists:

- How to take care of one's mental health
- How to take care of one's financial health (i.e., banking, finance, debt management, investing, saving money, and monthly budgeting)
- How to deal with mistakes, failures, and rejection

- How to use social media safely and healthily
- How to meditate
- How to buy and maintain a car
- How to sustain relationships
- How to manage time and how to focus
- How to apply and interview for jobs
- How to communicate effectively
- How to grow a garden

A delightful combination of the totally practical (cars) and the abstract/psychosocial (failure).

I find the fact that the things in the above list are not taught to adolescents disappointing and frustrating.

We come out of school knowing the quadratic equation (although fewer than a third of eighth graders have grade-level math fluency) but not how to balance a checkbook. We know the internal organs of the frog but not how to apply for a job.

All this being said, there's an altogether different subset of skills that I believe every child should be not only taught but diligently encouraged to master: *spiritual virtues*. I mentioned the importance and relevance of virtues earlier in the book, remember? In the death chapter, when I discussed my idea for a revised Game of Life?

A brief refresher. From a completely spiritual perspective, virtues are those attributes of the divine that we seek to cultivate in our hearts and through our actions. They are ineffable traits that we take with us when we exit this material plane. Soul qualities. Characteristics that one thinks of when pondering God and the beautiful effulgence of His holiest of teachers, such as the Buddha and Jesus.

Here's a refresher: kindness, humility, compassion, generosity, mercy, trustworthiness, sincerity, tenderness, patience, wisdom. Love.

Spiritual attributes can also be categorized as qualities that describe *how* one pursues one's goals and undertakes actions. For instance:

determination, imaginativeness, confidence, cheerfulness, cleanliness, resilience, self-discipline, enthusiasm, flexibility.

I get why some might recoil when they hear the word "virtues." For some people the word might be associated with Sunday school or a certain brand of Christian philosophy and the way that orthodoxy was sometimes taught. Some might think some kind of religious indoctrination is associated with them.

For those of you who have this reaction, I simply ask that you reframe the phrase "spiritual virtues" by defining these same attributes as "character traits," "positive qualities," or even, for the more practically business-minded, "leadership skills."

Everyone loves a positive leadership quality, right? Regardless of whether one is religious or not. We like leaders who are honest, trustworthy, kind. We admire people who are courageous and humble. We emulate those in our lives who are wise and compassionate. Most people know someone with real "character" when they meet them. And I'm sure we all have people in our families who are naturally patient or curious or loving or creative.

I believe all children are born with these attributes to some degree. That's the miracle of these behavioral habits. I also believe they are universal. Although their importance might vary a bit from culture to culture, throughout the world humans are drawn to essentially the same list of positive character assets. It's why all parents—even those without religious affiliations—frequently report wanting to raise their children to be kind, loving, responsible adults.

Some of these virtues come naturally, and others we need to work on. My wife, for instance, is almost outrageously compassionate toward everyone. She deeply connects with how others might be feeling like she's some kind of alien empath. Me, not so much.

Some personality assets we might naturally develop over time. For instance, I'm much more gentle and less aggressive now than I was in my twenties or thirties. (But, then again, I'm super-duper old.)

However, it is a gross mistake to think that spiritual virtues can't be taught and that, instead of being trained or coached, they are learned through a kind of sociocultural osmosis. But, unfortunately, this is what the majority of the population seems to believe.

Sure, in school teachers might give the occasional lecture about how important honesty is when someone steals a couple dollars from the cupcake fund. And yes, parents involve themselves to varying degrees in the character development of their children. Some might occasionally work with their kids and point out positive qualities in others they have interacted with. Oftentimes certain virtues, such as cleanliness and courteousness, are highlighted regularly. Still others might teach through negative feedback: "Don't be so impatient!" "Don't call your sister names!" "Clean up your room!"

Aristotle defined it like this: "Virtue means doing the right thing, in relation to the right person, at the right time, to the right extent, in the right manner, and for the right purpose." And I believe that we can all learn to follow Aristotle's definition to an ever-increasing degree.

But collectively we seem to *not* believe that spiritual virtues or positive character traits are something that need to be actively cultivated through instruction and guidance.

I'm here to tell you they can be, and not only that, but it is also *imperative* that we turn our attention to a lifelong pursuit of spiritual virtues education, especially if we ultimately want a true spiritual Soul-Boom revolution.

Harvard philosopher Michael Sandel describes their use as similar to working out: "Altruism, generosity, solidarity and civic spirit are not like commodities that are depleted with use. They are more like muscles that develop and grow stronger with exercise. One of the defects of a market-driven society is that it lets these virtues languish. To renew our public life, we need to exercise them more strenuously."

I experienced this firsthand. I was involved for many years in helping to lead a diverse youth group in a fun, Baha'i-inspired series of empowerment courses called the Junior Youth Spiritual Empowerment

Program. In this terrific series of books that we used, we engaged young folk ages eleven to fifteen in many deep and difficult conversations around some profound moral quandaries.

A focus on character building through the lens of developing virtues was also a core part of the curriculum, and I witnessed that aspect of the program having a tremendous effect on the students. Let's say for example that our virtue of the week was generosity. We would study it. Learn about it. Read stories around it. Provide examples of times we had seen it in the real world. And then we would task the students with observing that same virtue throughout the course of the following week. When we would next meet, we'd go around the circle and share stories about generosity that we had witnessed. We would also share examples of times we were generous ourselves. And then, having that quality in our virtues toolbelt, we'd move on to another virtue for the upcoming week.

I was amazed over the course of a few months of doing this work how the language, energy, and power of this type of character education began to seep into all aspects of the work and the conversation at large. We would use the language of virtues on a regular basis. When we read a story, the first question we asked would be, "What spiritually rich personality traits were shown by the characters in the story?" If someone would ask a question, the kids would support them by saying something to the effect of "Great way of expressing curiosity!" If someone brought cookies to a fellow student whose cat had died, their compassion was complimented. If someone helped clean up, we would all comment on their quality of helpfulness.

Before too long we saw behavior improve and mature. We also witnessed regular evidence of the pleasure a young person might receive in being kind, respectful, joyful, and humble.

And where does this all lead? To values. To real identity. And ultimately? To *Character* with a capital C.

What do you value in others, and what do you value in yourself? What are your character defects, and how, by focusing on the spiritual virtue that needs attention, can you transform those deficits into character *assets*? By continuously using the language of virtues, we create a strategy for empowering the best in kids as well as in ourselves.

If we want a spiritual revolution, we need to arm ourselves, our children, and our youth with all the tools they will need in this endeavor as they walk along the *Kung Fu* path of the spiritual activist. These tools are not prioritized in our present-day world, but they should be—they work both on a mystical level, revealing the divine light of the Creator, and on an utterly practical one, making our lives richer and our efforts more successful.

It is important to note that virtues not only build character on an individual level but also create a social condition in which all human beings can flourish and live their very best and most vital lives. When one is in alignment with these special qualities—qualities that illumine the very best aspects of what it means to be a human—both children and adults become more fulfilled and the environment they inhabit becomes a safe and radiant space in which they can thrive. And isn't that what we truly need?

Of all these magnificent qualities, *compassion* may well be the most crucial, powerful, and transformative.

RADICAL COMPASSION

Infamous movie critic and cinema legend Roger Ebert once labeled films "empathy machines." In the stories we see on the screen, we see ourselves reflected right back at us. We're allowed to walk in another person's shoes for about 112 minutes and experience the world the way they do. In the best examples, we're allowed to take in the reality of what it's like to be in captivity in *12 Years a Slave*, or to be someone with facial abnormalities as in *Mask* or *Wonder*, or to be caught in the middle of a Jewish pogrom in stories as diverse in tone as *Fiddler on the Roof* and *Schindler's List*. Or, occasionally, to see the world as a frequently misunderstood, wildly attractive paper salesman/beet farmer.

But is film really an empathy machine? Does it work as one? Have we become more emotionally attuned to others over the last one hundred and some years since film was invented? We certainly know what it's like to be Michael Corleone or Forrest Gump or what choices we would have made in a Squid Game, but have we viewers changed our behavior in any way because of the insights film has given us into the consciousness, emotional and otherwise, of people who are different from us?

In a similar vein, virtual reality was supposed to bring about the advent of greater cognitive and emotional empathy. In fact, in France they recently did a trial use of virtual reality with men who were perpetrators of domestic abuse to try and increase their emotional understanding of what it might feel like to be a victim in those situations. They put the men right in the middle of a violent domestic conflict, but from the point of view of the woman or child. In 3D vision and surround sound. The results, from what I could determine, were inconclusive, but the idea is fascinating and has a great deal of potential.

I want to take this idea further than film and VR. What if we humans were able to build ourselves the ultimate compassion machine? Imagine if part of one's educational experience was an emotional empathy training program that involved an immersive experience of witnessing the life or consciousness of someone quite different from you vis-à-vis some kind of virtual device. An experience greater than a movie and even more effective than VR that fed *directly* into the sensory and feeling areas of your brain. Maybe it would require wires on your skull, perhaps it would be like sliding into an MRI tube filled with monitors, I'll let your imagination come up with the technology, but the result would be to experience the emotional life of another human in such a way that we physiologically and psychologically undergo the reality of their suffering and want to alleviate it.

And imagine if, as part of our educational journey, we were required to spend many hours in this Compassion Machine™, relating to dozens of different subjects all around the planet. People who are incredibly different from us. A queer kid getting bullied on a playground and crying around a corner, wiping their bloody nose. A Haitian laborer traveling to the Florida Keys on a makeshift raft in the noonday sun, longing to see his children back home. A woman giving birth in Sudan with no water anywhere around. A Ukrainian soldier who had lost his entire family, shivering in a trench, waiting for artillery to land. A scared child singing a song while hunting boar for the very first time in a remote jungle somewhere.

(You know what? Now that I think about it, this whole endeavor I describe could make a terrific sci-fi film!)

Imagine if, through this systematic, deeply virtual educational technology, humans were able to fundamentally conjoin with experiences outside of the normal ken of our daily lives and the lives of our local "tribe" and consequently emotionally mature. What if humanity, through this method, took a gigantic leap toward world peace with the help of our Compassion Machine? We would eventually get to a point where we simply could not stand to allow the suffering of any of our fellow human brothers and sisters.

Good news. We already have this machine! Each and every one of us. And guess what, at risk of being totally corny . . . it's called the *human heart*. If we *train* this pulsating muscle, use it more frequently, focus on it, harness its power, we can join in a very similar precious and profound union with someone less fortunate than us. Someone a world away.

Now you might notice that I've specifically been using the word "compassion" and not "empathy" or some other words that might seem to mean the same thing. Let's explore.

The Harvard Business Review's "Potential Project" actually published a breakdown of the words we use to describe our understanding of another person's experience. In a rough way, it's like this:

Pity is the lowest form of this understanding. It is the experience of "I feel *sorry* for you," which, to me, also implies someone holding oneself above others.

Sympathy is the sensation of "I feel *for* you"—the passive response of "that's rough" to someone's pain that feels superficial in its emotional connection.

Empathy is closer, expressing the idea of "I feel *with* you." But in my personal experience, empathy is a heart-based reaction to what another person might be going through (i.e., you cry when you see a friend cry because you feel their pain), but that's where it stops.

Compassion is described as "I feel with you, and I am *here to help.*" It captures the most significant willingness to provide support and *action* to relieve another's suffering. True compassion, in other words, transcends empathy because if you are experiencing compassion, you are driven to action to *alleviate* the pain. And that's *exactly* what humanity needs right now. I would argue this human/divine virtue is our most surprising superpower.

Radical compassion is somewhere between the divine and the practical. It's a pragmatic and commonsensical way to build emotional bridges between parties that wouldn't normally intersect. And at the same time, it's one of the most transcendent of spiritual qualities that cries out for a life-altering opening of the heart. Compassion is both the most human of emotions and the most sublime. And, like all virtues, it is a muscle in the chest that can be trained, nurtured, and honored.

If the Notorious G.O.D. is able to hold us in His gaze, in the palm of His hand (metaphorically), with nothing but utter love and forgiveness, my hope is that this is something we can emulate one to another right here on old planet Earth.

And why "radical" compassion? Because regular old compassion just ain't cutting it. We must expand the number of people we are able to deeply "feel with" and want to help, as well as increase the depth of the feeling itself. Until, finally, the intensity of that feeling, like water bursting through a dam, leads to real transformative action.

Regular compassion pauses at the point of empathy, while radical compassion demands action. And finally, seeking to relieve other people's suffering ultimately requires the pursuit of justice.

"The best beloved of all things in My sight is justice," writes Baha'u'llah. "Turn not away therefrom if thou desirest me."

The Dalai Lama is the living embodiment of this concept. He has a daily practice of compassion for the Chinese invaders who killed one million of his fellow Tibetans during their annexation of the territory, while at the same time forcing many of the residents to become atheist, to burn holy books and renounce their elders.

He says it perfectly: "Real compassion comes from seeing the suffering of others. You feel a sense of responsibility, and you want to do something for them."

And finally, his holiness sums the whole thing right up when he says, "If you want *others* to be happy, practice compassion. If *you* want to be happy, practice compassion" (italics mine).

Science confirms this wisdom to be true. In a study of one thousand people over seven years reported in the *Journal of Translational Psychology*, researchers found that higher levels of compassion toward others (versus toward self) predicted statistically better physical and mental health outcomes in nine out of ten adults.

As a matter of fact, Matthieu Ricard, a seventy-six-year-old Tibetan Buddhist monk, has been called the happiest man in the world. Why? Because during brain scans his happiness levels were off the charts and broke every previous record. And what was he doing when he achieved the highest recorded level of happiness? Why, a meditation that focuses on compassion for all of humanity, of course.

And there's the payoff. All this radical compassion for others, and the actions we then undertake, comes right back around and helps us with our own sense of inner bliss. A vitally needed source of individual and personal rocket fuel that can help kindle and sustain our desperately needed spiritual revolution.

———◆◆◆———

And there you have it, a compendium of some concepts we might draw on for our global, transformative revolution. Some spiritual solutions for some spiritual problems. Pillars to build on. As I said, we're really going to need a few dozen more of these that have been fleshed out to a far greater extent and to a far more exacting degree, but it's a start.

Because when I examine under the hood of the car of humanity, what I find is . . .

Dammit!

I just can't do it anymore. I need to find a better analogy.

(Pauses.)

OK, found one.

But you're going to need to read the conclusion to find out what it is.

IN CONCLUSION

When we try to pick out anything by itself, we find it hitched to everything else in the universe.

—*John Muir*

"In Conclusion"? Are you kidding me?! It's impossible to have some kind of "conclusion" to this Soul Boom thingamajig. There's no conceivable way to wrap up with a tidy little summary the topics we've been tossing about, mulling over, and digging around in for almost 254 pages. I mean, give me a break!

As proof of this, I offer a brief recap. We dove into God and '70s TV shows. Together, we tackled the entirety of religion and even tried to build a new, amazing one along the way! We explored all things profound: Consciousness! The sacred and the profane! The existential need for poetry! We dug into the spiritual phenomenon of death and what aliens might be saying about our civilization. And to top it all off, we examined global pandemics, diagnosed most everything that is broken about contemporary society, and laid out seven foundational concepts for a spiritual revolution!

There is simply no way on the Notorious G.O.D.'s green earth that I will be able to sum up the epic, rambling, sometimes profound and sometimes ridiculous conversation we've been engaged in.

But fine. I'll try.

In 1938, Harvard University's medical school began a study that followed a group of 268 men for eighty years. Called the Grant Study, this long-term, comprehensive investigation was focused on one question: *What makes a good life?* In the study, everything was accounted for. Data was gathered on health, psychology, marriage and children, behavioral choices, resilience in dealing with stress, diet, exercise, and, as the subjects got toward the end of their lives, retirement. All of it was sifted through and analyzed to try and determine what allows us to live happy, contented, and fulfilled lives. The data points and insights that were gathered were rumored to have filled rooms. There were many "aha" takeaways, but at the end of the day, the principal researcher, psychiatrist Dr. George Vaillant, summed up all the findings with a single sentence: "The only thing that really matters in life are your relationships to other people."

I find that summation incredibly powerful.

"Only connect," E. M. Forster once wrote. "Live in fragments no longer!"

Relationship. Connection. These words that hold such transformative power, along with several others (which, oddly, all begin with *C*) and that we've been pondering on our journey, such as *community, cooperation, consultation*, and *compassion*, bring me to my long-promised analogy. A metaphor far more apt and relatable than that stupid car one from the last chapter.

Here it is: *the human body*.

The human body is one of the most profound and intricate entities that we'll ever encounter. A far more complex and nuanced mechanism than a car. It is also a perfect example of a crucial spiritual concept (one we alluded to briefly in crafting SoulBoom the Religion): *unity in diversity*.

A body simply could not be any more diverse. A sloshy bag of skin that contains within it goopy liquids, gigantic bones, and tiny organs that determine all kinds of things. A pump and a bellows right smack-dab in the middle of the chest. A cauliflower brain sparked with electro-chemical impulses. Eyelashes. Nerve endings. Toenails.

All of these components could not be more various and distinctive from one another. And at the same time, they are harmoniously linked and operating (most of the time, hopefully) with incredible grace and fluidity. The body propels itself, meandering around a shopping mall or a park or a dining room, and meanwhile holds somewhere inside of it that miraculous flame of consciousness.

One could compare individuals to cells in the body. Independent, yes. But in service to their particular group. Pancreatic cells help a pancreas do whatever it does. Brain cells work together to help the brain do brain stuff. All thirty-seven trillion cells of the human body show flashes of independence, but at the end of the day, they are all working toward a larger unity—that of a body in space, moving, eating, sleeping, and pondering.

The natural systems of planet Earth work along analogous lines: oceans, rivers, mountains, forests, clouds. And the biosphere that inhabits those systems.

One could say all of humanity, too, is like a body—a single organism of eight billion cells (individuals), grouped into a myriad of divergent parts, components, and bits and bobs that must harmoniously balance to function as a civilization. Interdependent subsystems maintaining their wholeness while laboring toward an even greater wholeness.

Just as the health of the body depends on the various component parts all working together in balance, both our planet and our human society need an essential harmony to function with efficiency and grace.

Ultimately, I believe this entire crazy *Soul Boom* dissertation boils down to a single concept: *unity*. What we must seek in this spiritual revolution is a profound unity unlike anything humanity has ever experienced before.

The greatest illusion in this world is the illusion of separation.

—*Albert Einstein*

About ten thousand years ago, the current mythology of humans on planet Earth began to play out. Nomadic groups, village and cave dwellers, began to form civilizations that started separating from one another. We saw only differences between tribes and races. Then came remoteness and epochs of never-ending conflict.

At its center, this is the concept of duality. There is a thing and another thing and they are separate and different. The way the entire world works has been built on this illusion of separation for millennia. Much of humanity, living in this way for eons, has created a dualistic global culture: Mind versus body. Civilization versus nature. Spiritual versus material. Us versus them. Apart.

The result? Tribalism and the inherent separateness that comes with it.

In spiritual discourse, this tendency to separate is often defined as being fueled by ego, which Buddhists call the enemy of compassion. In religious thought, ego is the "persistent self" that is stubbornly seeking to win out, to assert and prove itself, to protect its insecurities.

In the human body, a single out-of-whack cell can lead to disease. Similarly, our cultural obsession with individualism—our ego-centered lives—is a factor in creating the imbalanced cells, systems, and pandemics that plague our collective well-being.

In recent years we've noticed a shift. As we've matured as a species and our technology has advanced, this myth of separateness has begun to transform. The world has become profoundly smaller with the advent of the modern age of cultural globalization—the telegraph, the steamship, the railroad, the airplane, the car, and, eventually, the internet. Although as a species we're still continuously wrestling with that ol' tribal separateness and collective ego, we're awakening to the truth of just how interdependent we are.

This interconnectedness became blindingly apparent when a virus that started in rural China swept through the world, affecting every country. Or when the tiny nation of Greece defaulted on its loans and upended stock markets globally. Or when supply chains seized up and car parts stuck on cargo ships affected automobile prices everywhere. (Also, remember when it seemed like everyone on planet Earth was watching *Squid Game* over the course of the exact same week?)

This, along with "The Blue Marble" photo phenomenon, has led, over the last fifty years, to an understanding of what many would term "planetary consciousness." We are all related. We need each other. Depend on each other. Affect each other. Tribalism must move toward community . . . a global community. Rugged individualism inevitably and necessarily inches toward vulnerable collectivism.

We are one human family, regardless of race or nation or class, sharing a rock in space.

As the Lakota say, "All my relations."

This realization/awakening is a crucial step along the path toward the inevitable maturation of our species. But wait! It isn't enough. There's another phase of evolution to go. There's a whole new story to tell.

One of my all-time favorite childhood jokes is about a Buddhist ordering a hot dog. He says to the vendor, "Make me one with everything."

In this case, a silly joke articulates something better than even Einstein could. If you continue with this evolutionary line of consciousness that I'm describing, you come to the inevitable conclusion that we are not only interconnected but that in actuality *we are one.* Any perception of isolation and disconnection is a mere illusion, as Einstein describes. We become like the Buddhist ordering the hot dog—limits, boundaries, and differences fall away and evaporate.

Picture yourself walking on a beach, watching the waves. You notice each wave crash to shore and dissolve into foam. You see new waves form and ride forward toward the sand. You observe the distinct curve and beauty of each individual crest and fall. Then something subtly shifts in your outlook. You notice that what you are actually taking in is the ocean itself. Your entire perspective slides and expands as you begin to consider the totality of the ocean—its depth and breadth, mysteries, currents and storms, its awesome beauty and its life-providing bounty. The fish that swim in it. The moisture that rises from it to form the clouds above you. You realize that you yourself are like a single wave on a much larger sea. And like a wave on the ocean, you are one small part of a much grander, more mysterious, powerful, and beautiful totality.

> Your souls are as waves on the sea of the spirit; although each individual is a distinct wave, the ocean is one, all are united in God. . . . We must not consider the separate waves alone, but the entire sea. We should rise from the individual to the whole.
>
> —'Abdu'l-Baha

As we rise from the individual to the whole, our fate can ultimately be a hopeful one.

We are like Kwai Chang Caine, like Basho the poet, wandering the earth, searching for the sacred, for meaning. Spiritual hopepunks on a journey to build community at the grassroots. As we suffer difficult tests, we draw upon that deep reservoir of wisdom from the world's great faith traditions. We know that the undefinable creative force that courses through every star and every cell is there to guide us. To quote the narrator of the Big Book of Alcoholics Anonymous, "We feel we are on the Broad Highway, walking hand in hand with the Spirit of the Universe."

This is the transformation that humanity is inevitably moving toward. A profound understanding that we are all linked. More than linked—in fact, we were never separated in the first place. We are interconnected like cells in a single body, alive only in relation to one another, bound together, as the poet Rumi describes, with the most powerful force in the universe:

> "Love is the whole thing; we are only pieces."

BOOKS THAT GREATLY INSPIRED ME AND THAT YOU SHOULD CONSIDER READING

(in no particular order)

Beyond the Culture of Contest by Michael Karlberg

A New Earth: Awakening to Your Life's Purpose by Eckhart Tolle

Black Elk Speaks by John G. Neihardt

The Family Virtues Guide by Linda Kavelin Popov, Dan Popov, and John Kavelin

The Second Mountain by David Brooks

High Conflict by Amanda Ripley

The Myth of Normal: Trauma, Illness, and Healing in a Toxic Culture by Gabor Maté and Daniel Maté

Zen and the Art of Saving the Planet by Thich Nhat Hanh

The Seven Mysteries of Life by Guy Murchie

Viral Justice by Ruha Benjamin

The More Beautiful World Our Hearts Know Is Possible by Charles Eisenstein

The Story of Our Time by Robert Atkinson

Global Unitive Healing by Dr. Elena Mustakova

What the Buddha Taught by Walpola Rahula

The Road Less Traveled by M. Scott Peck

How Should We Live? by Roman Krznaric

The God Equation by Michio Kaku

Einstein's God by Krista Tippett

What We Talk About When We Talk About God by Rob Bell

Team Human by Douglas Rushkoff

Help, Thanks, Wow by Anne Lamott

See No Stranger by Valarie Kaur

Plays Well with Others by Eric Barker

Narrow Road to the Interior by Matsuo Bashō

The Soul's Code by James Hillman

The Experience of God: Being, Consciousness, Bliss by David Bentley Hart

The Power of Myth by Joseph Campbell

New Seeds of Contemplation by Thomas Merton

The Awakened Brain by Lisa Miller, PhD

The Hidden Words by Baha'u'llah

ACKNOWLEDGMENTS

I know, I know—acknowledgments are boring and they suck and they all sound the same.

Too bad.

You're going to need to read this because I literally could not have written this book without a team of supporters, readers, editors, well-wishers, and people far smarter than me.

Be nice; take two minutes and join me in thanking them, please.

First off, to my partner and most important reader, author Holiday Reinhorn, who has the sharpest mind and biggest heart in the universe. I know it sounds corny, but everything I am and do I owe to you.

I could not have written this book without the push, guidance, and inspiration of the great Shabnam Mogharabi, a cofounder of SoulPancake and a fierce and demanding reader, editor, and idea bouncer.

My uncle, Dr. Rhett Diessner, who gave me exquisite help and feedback and a lot of love and laughter along the way.

Dr. Steven Phelps, who has a mind like no one else's.

Dr. Varun Soni, who is hella wise.

Dr. Reza Aslan, who has a big brain and a bigger heart.

Dr. Michael Karlberg, whose writings opened my mind to a new way of looking at the world. Thanks for sparking so many revolutionary ideas.

Phew, that's a *lot* of doctors! Here's a few more:

Dr. Todd Smith, Robert Atkinson, PhD, and Dr. Derik Smith for their guidance, help, support, and expert notes.

David Langness, for all his incredible help on the chapter that I ended up cutting. Sorry about that!

Aaron Lee, thank you as always.

Linda Kavelin-Popov, the virtues diva.

David Bentley Hart, everyone's favorite theologian, for helping me open my heart to the mystical Christian way of seeing the world. And God. Read his books.

Ken Bowers, may the Notorious G.O.D. bless you.

Brant Rumble at Hachette, you're a joy to work with and even nerdier than me! So grateful you got what I was trying to do from the get-go and guided me on the path.

My book agent, Richard Abate, who believed in this project before I did and provided the vision for it to come to life.

My son, Walter Wilson, who genuinely makes me laugh more than anyone else on the planet.

INDEX

ABOUT THE AUTHOR

Rainn Wilson is a three-time Emmy nominated actor best known for his role as Dwight Schrute on NBC's *The Office*. Besides his many other roles on stage and screen, he is the co-founder of the media company SoulPancake and host of *Rainn Wilson and the Geography of Bliss* on Peacock. Rainn is the author of *The Bassoon King: My Life in Art, Faith, and Idiocy*, as well as the coauthor of *SoulPancake: Chew on Life's Big Questions*, a *New York Times* bestseller. He lives in Oregon and California with his family and a lot of animals.

READING GROUP GUIDE FOR *SOUL BOOM*

DISCUSSION QUESTIONS

1. How does Wilson define spirituality? What are its essential component parts? What is the soul? What is its relationship with Wilson's idea of spirituality?

2. Consider the abstract definition of spirituality and the experience of spirituality. How are they similar or different? How is an experience of the spirit as Wilson discusses it related to, involved with, or separate from our physical, emotional, and intellectual capacities?

3. What are the important differences between spirituality and organized religion?

4. Wilson takes the time to articulate a "plethora of pandemics" that exist in contemporary societies around the world. What are these? In what powerful way does each involve the concept of *otherness*? What does Wilson mean when he says that all these complex societal problems, while also emotional, economic, and political, are "actually spiritual in nature"?

5. Consider the extensive list of virtuous qualities mapped out near the end of Chapter 3. Which are most important to you personally? Which do you enact most successfully? Which virtues don't come easily to you? Why might this be?

6. In what ways is the work of an artist—actor, painter, poet, etc.—personally or culturally relevant to the experience of spirituality? What is the relationship between spirituality and beauty? What might it mean to, in Basho's words, "live poetry"?

7. What might Wilson mean when, speaking of conceptions of God, he says, "perhaps we ought to spend less time thinking of this creative force as a *what* and more like a *how*"? How might such a shift affect how people think and behave?

8. What essential qualities do holy or sacred spaces seem to have? What might explain Wilson's profound feeling that "the world had shifted" after he visited the Shrine of Bahji? What sacred spaces, natural or made by humans, have you experienced? What effects did they have on you?

9. What, according to Wilson, is the proper, most effective relationship between science and spirituality?

10. Why is it so fundamentally important to be aware of and concerned about the suffering of others—to cultivate compassion? In a contemporary American culture so rich in individualism and alienation, how might one go about genuinely cultivating such an awareness of and concern for others?

11. Why are stories—factual or fictional—so powerful and important? What's important and effective about poetic and figurative language (metaphor, simile, etc.), particularly when examining or articulating spirituality?

12. How are mythologies created? Which modes of storytelling and teaching are most powerful in the modern world? How might they be harnessed to tell new stories about humanity and spirituality?

13. What is joy? How is it different from pleasure or happiness? How can one cultivate or create joy, even if not feeling well emotionally or physically? How can one apply it as a service to others?

14. What is hope? Why is it so essential to Wilson's view of spiritual growth? How does one prevent hope from being naive or passive? What is the danger of cynicism?

15. Why do "people *need* a movement"? How might people decide which causes and movements are best for them and best for humanity?

16. In what ways did Wilson's parents influence his awareness and experience of spirituality? What is important to convey to children about spirituality? How might one present ideas about spirituality to children without simply indoctrinating them?

17. What was Wilson's experience of family like? How might one explain the simultaneous presence of what seems like a profound teaching about the soul and also "a piss-poor fumbling love"?

18. How is it that many religious organizations throughout history, despite being founded on ideas of love and peace, have done harm? Where and how do such good intentions break down?

19. Growing up, Wilson was powerfully moved by two television programs, *Kung Fu* and *Star Trek*. How is each show relevant to Wilson's complex ideas about spirituality? What are the potential benefits and risks or limitations of disseminating such profound content via television? Which television shows have spiritual meaning for you?

20. How does Wilson define the complex, subjective experience of consciousness? What is its relationship to spirituality?

21. How does Wilson explain the existence and even potential value of human suffering?

22. What is it about Jerusalem and the various sites within that make Wilson adamantly encourage people to visit?

23. What is valuable about Black Elk's idea that all—people, places, animals, things—is spirit? Why was such a concept so unacceptable or even threatening to the early Christians in America? Which other ideological positions conflicted with such a pervasive, unified idea of spirituality?

24. What do the ideas of Carl Jung and those of modern depth psychology add to the discussion of spirituality? What is the psyche? What does quantum mechanics suggest about the relationship between matter and the expansive, spiritual realms?

25. In what ways might it be true that in the United States "*sports* is our religion"? What powerful religious or spiritual experiences are generated? What might be spiritually lacking in this version of worship and awe?

26. What is the difference between prayer and meditation, according to Wilson? Why is it important to him to practice both?

27. What is the importance of solitude in the pursuit of the spiritual? How might one mitigate the risk of becoming overly self-centered? Why is being quietly alone so difficult for many?

28. What, according to Wilson, are the ten universal commonalities of nearly all religions? How does SoulBoom envision each of these?

29. In what ways does advertising powerfully use storytelling, imagery, and creative language to influence people in ways that might be contrary to the values and goals of SoulBoom?

30. What might explain why throughout religious history women and the feminine were removed from almost all positions of power and denied equality with men in both the mythic stories and the real-world practice? What does Wilson suggest be done to repair this?

31. Wilson offers an additional ten principles in SoulBoom "to show how this new faith community will embrace the ideals needed to remake and progress our modern world." Why is each important?

32. Why is it important to Wilson that people understand that "destruction and evolution are happening *at the exact same time!*"? Integration and *dis*integration?

33. What are Wilson's Seven Pillars of a Spiritual Revolution?

34. What are the powerful effects of political protest? What are its most effective forms? What are the limitations of such actions regarding making change? What does Wilson suggest should always accompany or follow protest?

35. What, according to Wilson, is virtuous education? Why has the teaching of virtues largely been left out of modern schools? What are Wilson's suggestions for how to teach virtues while avoiding religious indoctrination?

36. What is compassion? Why is it so central to Wilson's complex ideas about a spiritual revolution?

WRITING FOR PERSONAL SPIRITUAL EXPLORATION

SACRED SPACES

Think of all the sacred spaces you've experienced. Make two lists, one of any naturally formed sacred spaces, another of any that were made or built by humans. What do these two types of spaces have in common? In what ways are they different? Choose the most powerful sacred place you've ever been in and take the time to describe it in as much detail as possible. Much of this might be visual, but be sure to move through all your senses as you describe it. When you're finished, read back through what you've written. How do you feel?

Write about what creating a sacred or holy space in or near your home would be like. How can we more effectively find that transcendent state of the sacred in our daily lives?

A VIRTUES JOURNAL

Begin keeping a Virtues Journal. Using the extensive list of virtuous qualities in Chapter 3 of *Soul Boom*, take a few minutes each day to list any virtues you saw enacted in the world or that you enacted yourself (and, no, it's not conceited to humbly list your own virtuous actions! It's essential).

Randomly pick a virtue and, each day or each week, seek to notice it in both your own and others' behavior. At the end of the week, write about the impact cultivating that character asset had on you.

If there's a virtue you value but don't see often enough in your own behavior or that of others, use your imagination to make a list of ways such a virtue could be enacted in the world. Stay open to the small or subtle gestures because they are often very powerful.

YOUR SPIRITUAL FOUNDATION

Write a letter to yourself. If you feel disconnected from or unsatisfied with your experience of spirituality, perhaps as one of the "spiritual but not religious," take the time to write out what you wish for in religion, faith, or spiritual practice. Which elements of your spirit feel alive and powerful? Which values or spiritual experiences would you like more of in your life? What would a daily practice look like? Which spiritual tools would this practice utilize? What might that look like in action?

EXPRESSIVE COMPASSION

Write a card or note to someone you believe could use some compassion. You can keep this simple. Just express that you are thinking of the person, have made an effort to feel at least some of what they must be feeling, and that you are there for them. Send it. Notice how this act makes *you* feel. Then do it again.

When you find yourself angry or frustrated with someone, pause and write about them. View them and their behavior through the lens of ultimate compassion. Seek to see the world through their eyes and write about the experience from their point of view. See whether this effectively increases your compassion for others.

MYTH MAKING

Write a short story or fable that powerfully demonstrates a hardship you've experienced and the values and qualities you, the hero, used to transform the conflict into some kind of resolution. Your characters can be anyone or anything. Keep in mind this isn't about everything working out alright. No need for a simple "happily ever after." This is about imagining someone (or something!) demonstrating Character in the face of challenge. Use your imagination!

ALIEN OBSERVERS

Create your own alien characters that are observing human activity on planet Earth. Write a dialogue, in the same vein as Wilson's, discussing what these aliens notice about the hypocrisies, struggles, and oddities of *Homo sapiens* as they live a contemporary life on Earth. Give the characters memorable names. Have fun! Here's your chance to really dig into humanity's many foibles and dichotomies.

YOUR NOTORIOUS G.O.D.

Wilson says to his atheist friends, "I don't believe in the God that you don't believe in." Write a series of lists focused on what God is *not* in both your mind and your heart.

Wilson contends God is more approximate to Beauty, Love, and Music than any kind of "sky-daddy" deity. Journal about your Higher Power. What is most approximate to *you* when you think about God? Write a job description for a Higher Power, like an ad that might be placed in an old-fashioned local newspaper. What are the qualifications for the role of Higher Power in your life? Get detailed! What are some obstacles you have to understanding the Notorious G.O.D.?